The I Hate Ann Coulter, Bill O'Reilly, Rush Limbaugh, Michael Savage, Sean Hannity ... R·E·A·D·E·R

The

I Hate

Ann Coulter,

Bill O'Reilly, Rush Limbaugh, Michael Savage, Sean Hannity ...

R·E·A·D·E·R

THE HIDEOUS TRUTH ABOUT AMERICA'S UGLIEST CONSERVATIVES

EDITED BY CLINT WILLIS

THUNDER'S MOUTH PRESS
NEW YORK

THE I HATE ANN COULTER, BILL O'REILLY, RUSH LIMBAUGH, MICHAEL SAVAGE, SEAN HANNITY . . . READER: *The Hideous Truth About America's Ugliest Conservatives*

Published by
Thunder's Mouth Press
An Imprint of Avalon Publishing Group Incorporated
245 West 17th St., 11th floor
New York, NY 10011-5300

AVALON
publishing group incorporated

Compilation copyright © 2004 by Clint Willis
Introductions copyright © 2004 by Clint Willis

Library of Congress Cataloging-in-Publication Data is available.

ISBN 1-56025-614-1

Interior design by Paul Paddock

Printed in the United States of America
Distributed by Publishers Group West

For their victims

CONTENTS

INTRODUCTION

I have edited four books that feature the words "I Hate" in their titles—and it bothers me. I keep doing it because people keep buying the books; apparently, hatred sells. Then again, I like to think that I'm selling love, if in a kind of roundabout way—and I believe that love ultimately outsells its opposite.

The great religious traditions arose from our desire and our need for connection and community. These traditions have been exploited by fools and villains of every stripe— from Pat Robertson to Osama bin Laden. Even so, the essential wisdom of Islam, Judaism, Christianity, Buddhism and other religious traditions speaks to billions of us (including many secularists). We may or may not believe in God, but we feel the need to find an altar and worship at it.

Some of us worship at the altar of democracy, another institution that grew from a wish for connection and community—from a wish to nurture the ties that bind us as human beings. The pursuit of individual liberties is a spiritual one, founded on the notion that each person matters as much as any other. The pursuit of democracy is the quest for a community that is true to this notion— which is to say that democracy is founded on love; that democracy is by nature tolerant and peaceful.

These are treasonous ideas in the eyes of Ann Coulter or Rush Limbaugh. They will tell you that democracy must be defended by force; they'll cite World War II and the Cold War and the recent wars against Iraq.

And yet it is worth asking how the people of Poland

benefited from World War II; how the people of the Sudan benefited from the Cold War; how the people of Iraq—let alone Palestine or Israel or the United States—have benefited from the recent invasion of Iraq. The answers are more complex than Rush or Ann may wish to believe.

More to the point, it is worth asking how the people of the world—including you and me—might have benefited from an American foreign policy designed to foster true democracy in all nations. Such a policy would be characterized by enormous spending on global humanitarian aid and economic development and by more modest investments in weapons and wars. Such a policy would be characterized not by fear (and thus hatred) but by curiosity, understanding and love.

Those motives—curiosity, understanding and love— can be of use to us as we review the work of today's well-known right-wing demagogues.

Their words can easily summon up old-fashioned righteous anger—as we read Ann Coulter's latest screed against liberal "traitors"; as we watch Bill O'Reilly bully the courageous son of a 9/11 victim; as we listen to Rush Limbaugh compare prisoner abuse at Abu Ghraib in Iraq to fraternity hazing in America.

Anger is only one possible response; it is not a satisfactory one. We may also feel a certain despair: Coulter's most recent book has sold nearly a million copies; O'Reilly hosts the most popular news program on cable; Limbaugh has almost 20 million listeners.

Our despair may lead us to curiosity (an alien emotion to the loudmouths on the Right): How do Coulter and her ilk manage to make up such outrageous lies and defend them, day after day? Why do they do it? And why are their lies and rants so popular?

Here are some answers: They can lie and keep lying because they lack integrity; they don't know the difference between right or wrong; they don't know who they are; they are afraid.

Their fear makes them desperate—and this answers the second question: They lie because they need power and their lies help them to get it.

And why are they popular? Their lies appeal to other people who are also afraid; people willing to listen to lies that comfort them, lies that say they are stronger than they are. Rush tells his listeners that America is the greatest country in the world—whatever that means—and his listeners are glad to hear it; they are Americans, therefore they are great—no matter what the actual experience of their lives may tell them.

The irony is that the lies of Ann Coulter and Bill O'Reilly and Rush Limbaugh help keep their fans powerless. Such lies support the power of institutions—the likes of Enron and Wal-Mart—over the power of individuals.

When we consider these facts, we may start to feel a genuine connection to the people who read Ann Coulter and watch Bill O'Reilly and listen to Rush Limbaugh. This connection can be our greatest weapon, because it furthers the process of forming a truly democratic community. We begin to recognize that we are in this together—liberals and conservatives alike.

We are all victims of the concentration of economic power that exists in this country and in the world. Corporations ranging from drug maker Pfizer to retail behemoth Wal-Mart increasingly dictate government policy in ways that harm us all—leading to poverty and pollution, unemployment and inflation, terrorism and war.

Once we acknowledge our common plight, we begin to see that each of us has a stake in redistributing power—in creating democracy. This stake binds us together whether or not we recognize the connection. When we do recognize it, we begin the process of building a community that can benefit us all.

When we see that we're all in this together, we don't need to lie. When we understand our connection to one another, we begin to find our integrity—we discover that we are meant to be true to this connection, to our community. We find that we are meant to resist the concentration of power and resources that leads to violence and suffering on our shared planet. We begin to acknowledge that we must share our resources with the powerless; that we must invite them into our community—that we must offer schools to the poor, food to the hungry, treatment to the sick, compassion to the cruel.

If we fail to do this, we will find ourselves living behind walls that can't protect us. Democracy will die, and with it our best chance to connect with each other—to serve each other.

Meanwhile, how should we live in a world that rewards and encourages the lies of Ann Coulter and Bill O'Reilly and Rush Limbaugh? The Buddha offers this:

> The thought manifests as the word;
> The word manifests as the deed;
> The deed develops into habit;
> The habit hardens into character.
> So watch the thought and its ways with care,

And let it spring from love
Born of concern for all beings.

The *Desiderata* offers this:

Avoid loud and aggressive persons; they are vexations to
the spirit.

—Clint Willis

ANN COULTER

*with a quote by Ann Coulter;
a short take by* The Beast *staff;
and anagrams*

Ann Coulter is an extreme version of the political hatchet man (hatchet woman?)—an opportunist who gives up her own humanity to do the dirty work of her party. She says the things Bush and Cheney and even Rush Limbaugh won't say but want said. Her reward is some spending money and the cheap notoriety of a vicious hack. Meanwhile, even the people she serves despise her—though not as much as she despises herself.

Coulter's second book, Slander: Liberal Lies About the American Right, *appeared in 2002.*

Ann Coulter

from *What Liberal Media?* (2003)

Eric Alterman

I first met Ann Coulter in 1996 when we were both hired to be pundits on the new cable news station, MSNBC. Still just a right-wing congressional aide, she had been hired without even a hint of journalistic experience but with a mouth so vicious she made her fellow leggy blond pundit, Laura Ingraham, look and sound like Mary Tyler Moore in comparison. Coulter was eventually fired when she attacked a disabled Vietnam veteran on the air, screaming, "People like you caused us to lose that war." But this was just one of many incidents where she had leaped over the bounds of good taste into the kind of talk that is usually reserved for bleachers or bar fights. In her columns, published in one of the most extreme of all conservative publications, *Human Events*, she regularly referred to the president of the United States, Bill Clinton, as a "pervert, liar, and a felon" and "a flim-flam artist." She termed the first lady to be "pond scum" and "white trash" and the late Pamela Harriman a "whore." Coulter said these things all the while appearing on air in dresses so revealing they put one in mind of Sharon Stone in the film *Basic Instinct.*

The greater Coulter's fame, the more malevolent grew her hysteria. In her 1998 book, *High Crimes and Misdemeanors: The Case Against Bill Clinton,* she wrote, "In this recurring nightmare of a presidency, we have a national debate about whether he 'did it,' even though all sentient people know he did. Otherwise there would be debates only about whether to impeach or assassinate." Such was the wisdom of the alleged "constitutional scholar" whose work George Will quoted on ABC's *This Week*. (Will is not very particular about his sources. I counted exactly one work of history in Coulter's copious footnotes. Coulter has also been accused of plagiarism by a former colleague, but denies the charge.)

Shortly after 9/11, Coulter became famous again when she suggested, in a column published by National Review Online, after seeing anti-American demonstrators in Arab nations, that we "invade their countries, kill their leaders and convert them to Christianity." Coulter's column was dropped by the magazine, but not because the editors objected to its content. Editor Jonah Goldberg explained, "We ended the relationship because she behaved with a total lack of professionalism, friendship, and loyalty." (Coulter had called the editors "girly boys.") Coulter remained unbowed. At a meeting of the National Political Action Conference, speaking of the young American who converted to militant Islam and fought for the Taliban, Coulter advised, "We need to execute people like John Walker in order to physically intimidate liberals, by making them realize that they can be killed too. Otherwise they will turn out to be outright traitors." She also joked about the proposed murder of the U.S. secretary of transportation, Norm Mineta.

In her second book-length primal scream, published in the summer of 2002, Coulter compared Katie Couric of the *Today* show to Eva Braun. (She would later add

Joseph Goebbels after Couric challenged her in an interview.) She termed Christie Todd Whitman, the former governor of New Jersey and then head of the Environmental Protection Agency, a "dimwit" and a "birdbrain." Sen. Jim Jeffords is a "half-wit." Gloria Steinem is a "termagent" and "deeply ridiculous figure," who "had to sleep" with a rich liberal to fund *Ms.* magazine. But the errors are even more egregious than the insults, and her footnotes are, in many significant cases, a sham. The good folks at the *American Prospect's* Web log "Tapped" went to the trouble of compiling Coulter's errors chapter by chapter. The sheer weight of these, coupled with their audacity, demonstrates the moral and intellectual bankruptcy of a journalistic culture that allows her near a microphone, much less a printing press.

Coulter's view of the U.S. media can be summed up as follows: "American journalists commit mass murder without facing the ultimate penalty, I think they are retarded." In the *New York Observer*, published in one of the two cities attacked on 9/11, Coulter joked about how wonderful it would have been if Timothy McVeigh had blown up the *New York Times* building and murdered all of its inhabitants. Apparently nothing—not even the evocation, serious or not, of the mass murder of journalists—could turn Coulter's love affair with the SCLM (so-called liberal media) sour.

For such comments, she is celebrated and rewarded. While promoting *Slander*, Coulter was booked on *Today*, *Crossfire* (as both a guest and guest host), *Hardball*, *The Big Story with John Gibson*, and countless other cable and radio programs. She was lovingly profiled in *Newsday*, the *New York Observer*, and the *New York Times* Sunday Styles page, while also enjoying a seat at the White House Correspondents Association Dinner as a guest of the *Boston Globe*. She was even invited on ABC's *Good Morning America* as an election analyst in November 2002. In the *Wall Street Journal*—a newspaper that had actually been destroyed by terrorists, and whose reporter, Daniel Pearl, had been murdered by them—Melik Kaylan defended her comments in Coulter-like fashion. He argued, "We have been programmed to think that such impassioned outrage, and outrageousness, are permissible only on the left from counter-culture comedians or exponents of identity politics." He also compared Coulter's alleged "humor" to that of Lenny Bruce, Angela Davis, and the Black Panthers. Too bad, therefore, as Charles Piece pointed out, the conservative media darling has yet to be "arrested and jailed for what she said (Lenny Bruce), prosecuted in federal court (Angela Davis), or shot to ribbons in her bed (the Black Panthers)."

The American Prospect's *web log (Tapped) ran this series of commentaries on Ann Coulter's . . . what to call them? Errors? Distortions? Bald-faced lies? Yeah, that's it.*

Fact-Check Ann Coulter

from The American Prospect (July 2002)

The American Prospect staff

Herewith, compiled, are Tapped's fact-checks of Ann Coulter:

1. ANN COULTER READER CONTEST! We'd almost run out of things to say about that nutty gal, Ann Coulter. But then she went and wrote another book (*Slander: Liberal Lies About The American Right*). But it may not be much of a book. Tapped reader U.R. reports that one chapter into Coulter's book—"I only managed to get through the first chapter," he writes, because "I can't read the book more than a few minutes at a time"—he's already found two obvious factual errors. On page 7, Coulter writes that Jim Jeffords "opposed Reagan's tax cut, supported the elder Bush's tax hike, supported Clinton's tax hike, and opposed the younger Bush's tax cut." She's right about the first two. But we checked, and Jeffords—like all Republicans at the time—voted *against* Clinton's 1993 budget (which included the tax hike) and *for* George W. Bush's recent tax cut. The latter is a pretty glaring error, both because it was so recent and because Jeffords' refusal to oppose the cut was a major blow to liberals who thought his party switch would help them defeat it.

(On the same page, Coulter also writes that Jeffords "voted against Clinton's impeachment"—which is impossible, as the Senate never voted on impeachment. The House has the power to impeach; the Senate only votes on whether or not to convict. Jeffords did, however, vote against conviction. So maybe we're quibbling.)

If Coulter is going to title her book *Slander*, it would be nice if she would also go to the trouble of proofreading it. But maybe she didn't have time. (She is, after all, a busy girl.) So we've decided to help Coulter out. Starting today, Tapped will hold a reader contest: Fact Check Ann Coulter. We invite our readers to slog their way through *Slander* and email Tapped with examples of factual errors. Include the page number; we'll take a look in our own copy and post the ones we can verify. As a reward for this difficult, dirty task, the Tapped reader who emails in the most examples will get a free year's subscription to *The American Prospect*. Let the fact-checking begin!

2. TIME STANDS STILL FOR ANN COULTER. Okay, this isn't exactly a "fact check" of Coulter's new book. It's almost too obvious for that. Nevertheless, we couldn't resist pointing out something this glaring. On page four of her book *Slander*, Coulter writes that "after the September 11 attack on America, all partisan wrangling stopped dead," and soon continues:

> The bipartisan lovefest lasted precisely three weeks. That was all the *New York Times* could endure. Impatient with the national mood of patriotism, liberals returned to their infernal griping about George W. Bush—or "Half a Commander in Chief," as he was called in the headline of a lead *New York Times* editorial on November 5, 2001. From that

moment on, the left's primary contribution to the war effort was to complain.

Sorry, Ann, but last we checked, November 5 was just under *two months* after September 11.

3. FACT CHECK ANN COULTER!: SHOOTING BLANKS ON *CROSSFIRE*. Okay, this isn't from *Slander*. It's from Coulter's appearance on *Hardball*, guest-hosted by Mike Barnicle. We missed this gem, but reader R.L. passed it along:

> I will guess that the judges who said the Pledge of Allegiance violates the constitution were appointed by Democrats and not Republicans. I haven't looked at the decision. I haven't even heard about the decision because I've been busy today, but that's a wild guess I'm going to make. . . .Oh, I'm just waiting to see if anyone will take any bets on me on whether the judges who wrote the decision were appointed by a Democrat or Republican.

We think we can safely assume the implication here. In actuality, of course, only one of the two judges was appointed by a Democrat—Judge Stephen Reinhardt, a Carter appointee. The other was Judge Alfred T. Goodwin, who was appointed by that great liberal, Richard Nixon. This really speaks volumes about just what a hack Coulter is; it requires no elaboration on our part. But perhaps now the chat shows will stop billing Coulter as a "constitutional lawyer." No wonder the profession is held in such low regard.

4. FACT CHECK ANN COULTER!: LEXIS-NEXIS ABUSE. On page 15 of

Slander, she writes: "In the *New York Times* archives, 'moderate Republican' has been used 168 times . . . There have been only 11 sightings of a 'liberal Republican.'" Coulter does not footnote her methodology in "discovering" this nugget, but we checked using both the *Times*'s own free search page and Lexis-Nexis. Our results? Our *Times* search reveals twenty-two hits for "liberal Republican" since 1996—that is, in just the last seven years. For Lexis, we searched for "liberal Republican" in the *New York Times* over "all available dates"—and got 524 documents. Coulter's claim is obviously false. But stay tuned—Tapped spent all weekend reading *Slander* and there's *lots* more to come.

P.S. We also have another non-*Slander* error, courtesy of reader J.O. In Coulter's latest column on Townhall.com, she writes:

> If Arabs were being stopped at airports before Sept. 11—and that's a big if—that was probably wrong. There had been only one terrorist attack here in America by Arabs—the bomb at the World Trade Center in 1993. (This is excluding Sirhan Sirhan, the first Muslim to bring the classic religion-of-peace protest to American shores, when, in support of the Palestinians, he assassinated Robert Kennedy.)

But Sirhan Sirhan was, in fact, a Christian of Arab descent, not a Muslim. For a relatively recent source on this, you can check out the historian Godfrey Hodgson's 1995 review of Dan Moldea's *The Killing of Robert F. Kennedy* in *The Washington Post*. We found it on Lexis, but a quick Google search led us to the citation. Hey, Jonathan, is Coulter phoning it in or what?

5. FACT CHECK ANN COULTER: THE "GORE LIED" LIE. Today's first installment concerns Al Gore's reputation as a lying, exaggerating braggart, gleefully perpetuated by Ann Coulter in her new book, *Slander*. Coulter eeks out impressive mileage from Gore's supposed lie about having been "the inspiration" for *Love Story*, Erich Segal's 1970 bestselling-romance-novel-turned-Oscar-nominated-film. She refers to the alleged *Love Story* lie a whopping four times in Slander—on pages 145, 154, 159, and 160. But this one has been debunked by Eric Boehlert in *Salon*, Bob Somersby in the *Daily Howler*, Robert Parry in *The Washington Monthly*, and Sean Wilentz in *TAP*.

The truth is that Gore *was* the inspiration for the book's hero, Oliver Barrett IV, according to Segal. Segal's reported "denial" of Gore's claim was no denial at all. Speaking to the *New York Times*'s Melinda Henneberger for a follow-up story, Segal said that Oliver Barrett was based on Gore and his Harvard roommate, actor Tommy Lee Jones. He only denied that the female lead, the fiery musician Jenny Cavilleri, was based on Tipper Gore. And even that wrong detail was not Gore's mistake.

What actually happened? On a late-night plane ride in late 1997, shooting the breeze with *Time*'s Karen Tumulty and the *Times*'s Rick Berke, Gore mentioned that the main characters in Love Story were based on him and Tipper. At any rate, Gore said, that's what Segal had told the *Nashville Tennessean* years ago on his book tour. Segal met Gore and Jones when they were students at Harvard together and Gore was dating Tipper, then a student at Boston University. Tumulty reported this comment in *Time* but neglected to include in her story the fact that Gore had said explicitly that his only source on *Love Story* was what the *Tennessean* had reported some seventeen years prior. But the *Tennessean*, it turned out, has misquoted Segal, who had said nothing about Tipper.

In Henneberger's follow-up, Segal himself defended Gore: "Al attributed it to the newspaper . . . They conveniently omitted that part. *Time* thought it was more piquant to leave that out."

So did Coulter.

DEGREE OF DISHONESTY: 6
ANALYSIS: It's a small detail, but Coulter uses it so often—and so flagrantly disregards the truth—that we're giving this one an above-average score.

6. FACT CHECK ANN COULTER: THE SELMA LIE. Live by LexisNexis, die by LexisNexis. That certainly seems to be the case with Ann Coulter's latest book, *Slander*. Yesterday we exposed a blatantly false statement in her book about the use of the phrase "liberal Republican" in the *New York Times*, and today we expose another. Here is the relevant passage, from p. 199 of *Slander*:

> Since abortion is not the left's proudest moment, liberals prefer to keep reminiscing about the last time they were giddily self-righteous. Like a senile old man who keeps telling you the same story over and over again, liberals babble on and on about the "heady" days of civil rights marches. Between 1995 and 2001, the *New York Times* alone ran more than one hundred articles on "Selma" alone. I believe we may have revisited this triumph of theirs sufficiently by now. For anyone under fifty, the "heady"

days of civil rights marches are something out of a history book. The march on Selma was thirty-five years ago.

Tapped smelled a rat here. Maybe it was Coulter's repetition of the word "alone"; or maybe it was the fact that the famous 1965 "Bloody Sunday" march was *from* Selma to Montgomery, not a march "on" Selma. So we searched the *New York Times* archives on LexisNexis for the word "Selma" for the years 1995–2001. This produced 776 total hits. Of these, 424 were death notices, 18 were wedding announcements, 25 were other sorts of paid notices, 5 were in photo captions, and 234 were either: a) contents listings; b) people with the name Selma; c) references to Selma, California; or d) references to Selma, Alabama that had nothing to do with civil rights (b, c, and d include letters and op-eds as well as regular articles). Of the remaining 70 items, in our judgment only 16 were centrally concerned with historic happenings at Selma from the civil rights era. The other 54 contained brief mentions of Selma and civil rights but appeared in articles on different topics. Once again, Coulter's dubious claim—that "between 1995 and 2001, the *New York Times* alone ran more than one hundred articles on 'Selma'"—is false.

DEGREE OF DISHONESTY: 5
ANALYSIS: Another misdemeanor for Coulter. It's hard to tell whether this one resulted from deliberate deceit or incorrigible stupidity.

7. FACT CHECK ANN COULTER: LIBERAL CHEAP SHOTS. As Tapped readers know, we've been fact checking Ann Coulter's new

book with some regularity lately. And we've got some more on this today, but first, a couple of asides. Lest we be accused of bias against Coulter—as opposed to mere animus—let us note that she actually isn't wrong about *everything*. Yes, we know it's a shock.

Now that that's said, though, we'd like to get on to the various problems with Coulter's book. Coulter, herself a paragon of high-minded political dialogue, charges that the left resorts to *ad hominem* low blows and cheap shots on conservatives, especially women. On p. 17 of *Slander*, she asks rhetorically: "[W]hich women are constantly being called ugly? Is it Maxine Waters, Chelsea Clinton, Janet Reno, or Madeline Albright? No, none of these. Only conservative women have their looks held up to ridicule because only liberals would be so malevolent."

Coulter apparently forgot John McCain's notorious joke about Chelsea Clinton: "Why is Chelsea Clinton so ugly? Because Janet Reno is her father." And let's not forget Jay Leno calling a man dressed as Reno an "ugly bitch."

Now, is this a "fact check"? Well, note that Coulter says categorically, "No, none of these"—i.e., none of these women are frequently being called ugly. Coulter's point about low blow attacks is well taken, but her comment plainly isn't true.

DEGREE OF DISHONESTY: 6
ANALYSIS: How could anyone honestly claim that Chelsea Clinton hasn't suffered slights based on her appearance? If Ann Coulter had a movie made about her, it would have to be titled "Say Anything."

8. FACT CHECK ANN COULTER: RONALD REAGAN, COLD WAR HERO.

In her new book, *Slander*, Ann Coulter repeats herself a number of times on a number of points (and we use the term "points" here loosely). Her most beloved mantra, however, is Ronald Reagan's heroic Cold War victory. Coulter returns to Reagan as a sacred mantra, reiterating at least ten times her assertion that Reagan "won the Cold war" (see pp. 16, 33, 34, 125, 130, 132-33, 134, 145, and 197).

Now, mind you, Coulter's book isn't about Reagan. She simply uses Reagan's Cold War victory as the ultimate trump card against liberals who criticized Reagan, then and now. How can they call him stupid, she asks—and fiscally irresponsible, and a supporter of brutal third-world regimes—when "the ripe old fellow single-handedly won the Cold War, ending the forty-year threat of nuclear annihilation"? (Aside: Will someone please tell India and Pakistan to get with the program? Nuclear brinksmanship is so fifteen years ago—it went out with shoulder pads and good punk rock.)

The obvious objection to Coulter is that both the collapse of the Berlin Wall and the end of the Soviet Union took place while Bush Sr. was president. So at the very least, she ought to explain how they're Reagan's doing (she doesn't). More importantly, though, the frequently-touted argument that Reagan deserves credit for exhausting the Evil Empire through huge increases in military spending (with which the Soviets were forced to keep pace) is flawed. Soviet documents released in the 1990s reveal that Reagan's defense policies had little effect on Soviet spending (see, for example, Jonathan Kwitny's *Man of the Century*). The Soviet Union was going to collapse under its own weight no matter how many peasants U.S.-trained death squads murdered in El Salvador. Reagan deserves credit for disarmament efforts, but those certainly had support from Democrats—as, to be fair, did huge budget deficits.

DEGREE OF DISHONESTY: 5
ANALYSIS: Cold War debates are always murky, and Coulter isn't the first to lionize Reagan, so she isn't lying. Still, Coulter never bothers to back-up her claim with any historical argument, even a flawed one. She glibly refers to Reagan's "winning" as though it were common knowledge, substituting soggy repetition for evidence.

9. FACT CHECK ANN COULTER: MEDIA DARLING AL GORE. This, gentle reader, is the mother of them all. Make sure you're sitting down. Thanks to Coulter whistle-blower K.M.

On page 139 of her new book, *Slander*—now a bestseller— Ann Coulter describes how cruelly the media treated George W. Bush during the election. By contrast, she reports:

> [T]he press maintained radio silence on stories embarrassing to Gore. For example, . . . Al Gore couldn't pick George Washington out of a lineup. In a highly publicized stop at Monticello during Clinton's 1993 inaugural festivities, Gore pointed to carvings of Washington and Benjamin Franklin and asked the curator: 'Who are these guys?' He was surrounded by reporters and TV cameras when he said it. Only one newspaper, *USA Today*, reported the incident.

Coulter isn't wrong if, by "only one newspaper," she actually means "dozens of newspapers." In the immediate aftermath of the incident, references to Gore's gaffe appeared in *USA Today*, *Newsday*, *The Washington Times*, London's *Evening Standard*, and, the coup de grace, *two articles* in Coulter's favorite bulwark of liberal bias, the *New York Times*. The Associated Press also ran a story with the incident in its headline, so many local papers probably picked it up.

But wait! There's more! The authors of one of the *New York Times* articles were none other than Maureen Dowd and Frank Rich, two of Coulter's most reliable liberal scapegoats, who were both reporters in 1993 when the incident occurred. If these two are co-leaders of the vast, left-wing conspiracy, they sure dropped the ball.

Had enough of the love? We're still not done yet because . . . Coulter also misquoted Gore! His actual words were "Who are these people?" not "Who are these guys?" It's a small error, but it obviously makes Gore sound more disrespectful of the founding fathers, and even the *USA Today* article Coulter did find got the quotation right.

DEGREE OF DISHONESTY: 7

ANALYSIS: Either Coulter is purposefully lying, or she is breathtakingly incompetent, even using her favorite research tool, LexisNexis. Have you no sense of decency, madam, at long last?

Blaming of the Shrew

from *The Washington Post* (8/15/02)

Richard Cohen

May I say something about Ann Coulter? She is a half-wit, a termagant, a dimwit, a blowhard, a worthless silicone nothing, physically ugly and could be likened to Eva Braun, who was Hitler's mistress. As it happens, these are all descriptions or characterizations Coulter uses for others in her book, *Slander*. It ought to be called *Mirror*.

The book is now the No. 1 bestseller in the nation. If I were writing this column as she has written the book, everything I wrote above would be footnoted. For instance, the deft Eva Braun crack was aimed at Katie Couric. Coulter calls the "Today" host "the affable Eva Braun of morning TV." You can, as they say, look it up.

In fact, you can look up almost anything you want in this book. It has 780 footnotes and makes frequent references to LexisNexis, the computerized research service. The effect is to give the book a scholarly air, but the method is to cast as wide a net as possible for every idiotic remark made by anyone—and I do mean anyone —on the left or who happens to be pro-choice or, worse, a feminist.

Thus, Christie Todd Whitman, the former governor of New Jersey and the current head of the Environmental Protection Agency, is called a "dimwit" and a "birdbrain." Sen. Jim Jeffords (I-Vt.) is a "half-wit." Gloria Steinem is a "deeply ridiculous figure" who "had to sleep" with a rich liberal to fund *Ms.* magazine— all of which makes her a termagant, which is a shrew. For some reason, though, someone found her attractive.

On the other hand, conservatives—real, true, authentic conservatives like Coulter—are the sweetest, nicest, most moral people alive. No one could put it better than Coulter herself: "The point is that conservatives are the most tolerant (and long-suffering) people in the world."

This may explain how Coulter came up with a really tolerant way of dealing with the Islamic world: "We should invade their countries, kill their leaders and convert them to Christianity," she wrote last fall in her National Review Online column. For some reason, the intolerant *National Review* fired her.

Is it time for an intervention? I ask this because such anger, such intolerance, such rage, such a compulsion to denigrate and to distort is hardly based on any reality. If, as Coulter says, liberals control the media and much of the animal and plant kingdoms, then how is it that the president du jour and others of recent times—Eisenhower, Nixon, Ford, Reagan and Bush the Elder—happen to be conservatives? I must be missing something here.

Such harrumphing says something not only about Coulter but about her audience. Who are the people who read such tripe, who listen to talk radio and its chorus of conservatives (nary a liberal on the air) and who buy books such as the one under examination today?

What explains their rage and, while I am asking questions, could you think of another commentator—especially one on the left—who could have written what Coulter did about Muslims and go on to bestsellerdom? Being conservative is like being criminally insane: You can't be held accountable.

Could it be—is it remotely possible—that the anger and demagoguery Coulter assigns to liberals is really what the shrinks call "projection"? I mean, almost everything Coulter says about her ideological enemies could be said about her.

She is the master of the half-fact and the semi-story. She blames the liberal press for not revealing that Bob Packwood was forever hitting on his female staffers, but then neglects to mention it was the odiously liberal *Washington Post* that broke the story. She uses David Brock's book on Anita Hill to skewer Clarence Thomas's critics, but fails to mention that Brock himself renounced the book.

Ah, but I am one of the people she skewers—maybe one of the "pathetic little parakeet males" who are always liberals. (For some reason, Coulter has a need to question the manliness of liberals; against all evidence, she even refers to Bill Clinton as "IMPOTUS.") And yet, some of what she writes about me is true. I have not always been wise and at times I have strayed from liberal orthodoxy.

I concede that at one place in the book I scribbled "good point!" in the margin. I tell you that so you can turn to that page in the bookstore and skip the painful rest.

See, Ann, liberals can be compassionate.

"When contemplating college liberals, you really regret once again that John Walker is not getting the death penalty. We need to execute people like John Walker in order to physically intimidate liberals, by making them realize that they can be killed, too. Otherwise, they will turn out to be outright traitors."
—Ann Coulter, February 2002

When Right-Wing Fembots Attack

from Salon.com (6/27/02)

Charles Taylor

Golly, it's tough being a conservative! Here's a typical day that a member of the American right must endure as imagined by Ann Coulter in her new screed "Slander: Liberal Lies About the American Right." Wake up to Katie Couric haranguing Charlton Heston about gun control or claiming hate speech is what killed Matthew Shephard. Flip the channel to Bryant Gumbel—but not before you put Aunt Tillie back to bed to keep her from seeing "smut peddler" Hugh Hefner asked his views on the presidential campaign. Pick up the *New York Times* and read trumped-up articles about the alleged threat of the religious right or something derogatory about President Bush.

If that doesn't have you ready to crawl back in the hay with Aunt Tillie and you still manage to summon the strength to make it through the day, there's more to be endured at the end of it. In the evening, you've got to face Dan Rather "falsely accusing Republicans of all manner of malfeasance." If you decide to relax by taking in a movie you'll see "kind-hearted abortionists, Nazi priests, rich preppie Republican bigots, and the dark night of fascism under Senator Joe McCarthy." Gee willikers, what's a right-winger to do?

Coulter could probably have a day much more to her liking by skipping the TV and heading straight for the radio, tuning in to hear Rush Limbaugh talking about "feminazis" or G. Gordon Liddy giving instruction on the most effective way to kill federal agents ("aim for the head"). She could pick up the *Washington Times* or the Op-Ed page of the *Wall Street Journal*. She could change channels to Fox News and listen to the headlines of the day from Brit Hume. Or tune in to Alan Keyes on MSNBC or Bill O'Reilly (though, Coulter tells us, he's not really a conservative since he's against the death penalty). If she felt like an evening out, she could go see *The Sum of All Fears* and relive the thrill of the Russian threat, or rent *The Patriot* and groove to its vision of government as an alien force that will burn your home and kill your children. Or, if a quiet evening is more to her taste, she could relax with her vintage collection of Everett Dirksen records, or perhaps peruse such literary classics as "Six Crises" or "God and Man at Yale." It's her choice.

But just like the liberals she hates—the ones who think Fox News is a threat to the nation or who want to keep Eminem's "hate speech" off the radio and MTV—Coulter knows the rhetorical value of crying coercion. The easiest way to protest speech that offends you is to act as if you are forced to listen to it. Rather than doing the work of finding media in tune with your views—not especially hard for either a conservative or a liberal—it's more dramatic to portray yourself as an oppressed victim à la "1984" enduring the lies of "newspeak."

Coulter, an attorney and one of the "elves" who aided Paula Jones in her lawsuit against Bill Clinton, is too combative to ever envision herself as a hapless Orwellian drone. The self-portrait that emerges from "Slander" and from her regular TV appearances (which must have somehow been arranged when the liberal ayatollahs who control the media were asleep on the job) is of a freedom fighter in Manolo Blahniks, tirelessly pointing out the liberal propaganda that threatens free speech and the Republic itself, preferably in a chic and simple outfit that will take her from policy meetings to television interviews to cocktail parties without missing a beat of her busy day.

Coulter is the most visible and vociferous of the conservative fembots (hereafter known as the CFs) who have emerged in the last few years. Her mob-hit style of discourse is captured by David Brock in his tinny, gossipy mea culpa *Blinded by the Right* when he quotes her, speaking in reference to Bill Clinton, wondering whether it would be better "to impeach or assassinate." Some of her colleagues seem to have fallen out of the spotlight, depriving conservatives of media heroes and liberals of favored targets ("Coo, coo, ca-choo, Laura Ingraham, the Nation turns its lonely eyes to you"). But there are still enough around to make the soon-to-be-late "Politically Incorrect" look like "The Dating Game" as fantasized by the Young Americans for Freedom.

Besides Coulter there's the likes of Kellyanne Conway (nee Fitzpatrick), Lisa Pinto of the Oxygen Channel's "SheSpan" (catchy) and Dr. Monica Crowley. We have yet to see their glamorous equivalent among young male conservatives where the closest thing to a star is Tucker Carlson on "Crossfire," playing Jimmy Olsen to Robert Novak's cranky Perry White ("Great Goldwater's Ghost!"), who in turn is on guard against James Carville's Lex Luthor.

The media stardom of the CFs is a perfectly logical phenomenon, one that actually started before the trend of TV news outlets (like CNN and CNN Headline News) making the move to younger, "camera-friendly" anchors. The CFs' demeanor and presentation is carefully calculated to counter the traditional image of Republicans as uptight, cigar-chomping fat cats. And probably some of the resentment against these young women has come from liberals who wish that the left could be represented by their own spangly equivalents. (To anybody who doesn't think liberals could use some pizazz, I offer these four words: Sex God Warren Christopher.) Be careful what you wish for.

The views of the CFs emulsify like a perfect mayonnaise, but what they share apart from ideological consistency is a uniformity of attitude. I don't know the social background of Coulter, Ingraham, Conway or Pinto, but I've encountered their type before. They are the essence of the white, privileged kids at the small New England college I attended during the conservative heyday of the early Reagan years. What characterized those kids and what characterizes the CFs is that they seem unaware that not everyone shares their privileged existence, or seem to believe that anyone who doesn't has only themselves to blame. It's a small world, after all, and the CFs are absolutely secure about their place in it and the rightness of their views.

Nobody does smug like Ann Coulter. Like the other CF sorority gals, she is always ready to flash a look of incredulity at anyone stupid enough to hold beliefs different from her own. It's a look of self-satisfied disdain, and she's got it down as perfect as Edgar Kennedy's slow burn. For all of her jibes at the snobbishness of liberals who patronize the people they purport to be championing—and she is often quite right about that—Coulter doesn't project a sense that she is speaking for anyone beyond her little clique. She has none of the populist demagogue's gift for humor (sarcasm isn't the same thing) or geniality, two of the things that made Rush Limbaugh so popular. (The guy conducts his show something like the DJ he once was, performing his political rants as patter. You half expect him to segue into an ad for drag-racing or spin "a hot new platter from the Shirelles.")

There's no point arguing with someone like this, no matter what side she's on. And predictably, "Slander" is not an argument for balance in the media or for civility in political discourse, even though it pretends to be. "Instead of actual debate about ideas and issues with real consequences," Coulter fumes, "the country is trapped in a political discourse that increasingly resembles professional wrestling." If you can read that sentence coming from the Chynna of the far right and not wet your pants with laughter, you've got more control than I do.

Coulter complains because the New York Times likened Tom DeLay's efforts to turn the nation into a theocracy to the Crusades and the Salem Witch Trials. She steams up at Ted Kennedy for saying that the logical extension of Robert Bork's constitutional vision, judging from his previous judicial opinions, would bring about the return of segregation, a decrease in rights for women and extraordinary powers to the police to override any right to privacy. She gets her thong in a bunch over commentators who point out similarities between Timothy McVeigh's anti-government beliefs and the demonizing of the very idea of government that came out of Newt Gingrich's 1994 Congress.

All of this she considers unforgivable rhetorical exaggeration, yet she has no trouble calling Bill Clinton a rapist. She compares liberals who favor affirmative action to the Ku Klux Klan (they're both practicing racial separatism). She derides as disingenuous liberals who claim people they disagree with have a right to say what they want (even though she herself begins a later sentence "The New York Times has every right to . . .").

In short, Coulter can call any liberal any name that strikes her fancy and yet pretend she still wants "actual debate about ideas and issues." And if you can't take her hard knocks, you're a "pantywaist" or a "girly-boy," as

Coulter called the editors of the *National Review* after they shit-canned her following an editorial in which she wrote, of Muslim nations, "We should invade their countries, kill their leaders and convert them to Christianity." That column provoked an outcry on the right as well as the left. When the *National Review* declined to run a follow-up in which Coulter argued, "We should require passports to fly domestically. Passports can be forged, but they can also be checked with the home country in case of any suspicious-looking swarthy males," Coulter, accused her editors of censorship, even though she'd ridicule any liberal who claimed the same thing. *National Review Online* editor Jonah Goldberg commented, "It's called editorial judgment, and there's a world of difference," proving himself able to make a distinction that's beyond many liberals and conservatives.

Coulter has a lot in common with the liberals she despises. Just as, for some liberals, there is no such thing as a principled conservative, in Ann Coulter's world there is no such thing as a principled liberal. And it seems there aren't even that many principled conservatives. To determine who passes muster and who doesn't, she applies standards of ideological purity that Stalin would admire. Phyllis Schlafly makes the grade, but not Bill O'Reilly. John McLaughlin passes, but not William Safire ("voted for Clinton"). Jerry Falwell squeaks by, but not Pat Robertson (wanted to drop the impeachment and spoke in favor of China's one-child policy). In the book's most hilarious moment she lauds the unshakable conservative credentials of right-wing publisher Henry Regnery by telling us he was deemed "the most dangerous man in America." Where? Why, in Pravda.

Getting mad at Coulter is exactly the reaction she sets out to provoke. Debating her on her "ideas" does about as much good as kicking a retarded puppy. She has no ideas and she's not a thinker. Here are a few of the plums awaiting any Little Jack Horner who sticks his thumb into "Slander":

- The "religious right" is a nonexistent creation of liberal paranoia.

- There was no conflict of interest when Fox News allowed Bush's cousin to call election night results.

- Rush Limbaugh's epithet "feminazis" is accurate because it refers only to the women who prefer abortion over childbirth.

- Television, newspapers, and magazines can inflict liberals on the public because, unlike radio, books and the Internet, they don't operate in the free market.

- "Liberals don't believe there is such a thing as 'fact' or 'truth'."

I could go on, citing claims and quotes, but since I do believe in fact and truth, I don't believe anything Ann Coulter says without seeing it in its original context. The following passage gives a good example of how "Slander" works:

"After Supreme Court Justice Clarence Thomas wrote an opinion contrary to the *clearly* expressed position of the

New York Times editorial page, the *Times* responded with an editorial on Thomas titled 'The Youngest, Cruelest Justice.' That was actually the headline on a lead editorial in the Newspaper of Record. Thomas is not engaged on the substance of his judicial philosophy. He is called 'a colored lawn jockey for conservative white interests,' 'race traitor,' 'black snake,' 'chicken-and-biscuit-eating Uncle Tom,' 'house Negro' and 'handkerchief head,' 'Benedict Arnold' and "Judas Iscariot'."

The passage is conveniently phrased to make it look as if the quotes, as well as the headline, appear in the *Times* editorial. They don't (notes in the back of the book identify the sources as former Surgeon General Jocelyn Elder's interview in *Playboy*, and Joseph Lowery at a meeting of the Southern Christian Leadership Conference quoted in the *New Yorker*). Coulter sets up the passage to give the impression that the *Times* called Thomas a "lawn jockey" and a "house Negro" and hopes that we won't notice that she's fudged it.

Convenience is Coulter's m.o. Dismissing the claim that echoes of the rationale for the Oklahoma City bombing can be heard on conservative talk radio, she neglects to mention G. Gordon Liddy's comments on how to effectively kill federal agents. A list that is meant to demonstrate that "liberals have been wrong about everything in the last half-century" includes the Civil Rights Act. She's not against it, but she labels the segregationist Southern Democrats who opposed it as "liberals." She omits the fact that the act was pushed through Congress (as was the Voting Rights Act a year later) by a Democratic president, a product of those segregationist party politics, who understood the moral necessity of the measures and fought like hell to achieve them.

Coulter cites numerous examples of conservative books described as "surprise bestsellers" in the press to demonstrate the media's inability to imagine anyone would want to read them. But what surprised people about the success of "The Closing of the American Mind," "Illiberal Education" or "The Bell Curve" was that the bestseller lists are not usually the province of dense, academic cultural studies, policy discussions or scientific (or, I should say, junk-scientific) theory. After all, no one expected Michael Harrington's "The Other America" or Camille Paglia's "Sexual Personae" to become bestsellers, either.

Coulter isn't wrong about everything. She scores some real hits when it comes to left-wing condescension toward the working class and the religious. In one of several examples, she cites a 1993 *Washington Post* report saying the "Gospel lobby" is made up of the largely "poor, uneducated, and easy to command" (i.e., dumb Southern "white trash," a phrase John Waters has rightly called "the last politically correct racist phrase"). She calls Michael Moore's dodgy documentary "Roger & Me" on the carpet for setting up the people it supposedly sympathizes with as hicks and rubes and fools.

And though she goes too far, she's got a point when she says, of the left's reaction to Sept. 11, "Here the country had finally given liberals a war against fundamentalism and they didn't want to fight it." The Taliban enacted the left's worst nightmare vision of the American religious right, yet waging war on them was denounced as xenophobia. With a few exceptions, Michael Walzer in *Dissent* prominently among them, the left's intellectual reaction to Sept. 11 was embodied by those two quislings Noam Chomsky and Susan Sontag, whose implicit view was that

America is too morally dirty to ever be justified in defending itself or retaliating against attack.

This inability to come up with new political frameworks to deal with new political realities was, Coulter points out, embodied in liberal complaints about "flag-wavers." It was as if showing solidarity with your country after 3,000 of your fellow citizens had been killed was equal to the worst, love-it-or-leave-it chauvinism. (At the College of the Holy Cross in Worcester, Mass., a faculty member who was a friend of Todd Beamer, the man killed in the plane that crashed in Pennsylvania, was prevented by her department members from placing a flag outside her office.)

Of course, Coulter can't leave one of her few cogent points alone. She has to push it to an absurd extreme and say that if Islamic terrorists had devoted as much energy to hating America as American liberals do, "they'd have indoor plumbing by now." (But, then what would swarthy males want with indoor plumbing?)

Toward the end of "Slander" comes a passage that can stand for the limitations of Coulter's intellect. "Between 1995 and 2001, the *New York Times* alone ran more than one hundred articles on Selma alone. [This sentence copyrighted by your Department of Redundancy Department.] I believe we may have revisited this triumph of *theirs* [emphasis added] sufficiently by now. For anyone under 50, the 'heady' days of civil rights marches are something out of a history book. The march on Selma was 35 years ago."

"History," in that passage, means the same thing as "dead." The triumphs of the civil rights era didn't occur in Coulter's lifetime, so it's past, done with (she may as well be saying, "Oh, not that tacky old Negro stuff again!"). That's a very strange notion for a conservative to espouse, one that goes against the very meaning of the word "conservative." And funny that an affirmation of the American principles of liberty and justice for all is "their" triumph (meaning, I assume, blacks and liberals) instead of a triumph for all Americans.

It's a definitive moment, the essence of the shallowness and insularity that the CFs epitomize. It's politics and history and culture as a clique, a coffee klatch, a night spent mooning with your girlfriends over "An Affair to Remember." And it's fatal to Coulter's efforts to represent herself as a thinker. Even those in opposition to a culture have to be able to engage it rather than shut it out or sarcastically dismiss it.

We all know that liberals hate Ann Coulter and her sisters. But what about conservatives? Do they really want to be represented by this nonthought, this conscious shunning of history? There's no reason conservatives shouldn't be as susceptible to media glitz as everyone else. So it's no surprise and no sin that the notion of young, glammed-up women touting conservative ideology holds some appeal for them. But the smugness and conspicuous lack of experience and seasoning in these telebimbos should give conservatives pause. Coulter and her brood could benefit from a little conservative ideology themselves. Arguing with them is like paying attention to disobedient children. They should be treated like spoiled brats who mouth off. Put them over the knee, paddle their fannies, tell them to wipe that smirk off their face and to speak up only when they've learned something about the world.

ANAGRAM

Ann Coulter
Real con nut

The Wisdom of Ann Coulter
from *The Washington Monthly* (10/2001)
The Washington Monthly staff

After the September 11 attack masterminded by a terrorist hoping to spark a religious war, virtually every official and pundit knew better than to take the bait. Except for conservative commentator Ann Coulter, who wrote in a syndicated column on September 12 that in responding to terrorists "we should invade their countries, kill their leaders and convert them to Christianity."

The column outraged the public, but conservatives, including *National Review* editor Richard Lowry, ascribed Coulter's column to grief over the loss of a friend in the attacks. But the following week, Coulter was at it again: "Congress could pass a law tomorrow requiring that all aliens from Arabic countries leave. . . . We should require passports to fly domestically. Passports can be forged, but they can also be checked with the home country in case of any suspicious-looking swarthy males." This time Lowry spiked her column. Coulter responded by calling Lowry and his staff censorious "girly boys." Lowry then dropped her as a contributing editor. Other conservative leaders also condemned her comments.

What's curious is that Coulter's comments aren't all that different, in tone and style, from hundreds of others she's made over the years. But in the past, her ire was directed at her domestic political enemies—for which she drew fulsome praise from conservatives. Last year, the Media Research Center presented Coulter with its "Conservative Journalist of the Year" award. The Clare Boothe Luce Policy Institute bestowed upon her its annual conservative leadership award "for her unfailing dedication to truth, freedom and conservative values and for being an exemplar, in word and deed, of what a true leader is."

Coulter is spinning her downfall as a new kind of terrorist-war McCarthyism. "People are hysterical about speech right now," she told The Washington Post's Howard Kurtz. "Everyone's comments are being taken out of context and wildly misinterpreted." At the risk of further decontextualization, here are some of Coulter's past comments:

"[Clinton] masturbates in the sinks."
—Rivera Live 8/2/99

"God gave us the earth. We have dominion over the plants, the animals, the trees. God said, 'Earth is yours. Take it. Rape it. It's yours.'"
—Hannity & Colmes 6/20/01

The "backbone of the Democratic Party" is a "typical fat, implacable welfare recipient"
—Syndicated column 10/29/99

To a disabled Vietnam vet: "People like you caused us to lose that war."

—MSNBC

"Women like Pamela Harriman and Patricia Duff are basically Anna Nicole Smith from the waist down. Let's just call it for what it is. They're whores."

—Salon.com 11/16/00

Juan Gonzales is "Cuba's answer to Joey Buttafuoco," a "miscreant," "sperm-donor," and a "poor man's Hugh Hefner."

—Rivera Live 5/1/00

On Princess Diana's death: "Her children knew she's sleeping with all these men. That just seems to me, it's the definition of 'not a good mother.' . . . Is everyone just saying here that it's okay to ostentatiously have premarital sex in front of your children?" . . . "[Diana is] an ordinary and pathetic and confessional—I've never had bulimia! I've never had an affair! I've never had a divorce! So I don't think she's better than I am."

—MSNBC 9/12/97

"I think there should be a literacy test and a poll tax for people to vote."

—Hannity & Colmes 8/17/99

"I think [women] should be armed but should not [be allowed to] vote."

—Politically Incorrect 2/26/01

"If you don't hate Clinton and the people who labored to keep him in office, you don't love your country."

—*George* 7/99

"We're now at the point that it's beyond whether or not this guy is a horny hick. I really think it's a question of his mental stability. He really could be a lunatic. I think it is a rational question for Americans to ask whether their president is insane."

—*Equal Time*

"It's enough [to be impeached] for the president to be a pervert."

—*The Case Against Bill Clinton*,
Coulter's 1998 book

"Clinton is in love with the erect penis."

—*This Evening with Judith Regan*,
Fox News Channel 2/6/00

"I think we had enough laws about the turn-of-the-century. We don't need any more." Asked how far back would she go to repeal laws, she replied, "Well, before the New Deal . . . [The Emancipation Proclamation] would be a good start."

—*Politically Incorrect* 5/7/97

"If they have the one innocent person who has ever to be put to death this century out of over 7,000, you probably will get a good movie deal out of it."

—MSNBC 7/27/97

"If those kids had been carrying guns they would
have gunned down this one [child] gunman. . . .
Don't pray. Learn to use guns."
            —*Politically Incorrect* 12/18/97

"The presumption of innocence only means you
don't go right to jail."
            —*Hannity & Colmes* 8/24/01

"I have to say I'm all for public flogging. One type
of criminal that a public humiliation might work
particularly well with are the juvenile delinquents,
a lot of whom consider it a badge of honor to be
sent to juvenile detention. And it might not be such
a cool thing in the 'hood to be flogged publicly."
            —MSNBC 3/22/97

"Originally, I was the only female with long
blonde hair. Now, they all have long blonde hair."
            —CapitolHillBlue.com 6/6/00

"I am emboldened by my looks to say things
Republican men wouldn't."
            —*TV Guide* 8/97

"Let's say I go out every night, I meet a guy and
have sex with him. Good for me. I'm not married."
            —*Rivera Live* 6/7/00

"Anorexics never have boyfriends. . . . That's one
way to know you don't have anorexia, if you have
a boyfriend."
            —*Politically Incorrect* 7/21/97

"I think [Whitewater]'s going to prevent the First Lady from running for Senate."
—*Rivera Live* 3/12/99

"My track record is pretty good on predictions."
—*Rivera Live* 12/8/98

"The thing I like about Bush is I think he hates liberals."
—*Washington Post* 8/1/00

On Rep. Christopher Shays (D-CT) in deciding whether to run against him as a Libertarian candidate: "I really want to hurt him. I want him to feel pain."
—*Hartford Courant* 6/25/99

"The swing voters—I like to refer to them as the idiot voters because they don't have set philosophical principles. You're either a liberal or you're a conservative if you have an IQ above a toaster."
—*Beyond the News,*
Fox News Channel 6/4/00

"My libertarian friends are probably getting a little upset now but I think that's because they never appreciate the benefits of local fascism."
—MSNBC 2/8/97

"You want to be careful not to become just a blowhard."
—*Washington Post* 10/16/98

Short Take

Ann Coulter
The Beast staff

from BuffaloBeast.com (2002)

The phenomenon we all should have seen coming; the merger of bimbo sex appeal and neo-fascist vituperation. In an age when every Hollywood hero is a CIA administrator and people express their rebelliousness by playing the stock market, it only makes sense that we'd have a sex symbol who lobbies to massacre foreigners and forcibly convert the survivors to Christianity.

If Ann Coulter had been around for the Third Reich Ice-Cream Social, Eva Braun wouldn't have stood a chance. Every time this woman opens her mouth, hordes of winged demons fly out and rip the flesh from unsuspecting public school children. Only a paranoid fascist accuses more than half a nation of treason. It's rumored that the film *The Ring* is actually a biopic of her childhood.

ANAGRAM

Ann Coulter
Unclean rot

Coulter thinks she can lie on television with impunity, and she's often—but not always—right.

Ann Coulter Goes to the Movies

from *The Nation* (11/05/03)
David Corn

Don't read this if you like Ann Coulter.
Don't read this if you want to believe Ann Coulter gets her facts straight.

The other night I was enlisted to appear on MSNBC's *Hardball* to discuss the controversy over the CBS miniseries on Ronald and Nancy Reagan. On the other side was Coulter, the over-the-top-and-over-the-edge conservative author whose latest book literally brands all liberals as treasonous. Conservatives and Republicans have howled that the Reagan movie was a travesty, complaining it portrays Reagan as out of it in the White House and callous toward AIDS victims. On air, I noted that since the movie, as far as I could tell, does not detail how Reagan had cozied up to the apartheid regime of South Africa, the murderous dictator of Chile, and the death-squad-enabling government of El Salvador, it indeed has a problem with accuracy. But the miniseries' true sin seems to be its schlockiness. The available clips make it look like *Dynasty* meets *Mommie Dearest* set in the White House.

Coulter started more restrained than usual, though she predictably bashed Hollywood liberals for trying to undermine the historical standing of a president they despised by resorting to trashy revisionism. Perhaps she even had a point. Who could tell what the producers were aiming at? But then she jumped the tracks. She claimed that the movie *Patton* was made by Holly-libs with "hatred in their hearts" for George S. Patton, the brilliant but erratic World War II general. These film-makers "intended to make Patton look terrible," she maintained, but because they produced an accurate work, the movie ended up making "Patton look great and people loved him."

Was *Patton* a left-wing Hollywood conspiracy that backfired? Host Chris Matthews immediately challenged her in his subtle fashion: "You are dead wrong." He pushed her for proof, and she replied, "That is why George C. Scott turned down his Academy Award for playing Patton." Coulter was suggesting that Scott had spurned his Oscar because the filmmakers plan to destroy Patton's image by portraying the general "as negatively as possible" had gone awry.

Matthews wasn't buying. "Who told you that, who told you that?" he shouted. Her oracle-like response: "It is well known." She added, "Why did you think he turned down the award, Chris? You never looked that up? It never occurred to you?"

Matthews retorted, "Because he said he wasn't going to a meat parade, because he didn't believe in award ceremonies." And Matthews was right. Following the show, I took Coulter's advice and did look it up. I found a 1999 obituary of Scott that noted he had stunned Hollywood in 1971 for being the first person ever to refuse an Academy Award. He had explained his action by slamming such awards as "demeaning" and he had dismissed the Oscar ceremony as a "two-hour meat parade." (Matthews receives extra points for getting this quote correct.) Coulter had twisted this well-documented episode into yet more proof that liberals—especially those in Hollywood—are conspiratorial traitors.

After I described this exchange to someone who once worked with her, he said, "That's Ann. She lives in her own world and she just makes things up." This interlude concerned a small matter. (Who knew we would be debating one of my favorite movies?) But this minor dustup provided evidence to support a serious charge. As Matthews remarked while wrapping up the segment, "Facts mean nothing to you, Ann." If so, why continue to have her on?

Coulter was at her most odious in her attempts to discredit disabled war veteran Max Cleland.

Coulter and Cleland

from *The Nation*'s "Daily Outrage" message board

Matt Bivens

02/17/2004

We'll get to the loathsome likes of Little Miss Treason shortly, but first let's look at the man she has libeled: Max Cleland.

Cleland lost both legs and an arm in Vietnam, wounds that could have destroyed a lesser man. Instead, he not only kept his life together, he made it all the way to the United States Senate. In the fall of 2002, control of Congress hinged on his seat, and the GOP leadership poured its black heart into his defeat. President George Bush visited Georgia five times to campaign against him, and a Republican ad campaign likened Cleland to—of course—Osama bin Laden. Old-school Republicans like John McCain and Chuck Hagel, who both served in Vietnam, were appalled. But the new-school Bushies, morals all a-AWOL, were pleased to do whatever it took to pick up Cleland's seat.

Fast-forward 18 months. Today, George W. Bush is scrambling to put a good face on how he spent the Vietnam war. (To recap: States-side, in a cush gig brokered by his daddy just 12 days before he'd have again been eligible for the draft, he learned at taxpayer expense to fly a fighter jet, then announced he wanted to campaign for an Alabama pal of Richard Nixon's, stopped showing up, then declined to provide that embarrassing urine sample and so lost his flight status, then "arranged it with the military" to leave early to go get an M.B.A. Mission accomplished!)

Those asking harsh questions about the President's frivolous relationship with his military duties include Cleland. This is driving the Bush Republicans crazy. After all, it's embarrassing to have a true-blue war hero point out that your guy is a true-blue phony.

So the new strategy is the old strategy: Smear Cleland.

How dare he question our President!

He must be a traitor!

And he's certainly no hero, says Coulter. After a spit-fleckled rant against those who have permitted themselves to question the Great Leader's National Guard service, she says: "If we're going to start delving into exactly who did what back then, maybe Max Cleland should stop allowing Democrats to portray him as a war hero who lost his limbs taking enemy fire on the battlefields of Vietnam.

"Cleland lost three limbs in an accident during a routine non-combat mission where he was about to drink beer with friends. He saw a grenade on the ground and picked it up. He could have done that at Fort Dix. . . . Luckily for Cleland's political career and current pomposity about Bush, he happened to do it while in Vietnam. . . .

"Cleland . . . didn't 'give his limbs for his country,' or leave them 'on the battlefield.' There was no bravery involved in dropping a grenade on himself with no enemy troops in sight."

Coulter's account has already been applauded by someone named Mark Steyn who writes for *The Washington Times*. "As Ann Coulter pointed out in a merciless but entirely accurate column, it wasn't on the 'battlefield.' It wasn't in combat," Steyn writes. "[Cleland] was working on a radio relay station. He saw a grenade dropped by one of his colleagues and bent down to pick it up. It's impossible for most of us to imagine what that must be like—to be flown home, with your body shattered, not because of some firefight, but because of a stupid mistake." (The clear implication is that Cleland was stupid enough to blow himself up and has to live with that.) Steyn goes on to say Cleland is happy "to be passed off" as a hero, because that makes him "a more valuable mascot."

It's hard to know how to continue, because all I want to do is direct an awful string of insults and profanity at Coulter and Steyn.

Instead, I'll just lay out Max Cleland's record.

First of all, Cleland was wounded during the siege of Khe Sanh.

Khe Sanh, for Christ's sake!

I know the smug Bush Republicans are utterly ahistorical, but surely they've heard of Khe Sanh?

Let's help them out. Here is a fine timeline by PBS of the Vietnam war for 1968. I'll quote a three-month stretch of it here, February, March and April:

FEBRUARY 23, 1968—Over 1,300 artillery rounds hit the Marine base at Khe Sanh and its outposts, more than on any previous day of attacks. To withstand the constant assaults, bunkers at Khe Sanh are rebuilt to withstand 82mm mortar rounds.

MARCH 6, 1968—While Marines wait for a massive assault, NVA forces retreat into the jungle around Khe Sanh. For the next three weeks, things are relatively quiet around the base.

MARCH 11, 1968—Massive search and destroy sweeps are launched against Vietcong remnants around Saigon and other parts of South Vietnam.

MARCH 16, 1968—In the hamlet of My Lai, US Charlie Company kills about two hundred civilians. Although only one member of the division is tried and found guilty of war crimes, the repercussions of the atrocity are felt throughout the Army. However rare, such acts undid the benefit of countless hours of civic action by Army units and individual soldiers and raised unsettling questions about the conduct of the war.

MARCH 22, 1968—Without warning, a massive North Vietnamese barrage slams into Khe Sanh. More than 1,000 rounds hit the base, at a rate of a hundred every hour. At the same time, electronic sensors around Khe Sanh indicate NVA troop movements. American forces reply with heavy bombing.

APRIL 8, 1968—US forces in Operation Pegasus finally retake Route 9, ending the siege of Khe Sanh. A 77-day battle, Khe Sanh had been the biggest single battle of the Vietnam War to that point. The official assessment of the North Vietnamese Army dead is just over 1,600 killed, with two divisions all but annihilated. But thousands more were probably killed by American bombing.

April 8, 1968, was also the day that Captain Max Cleland lost both legs and an arm. He had less than a week earlier already earned commendations for heroism during some of the bloodiest combat of the whole Khe Sanh siege—combat missions for which he had volunteered, so as to relieve stranded Marines and Army infantry. The order in which the President awarded him the Silver Star reads:

"Captain Cleland distinguished himself by exceptionally valorous action on 4 April 1968, while serving as communications officer of the 2nd Battalion, 12th Calvary during an enemy attack near Khe Sanh, Republic of Vietnam.

"When the battalion command post came under a heavy enemy rocket and mortar attack, Capt. Cleland, disregarding his own safety, exposed himself to the rocket barrage as he left his covered position to administer first aid to his wounded comrades. He then assisted in moving the injured personnel to covered positions. Continuing to expose himself, Capt. Cleland organized his men into a work party to repair the battalion communications equipment, which had been damaged by enemy fire. His gallant action is in keeping with the highest traditions of the military service, and reflects great credit upon himself, his unit, and the United States Army."

Here, in a speech he was invited to give about character, is how Cleland himself tells what happened next:

> "I remember standing on the edge of the bomb crater that had been my home for five days and five nights, stretching my six-foot, two-inch frame, and becoming caught up in excitement. The battle for Khe Sanh was over, and I had come out of it unhurt and alive! Five terrible days and nights were behind us. In spite of dire predictions, we had held Khe Sanh. I had scored a personal victory over myself and my fears. . . . My tour of duty in Vietnam was almost over. In another month I'd be going home. I smiled, thinking of the good times waiting stateside.
>
> "On April 8, 1968, I volunteered for one last mission. The helicopter moved in low. The troops jumped out with M16 rifles in hand as we crouched low to the ground to avoid the helicopter blades. Then I saw the grenade. It was where the chopper had lifted off. It must be mine, I thought. Grenades had fallen off my web gear before. Shifting the M16 to my left hand and holding it behind me, I bent down to pick up the grenade.
>
> "A blinding explosion threw me backwards."

Ann Coulter, the facts be damned, calls this "a routine non-combat mission where he was about to drink beer with friends," and says "there was no bravery involved." Mark Steyn says Cleland is happy "to be passed off" as a hero. And both, incredibly, characterize Cleland's wounds as good fortune.

But just because these two hacks think losing limbs to

advance their Republican political careers would be a lucky trade—hell, they've already given away their souls, what's an arm or a leg?—doesn't mean the rest of us share their warped priorities.

I mean, Khe Sanh!

02/20/2004

Never one to let the facts get in the way of a good story, Ann Coulter is standing by her bizarre assault on Max Cleland, the former Democratic Senator. Coulter still insists he's not a Vietnam war hero.

True, Cleland lost both legs and an arm—but Coulter has done us the important service of noting that those three limbs were not *shot off*, one by one, with an AK-47 wielded by an actual screaming Viet Cong. Ergo, they aren't combat injuries.

Our political discourse is vastly improved for Ann Coulter's important contribution. This incisive distinction of hers ought to go down in history with such classic formulations as "I smoked marijuana but I didn't inhale."

Coulter also cleverly seizes upon remarks by Cleland and others expressing frustration at the random meaningless of his wounds: In essence he hopped out of a helicopter straight into an exploding grenade dropped accidentally by another American. Cleland has the humility and subtlety to say there was nothing heroic in that, it was just fate, bad luck; Coulter slyly twists such remarks into a blanket statement that Cleland is no hero, he's just a shmuck who blew himself up.

But wait. Once again, here is the US Army's own

description of how, four days before he lost his limbs, Captain Max Cleland "distinguished himself by exceptionally valorous action on 4 April 1968 . . . during an enemy attack near Khe Sanh, Republic of Vietnam.

"When the battalion command post came under a heavy enemy rocket and mortar attack, Capt. Cleland, disregarding his own safety, exposed himself to the rocket barrage as he left his covered position to administer first aid to his wounded comrades. He then assisted in moving the injured personnel to covered positions. Continuing to expose himself, Capt. Cleland organized his men into a work party to repair the battalion communications equipment, which had been damaged by enemy fire."

So in building her extremely worthy and important case that Cleland's no hero, how does Coulter finesse this?

By omitting it.

Entirely.

She titles her latest ramble "File Under: 'Omission Accomplished'."

No kidding!

The Army says that Captain Max Cleland, disregarding his own safety during one of the heaviest rocket and mortar attacks of the entire Vietnam war, ran out to save injured comrades, moved them back to cover, and then rallied his men to keep doing their job.

Just four days later, with his tour of duty in Vietnam near an end, Captain Cleland accepted one last mission. Here is how Cleland's commanding officer describes that mission:

"Max Cleland was with the Battalion Forward Command Post in heavy combat involving the attack of the 1st Cavalry Division up the valley to relieve the Marines who were besieged and surrounded at the Khe Shan Firebase. The whole surrounding area was an active combat zone . . . Max, the Battalion Signal Officer, was engaged in a combat mission I personally ordered to increase the effectiveness of communications between the battalion combat forward and rear support elements: e.g. Erect a radio relay antenna on a mountain top. By the way, at one point the battalion rear elements came under enemy artillery fire so everyone was in harm's way.

"As they were getting off the helicopter, Max saw the grenade on the ground and he instinctively went for it. Soldiers in combat don't leave grenades lying around on the ground. Later, in the hospital, he said he thought it was his own but I doubt the concept of 'ownership' went through his mind in the split seconds involved in reaching for the grenade. Nearly two decades later another soldier came forward and admitted it was actually his grenade. Does ownership of the grenade really matter? It does not."

Cleland's former C.O. adds: "This Ann Coulter has written real slime."

Coulter says she is responding to "insinuations that I 'lied' about Senator Max Cleland." Insinuations? For my part I'm not insinuating anything: Ann Coulter lied.

"It is simply a fact that Max Cleland was not injured by enemy fire in Vietnam," Coulter writes—a brilliantly trenchant and valuable observation, and undeniably true. She goes on to lie, "He was not in combat," and also to lie, "he was not in the battle of Khe Sanh, as many others [including, apparently, the US Army] have implied."

"He picked up an American grenade on a routine non-combat mission," she lies, "and the grenade exploded." Well, the officer who sent him on that mission calls it a combat mission at Khe Sanh; but Coulter long ago learned to cherry-pick what suits her off of Lexis-Nexis, so she knows it was a routine day of beer-drinking.

Coulter has become the thing she claims to hate—a caricature of a 1970s hippy spitting at men in uniform—because she wants us all to stop talking about George W. Bush's frivolous relationship to his National Guard service.

But Bush himself told *The Houston Chronicle* in 1994 he joined the Guard because "I was not prepared to shoot my eardrum out with a shotgun in order to get a deferment. Nor was I willing to go to Canada. So I chose to better myself by learning how to fly airplanes." That's pretty straightforward: He joined the Guard to stay out of Vietnam, a war he supported. (All the more ironic, then, that he now orders the Guard into harsh Iraq duty, and then sanctimoniously parries questions about *his* Guard days by noting how, thanks to his policies, service in the Guard is now quite dangerous.)

Coulter, for her part, takes Max Cleland's loss of his legs in Vietnam and turns it into a story of . . . George Bush's heroism: " . . . the poignant truth of Cleland's own accident demonstrates the commitment and bravery of all members of the military who come into contact with ordnance. Cleland's injury was of the routine variety that occurs whenever young men and weapons are put in close proximity—including in the National Guard."

Oh, it brings a tear to my eye! The commitment and bravery of our President pulling strings to join a Vietnam-era States-side "champagne" unit—especially after he had the poignantly cautionary example of Max Cleland's injuries!

ANAGRAM

Ann Coulter
Rectal noun

Ann Coulter driving a horse-and-buggy. It's a thought . . .

Anabaptist Coulter

from Soundbitten.com (February 2004)

Greg Beato

A few weeks ago, Elizabeth Coblentz, author of a 10-year-old syndicated newspaper column called "The Amish Cook," died at the age of 66. According to the *Fort Wayne News-Sentine*, Coblentz wrote about "the trips she took by horse-drawn buggy, the clothes she sewed by hand, the corn she canned. And, of course, she shared cooking tips and recipes." Over the years she garnered a loyal following: around 100 newspapers were running her column at the time of her death.

Because "The Amish Cook" was the brainchild of a 19-year-old college entrepreneur who started his own news syndication service, rather than an Amish cook, the column won't end with Coblentz' passing. The obvious choice to replace her: Ann Coulter, the Golden Geyser of Truth. Part Presbyterian, part Catholic, and all Christian,[1] Coulter already lives her life in the service of the Almighty. Once content to toil humbly in the clergy of the Law, she switched career paths only after the Lord ordained it. "I was just bumbling along practicing law," she explained to the *St. Petersburg Times.* "I never sought this for myself . . . God just decided, we've got enough lawyers, you are supposed to be on TV."

Thus inspired, Coulter commenced with her televisual uplift in 1996. "I have to say I'm all for public flogging," she preached on MSNBC. "Let's say I go out every night, I meet a guy and have sex with him. Good for me, I'm not married," she rejoiced on CNBC's *Rivera Live.* "God gave us the earth. We have dominion over the plants, the animals, the trees. God said, 'Earth is yours. Take it. Rape it. It's yours,'" she evangelized on Fox News' *Hannity & Colmes.*

Now, can't you just picture Coulter in the midst of Pennsylvania farm country, sexually harassing a cornstalk?

And who can argue that the Amish aren't in sore need of such fervor? As devout as they may be, a distinctly cool fire fuels their faith. And while their unwavering commitment to Pilgrim-wear often passes for patriotism, the truth is that English is their third language,[2] they don't pay Social Security tax, they're steadfast pacifists who make Gandhi look like Genghis Khan, and they're famously cliquish, sort of like Goths without make-up.

Like liberals (who also love beards), they reap all the benefits of U.S. citizenship, without taking on any of the responsibilities—driving SUVs, hating Democrats and foreigners, watching TV. For this, we subject them to regular harassment, but these days, when all Americans must come together as Republicans, buggy-burning and the occasional assault are no longer enough. Instead, we need passionate intervention, persuasion, someone who, in between baking loaves of Friendship Bread, can convince the Amish that it's not electricity that is their enemy, but rather Saddam Hussein and people who live in Manhattan.

Give Coulter three months in their camp, and the ideological cat o' nine tails will flog these peacenik, Marxist, paleo-hippie para-liberals into genuine U.S. citizens.

And, of course, Coulter will benefit from the association too. Even though she is forced to spend most of her professional time in New York, Vail, and Aspen,[3] and most of her free time in Vail, Aspen, and The Hamptons,[4] her heart belongs to the heartland, or as she lovingly describes it in *Slander*, the "land of pork rinds."

"I loved Kansas City!" she told the *New York Observer* recently. "It's like my favorite place in the world . . . In Kansas City, all the parties were always organized around, like, a softball game, waterskiing, going on a ski trip together. Oh, I so loved it."

In Amish country, the parties are exactly the same, except that instead of playing softball, waterskiing, or skiing, Amish teens drink beer and blast their boom-boxes while cruising the countryside in their horse-drawn buggies. Coulter, a bourbon-swilling, margarita-slurping, chardonnay-pounding tippler who has been hitting bars and nightclubs since she was in junior high,[5] would fit right in. Indeed, *rumspringa*, the Amish custom that allows Amish teens to experiment with booze, premarital sex, and all the other temptations the Devil's playground has to offer, seems to fit Coulter like a (mo)hair shirt designed by Versace.

And, who knows, the quadragenarian playgirl, engaged so many times she has lost count,[6] might even get a husband out of the deal. Amish men may not possess the virile locker-room magnetism of Matt Drudge, whom Coulter has dubbed "the sexiest man alive,"[7] but they do wear hats.

And while Amish men may be big, bearded girly-boys who prefer Ordnung to ordnance, they're also accomplished cervixian snipers who typically father enough children to populate at least two Sunday morning pundit shows. With a potent Amish farmer as her mate, the vehemently pro-life Coulter may one day finally have it all: a loyal husband, a beautiful house in the country, a popular column, and a half-dozen tow-headed anti-abortions playing in the yard.

Coulter may also find the communal spirit that informs Amish life appealing too. In 1998, Michael Chapman, a former colleague of Coulter's at the publication *Human Events*, cited numerous instances in Coulter's 1998 book *High Crimes and Misdemeanors* that closely resemble passages he wrote in "A Case for Impeachment," a special supplement that *Human Events* published in 1997. While some Coultersnipes have characterized these identical and paraphrased passages as plagiarism, it appears that the incident was really just a literary form of Amish-style house-building, where everybody pitches in to help. Chapman volunteered to ghost-write Coulter's book; Coulter's publisher hired another ghostwriter instead; eventually Coulter decided to ghost-write her book herself, and somehow in that process, a few of Chapman's passages wound up in the final product. The point? In Amish country, pitching in on group projects isn't foreplay for girly-girl whining about insufficient credit or plagiarism: it's just a way of life.

Of course, as much as Coulter seems suited to that life, her new vocation will require some changes on her part. Currently, Coulter sleeps until noon and works in her underwear.[8] As The Amish Cook, she'd have to wear a bonnet too, and get up earlier. She'd also have to give up watching her favorite TV shows, *elimiDATE* and *Change of Heart*.[9] Ultimately, though, these are small sacrifices, because Coulter now faces a career-threatening dilemma: overwhelming success. Like many satirists, she operates best from a position of disenfranchisement. Her marginalization to the furthest reaches of MSNBC, Fox News, CNN, CNBC, and ABC? Her ostracization by the publishing industry for a ceaseless, soul-crushing, almost unendurable two months?[10] Such discrimination simply gave Coulter more perspective, better aim, a bigger constituency. Pushed to the dusty outskirts of the elite media power grid, she spoke not only for Washington and New York insiders, as most pundits do, but also for underprivileged people of privilege everywhere.

Still, Coulter's public, the "grasping acquisitive middle class" as she calls it in *Slander*, isn't stupid. It may tolerate an advocate for conservative truth who lies about her age.[11] It may tolerate a careerist manizer who praises abstinence and marriage while safe-sinning[12] her way through an all-you-can-eat man-buffet of Muslims,[13] FBI agents,[14] conservative pundits,[15] and Bob Guccione, Jr. (Burp.) It may tolerate a fierce defender of the First Amendment whose greatest aspiration is to "censor ABC, NBC, and CBS, shut down the *New York Times*, the *Washington Post*, the *LA Times*, *Time*, *Newsweek*, *US News and World Report*." But it also knows the difference between an affluent child of privilege who insists she really isn't that well-off, [16] and a card-carrying member of the media elite whose best-selling success obliges her to admit, "I haven't seen the royalty checks yet, but I think I'm rich. Until now, I never thought of myself that way."

In other words, Ann Hart Coulter, daughter of hard-scrabble New Canaan, where the average household income is $272,500, has moved on up. Once able to command only $10,000 per speaking engagement, she recently raised her price to $25,000.[17] Like other arrivistes before her, she will now have to prove that, despite her ascendancy to the pinnacle of American news media, she's still the same Chardonnay-sipping, Vail-vacationing man-of-the-beautiful-people that she's always been.

To reinforce his Every-Schlub persona after he started making millions, Howard Stern had to keep not-fucking his Long Island hausfrau until she couldn't stand it any longer. To retain the disenfranchised outsider persona that fueled his 1999 masterpiece, "The Slim Shady LP," along with the commercial success it engendered, Eminem had to become the pre-*Slander* Ann Coulter of MTV—*allowed* there, yes, but not, you know, *liked*.

But now everyone loves Ann Coulter, even if they hate her. "I'm not anxious to have a TV show. Who's gonna give me a TV show?" she asked *The New York Observer* in August 2002. Two months later, she told the *Westchester WAG* that "I've been getting offers for years to have my own show. I'm just not sure about it." Can you believe that? She's so hot, she's even getting retroactive offers. Her next book, already finished, working title *Traitor!*, will no doubt command a hefty advance. But now that she charges more for a single lecture than many of the real American "coupon-clippers" whom she verbally dry-humps in *Slander*[18] earn in a year, how will she continue to connect with them? There's really only one solution: Coulter must become The Amish Cook.

1. Aileen Jacobsen, "Bait and Twitch: Ann Coulter says she's baiting liberals to read her book," *Newsday*, August 20, 2002. ("Her mother is Presbyterian, her father Catholic, and there were in her family 'huge religious wars . . . .I just consider myself a Christian.'")

2. Jay Golan, *Frommer's Philadelphia and the Amish Country*, John Wiley & Sons, 2001. ("They are a trilingual people, speaking Pennsylvania Dutch [essentially a dialect of German] at home, High German at worship services [the German of Luther's Bible translation], and English with members of the larger society.")

3. *Booknotes*, C-SPAN, August 11, 2002. In an interview with Brian Lamb, Coulter said that she "tried originally writing [*Slander*] from L.A., Vail and Aspen."

4. Emily Freund, "Ann Coulter: She May Be Right," *The Westchester WAG*, October 2002. ("During the summer, she frequents 'The Hamptons—I have lots of friends with places there—and Connecticut, where I visit with family.' For winter getaways, Coulter can be found on the slopes. 'Skiing is my biggest extravagance. I usually go to Aspen or Vail over New Year's.'") In her book, *Slander*, Coulter writes: "Nothing would make liberal environmentalists so happy as an entire country that looked like the Hamptons: beautiful rich people living in solar-powered homes staffed with a phalanx of obedient servants who can't afford SUVs."

5. Emily Freund, "Ann Coulter: She May Be Right," *The Westchester WAG*, October 2002. Included with this article is a sidebar with the following text: "Favorite Drinks: Chardonnay, margaritas, and bourbon." The article also explains how Coulter's oldest brother, John, used to bring her to bars and nightclubs in New York when she was still in junior high school.

6. Toby Harnden, "I Love to Pick Fights With Liberals," *London Telegraph*, July 19, 2002. ("Coulter is still searching for Mr Right-Wing. 'I've been engaged many times. Four, I think.'")

7. George Gurley, "Coultergeist," *The New York Observer*, August 26, 2002.

8. *Booknotes*, C-SPAN, August 11, 2002. In an interview with Brian Lamb, Coulter said, "I think I have a greater life than anyone in the universe in fact. I sleep until noon. I work in my underwear."

9. Emily Freund, "Ann Coulter: She May Be Right," *The Westchester WAG*, October 2002. ("I love the dumb dating shows—Change of Heart and elimiDATE—they're like watching a car crash.")

10. Coulter initially had a contract with HarperCollins to publish the book that would eventually become *Slander*. But when her editor at HarperCollins died, she says the company cancelled her contract, forcing her to look for another publisher. "For two months, my agent shopped it around and no one would buy it," she told Brian Lamb in her C-SPAN interview. Shortly after she told Lamb this, the length of her ordeal increased by one-third. "My original publisher (Harper Collins) dumped me, we had to refund the advance, and Joni had to spend three months shopping it," she told the *Westchester WAG*.

11. Aileen Jacobsen's *Newsday* article, cited above, includes this sentence: "Media accounts that she's 40 are wrong, she maintains." Toby Harnden's *London Telegraph* article, cited above, includes this passage: "An air of mystery surrounds Coulter's age. She says she is 38 but her publicist puts her at 40." On September 6th, 2002, *Washington Post* columnist Lloyd Grove reported that the birth date on file for Coulter at the New Canaan, Connecticut voter registration office was Dec. 8, 1961, which would make her 40.

12. Coulter's position on sex is somewhat complicated, sort of like her position on her age. "I will never say publicly that, as a Christian, I think God says it's OK to have premarital sex or to have homosexual sex," she told the *London Telegraph*. "You know, that is why Christians are the most tolerant people in the world— because we know there's original sin. We know people do bad things. But it seems to me it's a much worse thing to go around saying that it isn't a sin to commit a sin. I mean—at least feel guilty about it." In other words, if you're a "devout Christian" (as Coulter describes herself

in *People* magazine) but you want to fuck Bob Guccione, Jr. without actually having to marry him, just feel guilty about it afterward. While Coulter "sort of [jokes]" in the *Telegraph* article that gays will burn in hell for having sex, or maybe just for being gay, she doesn't explain what she believes the penance for heterosexual premarital sex is, other than fucking Bob Guccione, Jr.

13. Lynda Wright, *People*, 07/29/02. ("Although Coulter is a devout Christian, her most recent boyfriend was a Muslim; their first date was on a Sunday morning at her church.")

14. Howard Kurtz, "The Blonde Flinging Bombshells at Bill Clinton," *Washington Post*, October 16, 1998. ("Then she began seeing Bob Guccione Jr., the controversial founder of *SPIN* magazine, until becoming disenchanted in March. Now she's involved with an FBI agent.")

15. George Gurley, "Coultergeist," *The New York Observer*, August 26, 2002. ("I've dated [Dinesh D'Souza], I've dated every right-winger.")

16. How rich was Coulter before she started describing herself as "rich"? Well, rich enough to maintain dual residences in Manhattan and Washington, DC. In the early '90s, she used to make over $100,000 a year as a corporate attorney. In 1998, she explained to the *Washington Post*'s Howard Kurtz that "she took a two-thirds pay cut, to $35,000" in 1994 to work for Senator Spencer Abraham (R-Mich.). "I thought you got welfare benefits at that level," she joked then. More recently, Coulter complained to C-SPAN's Brian Lamb about the tough lot of a freelance writer. When she told him that her first book, 1998's *High Crimes and Misdemeanors*, sold approximately 250,000 copies, he remarked, "That's a lot of money." "It's never enough money," she replied. "No, in fact someone just

told me, I don't know if this is true, that the median income for a writer in America is about $2,000. If you want to make money, being a writer isn't the way to go . . . It was a bad year last year." Of course, back then she was making only $10,000 per speaking engagement.

17. Emily Freund, "Ann Coulter: She May Be Right," *The Westchester WAG*, October 2002. ("In fact, she is in such high demand [for speaking engagements] that 'I had to raise my price recently from ten thousand to twenty-five thousand. For students, the fee is negotiable.'")

18. Chapter Two of *Slander*, which the Gucci-loving, Hamptons-vacationing Coulter calls "The Gucci Position on Domestic Policy," is where she most emphatically champions the "acquisitive middle class," the "working class," "ordinary people," "working-class Americans," and the "coupon-clippers." She also reveals that liberals are "snobs" and suggests that Republicans are "aggressively anti-elitist" "working-class Americans" who have little interest in the trappings of snobby liberal elitism, like Gucci and The Hamptons. Except when they wear Gucci or vacation in The Hamptons, that is.

RUSH LIMBAUGH

with quotes by Rush Limbaugh;

a cartoon by Ruben Bolling;

a riddle;
and anagrams

Most Americans know that Rush Limbaugh is a big, fat idiot—but few people understand the depths of his wicked folly. His regular listeners derive false comfort from his rants, which pander to their worst instincts. People who don't listen to his show typically have only a vague sense of Limbaugh's astounding hypocrisy and the damage he does to our democratic discourse.

Rush Limbaugh
from *What Liberal Media?* (2003)
Eric Alterman

Edward Monks, a Eugene, Oregon, attorney, calculates that in his city, conservatives enjoy a 4,000-to-zero hour advantage over liberals on the radio. He wrote in *The Register-Guard*: "Political opinions expressed on talk radio are approaching the level of uniformity that would normally be achieved only in a totalitarian society. . . . There is nothing fair, balanced or democratic about it." Monk noted that as recently as 1974, such domination would have been not only inconceivable, but illegal. Back then, the Federal Communications Commission was still demanding "strict adherence to the [1949] Fairness Doctrine as the single most important requirement of operation in the public interest—the sine qua non for grant for renewal of license." This view was ratified by the U.S. Supreme Court in 1969 when it reaffirmed the people's right to a free exchange of opposing views, with roughly equal time given to all sides, if demanded, on the public airwaves. The doctrine was overturned by the Reagan-appointed FCC in 1987. The chairman then, Mark Fowler, made clear his view that "the perception of broadcasters as community trustees should be replaced by a view of broadcasters as marketplace participants." Meanwhile, media companies, together with cigarette and beer companies, working with Republican Senator Bob Packwood, set up the Freedom of Expression Foundation to fight the fairness doctrine in the U.S. Court of Appeals for Washington, D.C. The companies won in a 2-to-1 decision in which the two judges ruling in their favor happened to be Robert Bork and Antonin Scalia. President Reagan vetoed attempts by Congress to reinstate the doctrine, and the net result has been the complete far-right domination of the nation's airwaves, owing entirely to what analysts call "marketplace realities."

The amazing career of Rush Limbaugh owes a great deal to that moment in history. It is testament to just how well success succeeds in the U.S. media, regardless of accuracy, fairness, or even common sense. Limbaugh's legendary lies and mythological meanderings have been rewarded not only with legions of listeners, but also with incredible riches—a contract said to be worth $250 million over seven years. It has also won him the respect of the media establishment. Limbaugh, for instance, has been treated to laudatory coverage in *Time* and *Newsweek* and was invited by host Tim Russert of *Meet the Press* to be a guest commentator on what is certainly the most influential political program on television. And yet Limbaugh is, to put it bluntly, deranged. Fairness and Accuracy in Reporting has published an entire book of Rushisms that have turned out to be false, unsubstantiated, or just plain wacko. It is not just, as Maureen Dowd put it, his obsession with "feminazis," "environmental wackos," Anita Hill, Jesse Jackson, Hillary Clinton, Teddy Kennedy, Mario Cuomo, homeless advocates, dolphins, spotted owls, trees, "commie libs," and "the arts and croissant crowd." Limbaugh pushes the bounds of good taste in any medium, not to mention simple human decency, such as the time on his now-defunct TV show, he asked, "Did you know there's a White House dog?" and held up a photo of then-thirteen-year-old Chelsea Clinton. Another time, he showed a picture of Secretary of Labor Robert Reich that showed him from the forehead up, as though that were all of his frame that the camera could capture. (The diminutive Reich had a bone disease as a child.) Even when Limbaugh is not insulting the looks of young girls or making fun of childhood diseases, his ideological flights of fancy should leave any even remotely discerning listeners shaking their heads in disbelief.

Still, Limbaugh can have a real impact on issues, irrespective of the crackpot notions that inform his views. When, in June 2002, the Bush Administration gave up its Sisyphean battle to deny the reality of global warming—a fact of life accepted by the entire panoply of world governments as well as virtually every climatologist of note in all of these nations, Rush was aghast. He knew better.

> When I first became aware of this story Sunday night, I thought about what I would say on Monday's program: "Well, folks, guess what? I have been wrong about global warming. The president says it is happening and that human beings are causing it, so I've been wrong." I couldn't say that because I don't think I am wrong. There are too many scientists out there whom I implicitly trust who have proven to me these predictions are basically apocalyptic doom and gloom based on raw emotion. Even the global warming advocates, to this day, will not tell you it is definitively happening.

Recall that the Bush Administration was not actually proposing to do anything about global warming. It had, in fact, put itself in the absurd position of predicting horrific consequences of global warming and yet remaining politically unwilling or unable to avert them. One might therefore draw the conclusion that Bush's cabinet reluctantly came to their long-averted conclusion, particularly given the criticism the administration received for refusing to go along with the Kyoto Protocol, a treaty that all the other civilized nations of the world had signed. But Rush was not fooled. Bush and company had, for reasons he did not explain, caved into "the environmentalist wacko coalition." The president had morphed into "George W. Algore." (Within twenty-four hours the White House retreated, retracting the president's admission that global warming was, in fact, real. In related news, the White House also announced that gravity was just a theory, too.)

Limbaugh is also, surprise, surprise, not a terribly competent student of history. In July 2002, a liberal caller sneaked onto his phone lines, initially pretending to be a dittohead, and chastised Rush for what the caller believed was the hypocrisy in the disparity between his treatment of Whitewater and Bush's Harken Oil stock sale. Rush became furious and explained himself thusly: "Everybody knows that Bill Clinton was corrupt, everybody knows that Bill Clinton was a lying, scheming SOB, everybody knows that Bill Clinton violated the law, he was held in contempt of court. Everybody knows that he was having BJs given to him in the oval office by an intern while 19 rangers and Delta Force members were dying in Somalia. Now if you want to compare him to Bush, you go right ahead. . . ." The U.S. intervention in Somalia ended in 1993. The blow jobs began in 1995. But that's close enough for Rush.

Even more bizarre than these fusillades is the following transcript, taken from Limbaugh's program on July 20, 2001, in which he actually seemed to make a serious argument that Tom Daschle, leader of the Democratic majority in the Senate, was none other than the Fallen One, the Duke of Darkness, Satan himself. I quote from an extended transcript as published on the Web site, Spinsanity.com:

> I have a question for you, folks, and I know that this is going . . . you have to listen very carefully here, this is going to push the envelope. . . . How many different versions of Satan, the devil, have you seen in your life? I mean, the comic book devil with the red face and the horns, seen that one. We've seen the Satanic devil of the horror films. We've seen the devil portrayed as just an average man, a human being, in the movie *Rosemary's Baby*. We've seen the comic devil of TV shows. We've even seen the smooth, tempting devil in Hollywood movies. Is Tom Daschle simply another way to portray a devil?
>
> . . . There is no desire on Daschle's part to bring people together. There certainly is no bipartisanship flowing through his veins, nor is he leading any bipartisan effort. There is no working with the president of any of this. He's criticizing Bush, he's attempting to further the notion that Bush is illegitimate, incompetent, unintelligent. . . . Just yesterday, as Bush winged his way to Europe on a crucial mission to lead our allies into the twenty-first century, with Europe's flagging economy,

talking about mutual defense in the twenty-first century, realistic environmental solutions, solutions for world poverty, not this stupid Kyoto stuff and not allowing the United States to be robbed blind by the U.N. and the poor nations of the world, up pops "El Diablo," Tom Daschle, and his devilish deviltry, claiming that George Bush is incompetent, criticizing Bush at the very moment he is engaging in these efforts to improve our relationship with these world leaders. . . . Hang in there, folks. Now don't go bonkers—the devil comes in many disguises as we all know. . . . Let me stretch this analogy just a little bit farther. What would your reaction be if I were to say that I think Daschle has cast a spell on the media?

Listening to Limbaugh, the idea that he enjoys genuine power in the political life of the nation leaves you shaking your head in awe and amazement. But it is impossible to ignore. Limbaugh's radio audience is the largest any program on the medium has enjoyed since the advent of television. President George H. W. Bush invited him for a White House sleepover, as well as to be his honored guest at his State of the Union address, seated next to Barbara Bush, in a demonstration of fealty and respect. Shortly thereafter, in 1993, *National Review* termed him "the leader of the opposition." William Bennett averred that Limbaugh "may be the most consequential person in political life at the moment." When the Republicans took the House back in 1994 in a profound and humiliating rebuke to President Clinton, Limbaugh's broadcast received a lion's share of the credit. *Washington Post* media reporter Howard Kurtz even defended nonsense like the above as "policy oriented." As Newt Gingrich's former press secretary Tony Blankley noted,

> After Newt, Rush was the single most important person in securing a Republican majority in the House of Representatives after 40 years of Democratic Party rule. Rush's powerful voice was the indispensable factor, not only in winning in 1994, but in holding the House for the next three election cycles. At a time when almost the entire establishment media ignored or distorted our message of renewal, Rush carried (and often improved) the message to the heartland. And where Rush led, the other voices of talk radio followed.

This influence cannot be said to have diminished markedly during the past decade, even after Limbaugh lost his most-favored targets when the Clintons left the White House. Much to his chagrin as a McCain supporter, William Kristol credits Limbaugh with rallying conservatives behind Bush during the 2000 presidential primaries. "He helped make it the orthodox conservative position that McCain was utterly unacceptable and also that Bush was fine, neither of which were intuitively obvious if you're a conservative," Kristol said. McCain's South Carolina political adviser, Richard M. Quinn concurred, adding that the Arizona senator never recovered, in his opinion, from Limbaugh's repeated descriptions of the conservative Republican as a "liberal" in an extremely conservative state. "I never polled on the impact of Limbaugh," Quinn told the *New York Times*. "But anecdotally,

I heard it all the time. You would hear on the street repetition of what Rush was saying about McCain. There was a general sense in the campaign that Limbaugh was definitely hurting us." Blankley put it bluntly: "Given the closeness of the election, but for Rush Limbaugh's broadcasts, we would now be led by President Al Gore." In the 2002 midterm elections, NBC used him as one of its analysts. And on September 11, 2002, Vice President Cheney had just one planned interview on his schedule to mark the hallowed anniversary of the tragedy of a year before: a phone interview with Rush Limbaugh. Cheney canceled his appearance at the last minute, citing his removal from public view to a "secure location," under the raised state of alert declared by federal officials as the reason for his no-show. Apparently his "secure location" did not contain a telephone.

Who listens to Limbaugh, and why? Stephen Talbot grappled with the question back in 1995.

Wizard of Ooze

from *Mother Jones* (May/June 1995)

Stephen Talbot

As we approach the millennium, this is the astonishing reality of American political life: A radio talk show host occupies center stage. Rush Limbaugh is an unlikely man for the role: a college dropout, fired from four radio jobs, twice divorced, obese, and insecure. Yet he has become one of the most influential forces in the country. Even his mother can't believe it.

If you're skeptical, too, talk to the 73 Republican freshmen. They attribute their stunning victory to Rush Limbaugh, citing polls that show people who listen to talk radio 10 hours or more per week voted Republican 3-to-1.

Limbaugh is the national precinct captain for the Republican Party. And he works the precinct hard, five days a week, three hours a day. Like an electronic ward boss, Limbaugh explains the issues, offers the conservative GOP spin, rallies the faithful, and turns out the voters. It is a virtuoso performance, his harangue leavened by bursts of rock 'n' roll, bad-boy jokes, and moments of self-deprecating humor. It was no mistake that the Republican freshmen anointed Rush the "majority-maker" and inducted him as an honorary member of the 104th Congress at their orientation last December.

Another guy who started out in radio, Ronald Reagan, recognized Limbaugh's importance back in 1992, when he declared Rush "the number one voice for conservatism in our country." But the Democrats have been in denial. Before the Republican landslide last November, Democratic strategists shrugged off Limbaugh's clout. "People who listen to the radio in the morning are normal people," declared Clinton political adviser Paul Begala. "People who listen to Limbaugh in the afternoon are has-been, shut-in malcontents. I don't pay much attention to right-wing, foam-at-the-mouth radio because they just talk to each other. It's 20 million people telling each other how they hate Hillary." It's also 20 million voters, energized and mobilized by Mr. Limbaugh, as a chastened Begala discovered.

Liberals and progressives have consistently misunderstood, ignored, and underestimated Rush Limbaugh and his 20 million fans. That's fine, if you don't mind waking up one day to find Phil Gramm in the White House and an occupying army of Newts on Capitol Hill. But if Democrats and what's left of the Left have any intention of getting back in the game, their first step must be an accurate, clear-eyed assessment of Mr. Bombast and his loyal dittoheads.

THE EVOLUTION OF RUSH

When it comes to defining their enemy, Democrats are stuck in a time warp. They still criticize the in-your-face ranter who performed "caller abortions" on air, ridiculed "feminazis," and mocked people dying of AIDS. These hurtful, offensive routines helped Rush build an audience of angry white males, but they also sparked protests.

During a 1990 guest appearance on the "Pat Sajak Show," then CBS' late-night program, Limbaugh was rattled by ACT UP hecklers. To restore order, the entire audience was ushered out and a dejected Limbaugh delivered his final words to an empty studio. A CBS executive said, "He came out full of bluster and left a very shaken man. I had never seen a man sweat as much in my life."

Since then Rush has recalibrated his act. Recently, he criticized "anyone who takes pleasure" in the revelation that former Olympic diver Greg Louganis has AIDS. "It's just sad," he told his listeners. Rush will still resort to a fag joke now and then. He still makes fun of the homeless. He can still be reprehensible. But the new Rush is focused on partisan politics. His show is duller, more predictable, more strategic.

The transformation began in 1992 when the Bush campaign was shocked to learn how much political weight Limbaugh could throw around. In the New Hampshire primary, Rush endorsed Pat Buchanan, and the hard-line conservative scored 37 percent of the vote. The scared Bush team quickly invited Rush to spend the night at the White House and to join Marilyn Quayle in the vice president's box at the GOP convention in Houston. Rush loyally denounced Ross Perot, who appealed to many of his own listeners, and he hit the campaign trail, introducing Bush at a "victory rally" in New Jersey.

Even Rush could not save Bush. But after Clinton's victory, when conservatives were dispirited and leaderless, Rush played a crucial role, offering an optimistic voice that promised a conservative backlash. "I'll never forget those dreary, dark, depressing, despondent days after that defeat in 1992," recalls Bush's political director, Mary Matalin. "All we had to hold us together was Rush Limbaugh. And I can remember sitting in my apartment, by myself, day after day, for weeks on end, and [listening to Rush's radio program] was a centerpiece of my day." Matalin, who now hosts her own cable TV talk show, says Limbaugh was the "only voice in that huge defeat, in the arrogance of the Clintonistas rushing into town, that really kept us collected."

William Buckley's *National Review* proclaimed Rush "the leader of the opposition." It wasn't long before Newt Gingrich took notice, and he and Rush teamed up to become a heavyweight tag team body slamming the Democrats.

All the president's men are dazed and confused. "I haven't quite got it figured out," admits Paul Begala. "I don't know if it's Gingrich working for Rush, or if it's Rush working for Gingrich, but neither of them is working for America."

As *Mother Jones* first reported, Newt conspired to crush Clinton's lobby reform bill. At the 11th hour, Gingrich suddenly objected to language in the bill that he himself had added, declaring that it would muzzle grassroots activists. He then faxed Limbaugh, who dutifully warned his dittoheads that the lobby bill was a plot to stifle free speech. By the next morning, congressional phones were ringing off the hook. A Republican filibuster in the Senate finally killed the bill.

When the Clintons unveiled their health care plan and dispatched a bus tour across the country to rally support, Limbaugh and other conservative talk show hosts put their listeners on red alert, announcing the tour schedule, urging protests, and reporting—often with on-scene phone calls—the resulting confrontations. The bus tour, which had been such an effective technique during the Clinton/Gore campaign, was a fiasco.

Similarly, Rush ambushed the president's crime bill, which had seemed a sure winner. When Limbaugh denounced it as "social pork," Republican strategist Bill Kristol was delighted. He furiously faxed memos to congressional Republicans, urging them to create gridlock and deny the Democrats any legislative victories during the '94 campaign.

"I don't think in the old days we would have had much of a chance," admits Kristol. "The president of the United States said it was a crime bill. A fair number of state and local officials liked it because they got money from it. But Rush Limbaugh and several others were able to label it as pork."

"You cannot underestimate, and you cannot overstate, the power of Rush Limbaugh," insists Mary Matalin. "What he's saying is sinking in out there."

No wonder. Rush has the volume, and he's mastered the language his listeners like to echo. Radio consultants even have a name for Rush's format: "nonguested confrontation." The host is free to pontificate, entertain, and intimidate to his heart's content—with no guests and only a few heavily screened callers to challenge whatever he might say. And he repeats the format for half an hour each weekday on his nationally syndicated TV show. "No one has had this uncontested monologue of political advocacy in the history of U.S. television," complains media watchdog Jeff Cohen of Fairness & Accuracy in Reporting. "Never been heard of."

THE BEST-LOOKING AUDIENCE IN TV?

Democrats are slowly, belatedly figuring out Rush. But they still don't seem to have nailed his listeners. I regard Molly Ivins as a national treasure, like bluesman John Lee Hooker or the San Francisco 49ers. But she's behind the curve about the typical Rush Limbaugh listener. Rush may be blaring from the AM radio in Bubba's battered pickup as he bounces down some backwoods road on the way to an NRA meeting. But Bubba is only part of Rush's audience. To get a better sense of Rush's core followers, you have to look at his TV studio audience. There, Bubba would be a catfish out of water.

"Is this the best-looking audience in television or what?" Rush asks the adoring, cheering crowd in his New York studio. Most of them are white men—whiter than the Republican delegation in Congress—between the ages of

18 and 54. But they are not trailer park trash, survivalists in battle fatigues, or rednecked Klansmen. They are wearing suits, sports coats, and ties. A few are military men in dress uniform, clean-shaven and pink-cheeked. Women are welcome, as long as they behave. And on the surface anyway, these folks are not seething with anger and hatred. In fact, they appear to be happy, deliriously happy. And why not? Their side is winning.

So who are these people, and why are they listening to Rush? That's what I set out to discover last summer when I began producing the documentary "Rush Limbaugh's America" for the PBS series "Frontline." We crisscrossed the country, interviewing self-proclaimed dittoheads— people who say "dittos, Rush" as a shorthand expression of praise and agreement with their favorite talk show host. It might reassure Democrats to think of Rush's fans as poorly educated, gay-bashing morons. But dittoheads are not just marginalized hatemongers; they are a mainstream political force, and as such they are far more threatening.

A Times-Mirror survey last year split the right-wing electorate into three main groups: libertarians, moralists, and enterprisers. The enterprisers, who represent about 10 percent of American adults, are fiercely partisan Republicans who express the strongest anti-government, pro-business views. They hate taxes and regulations. They are suspicious of social welfare and the liberal media. They love Rush.

"The typical Limbaugh listener is a white male, suburbanite, conservative," says Times-Mirror pollster Andrew Kohut. "Better-than-average job, but not really a great job. Frustrated with the system, with the way the world of Washington works. Frustrated by cultural change. Maybe threatened by women."

These enterprising conservatives are salesmen, engineers, computer technicians, accountants, independent truckers, realtors, and owners of franchise food outlets. They want to make money. But they also tend to be civic-minded, and they vote. They are found in small towns and suburbs throughout the country, but the heart of "Limbaughland" is in the Midwest and the South, now the most populous region in the country.

If there is a quintessential Limbaugh listener, we found him in suburban Atlanta: a 33-year-old mortgage banker named B.J. Van Gundy. A graduate of Georgia Tech, a former bartender, Catholic, married, Van Gundy is a fiscal conservative who doesn't want the Republican Party to get bogged down in battles over abortion or school prayer. He's earnest, opinionated. He's comfortable in his business suit, regularly whips out his cellular phone, and drives a Jeep Cherokee with a bumper sticker that reads: "Visualize No Liberals."

Like all dittoheads, Van Gundy grimaces at the notion that he is the member of a cult. "Do I look robotic to you?" he asks. Well, a bit stiff perhaps, but a robot, no. "I think most of us out here listening to Rush like what he says because we already think these things. He's just incredible at saying it."

But what really seems to inspire Van Gundy is Limbaugh's personal success: "He was a loser 10 or 12 years ago. He didn't have two nickels to rub together. And for him to have done this is just phenomenal. I just want my turn next."

Limbaugh's fans are not country club Republicans. They are Kmart conservatives who consider Rush one of them, even if he did make $25 million over the last two years. Their demographics excite strategists like Bill Kristol, who sees in Rush a way to expand the Republicans' base. "He's a populist figure," says Kristol. "The Republican Party has changed an awful lot from the days when George Herbert Walker Bush was the example of a Republican. Conservatism today represents the common sense of the American people."

KING TUT

Rush's singular achievement has been to destroy the notion that "funny conservative" is an oxymoron. There had been strident right-wing voices on radio before— Father Coughlin, Joe Pyne, Morton Downey Jr.—but they were mean-spirited and shrill. When KFBK-AM in Sacramento hired Rush in 1984, they were looking for a kinder, gentler conservative. Rush played the angry white guy with a sense of humor. It seems obvious now, but no one had tried it before.

Rush's strength is that his humor and his conservatism both come naturally. Before there was Rush, there was Big Rush, his 300-pound father—a Goldwater Republican and "an imposing presence, physically and mentally," according to Rush's younger brother, David. "We were indoctrinated at an early age."

But Rush inherited his prankish humor from his mother, Millie. While the Limbaugh men are beefy, Millie is Long Tall Sally. She hails from Arkansas, her parents were Democrats, and she set out to be a jazz singer. "I was paid to be a singer for about four months of my life," she recalls with a smile, "and that's been the biggest joy of my life, besides my family."

When Rush, who always hated school, resisted his

father's pressure to follow in the family tradition and become a lawyer, Millie supported her son's efforts to become a Top 40 disc jockey. "He got his good sense from his dad and his nonsense from me," she says with a laugh.

At 16 Rush found his calling inside a booth, behind a microphone. He got an after-school show on a tiny radio station partly owned by his father. "It gave him a feeling of superiority," Millie recalls, "and made him feel like King Tut."

But Rush also bears the profound insecurity of a lonely, socially awkward fat boy who skipped his senior prom. He is still, acknowledges his brother, a man driven by old insecurities. The square, the nerd, the guy girls refused to kiss. His first two wives left him. David Limbaugh says it's because his brother is "sedentary." His mother confesses, "I can't imagine what it would be like to be married to him," and adds, "I think he needs a wife subservient to him."

Today, behind a microphone in his "Excellence in Broadcasting" studio, speaking to America over 650 radio stations, Rush Limbaugh is still King Tut. Some analysts speculate that Limbaugh might be tempted to run for office. His fans sell "Limbaugh for President" bumper stickers. But I doubt he'll ever risk it. Despite his immense popularity and political effectiveness, he remains an extreme, polarizing figure. And from what I observed of Limbaugh—he refused to be interviewed for either *Mother Jones* or for "Frontline"—he is simply too uncomfortable with people. Unlike Jack Kemp or Bill Clinton, Limbaugh hates to press flesh. He is a radio personality, magically transformed by a microphone, a man who prefers the security of his studio bubble to the uncontrolled environment of real life. Inside his bubble, Rush can make wild, unfounded assertions that would doom any politician. And he can avoid the debate that would deflate him in a campaign.

After six months of studying Rush Limbaugh, the image that lingers is of him at the freshman Republican orientation last December: A ponderously heavy man, sweating profusely, silent, uncomfortable, sitting alone in the midst of a noisy, celebratory crowd. At the moment of his political triumph, about to be honored by the Republican members of Congress who believe him responsible for their victory, Rush looks like a man who would rather be home on his couch channel-surfing. Then he rises, assumes his position behind the mike, and once again lacerates Clinton and warns Newt to hang tough. It makes me think of the Wizard of Oz, full of bluff and bluster, until Toto pulls back the curtain.

Rush Limbaugh
from deal-with-it.org
Gus DiZerega

The most remarkable things about Rush Limbaugh include the inaccuracies and even dishonesty of his arguments, combined with the trust his followers have in him. Here are a few examples of his views:

Limbaugh seems to have particular venom for environmental issues. Consider this passage from his book:

Here's what *The Washington Post* said in an editorial
on February 5, 1992. "Once again, it turns out that
the protective ozone layer is being destroyed faster
than even the pessimists had expected."

Then, on April 15, 1993 a front-page story had
this to say: ". . . researchers say the problem appears
to be heading towards a solution before they can
find any solid evidence that serious harm was or is
being done." . . . But have you heard Algore [Al
Gore] or any other ozone alarmist step up and
admit that he or she perpetuated (sic) a fraud on
the American people?

Rush didn't mention the story's second paragraph—
that the threat has been contained due to the Montreal
Protocol's phasing out of ozone destroying chemicals.
Because of environmentalists' pressures leading to action
by the Reagan administration, the ozone problem was
well on its way to disappearing. A success by environmentalists is termed a fraud by Limbaugh—because he doesn't
tell the whole story.

But truth has never mattered much to Limbaugh. Consider
some more of his statements:

* "A fact you never hear the environmentalist
wacko crowd acknowledge is that 96 percent of the
so-called 'greenhouse' gases are not created by man,
but by nature."

If Limbaugh ever read serious environmentalists,
he would know that this is well known and
acknowledged—and that these naturally produced

gasses are in rough equilibrium with the natural processes that absorb them. Human created emissions overwhelm natural re-absorption of these gasses. (Haimson, Oppenheimer and Wilcove)

* "It has not been proven that nicotine is addictive, the same with cigarettes causing emphysema [and other diseases]." (Radio show, 4/29/94)

Ronald Reagan's Surgeon General C. Everett Koop reported otherwise in 1988. The Encyclopedia Britannica's 1987 *Medical and Health Annual* states: "Today the scientific base linking smoking to a number of chronic diseases is overwhelming, with a total of 50,000 studies in dozens of countries."

* Misquoting President James Madison: "We have staked the future . . . upon the capacity of each and all of us to govern ourselves, to control ourselves, to sustain ourselves according to the Ten Commandments of God." (*I Told You So*, p. 73)

James Madison never said this. But he did say: "The number, the industry, and the morality of the Priesthood, & the devotion of the people have been manifestly increased by the total separation of the Church from the State." (March 2, 1819) Perhaps Limbaugh got his false quotation from Pat Robertson, who used it in an ad in *US News and World Report*, attempting to get money from people who didn't know any better.

* On Iran-Contra special prosecutor Lawrence Walsh: "This Walsh story basically is, we just spent seven years and $40 million looking for any criminal activity on the part of anybody in the Reagan

administration, and guess what? We couldn't find any. . . . There is not one indictment. There is not one charge." (1/19/94)

In fact, Walsh indicted 14 people, 11 of whom were convicted or pleaded guilty, including Bush appointee John Poindexter.

* Opposing gay marriage, he said "Marriage is about raising children. That's the purpose of the institution." (July 31, 2003)

Rush has been married three times and has no kids.

Limbaugh also brings a deep meanness, even viciousness, to his show, encouraging others to substitute nastiness for argument, just as he does. Consider:

* "Feminism was established to allow unattractive women easier access to the mainstream." Quoted in *Flush Rush Quarterly*, Summer, 1993.
* Molly Ivins reported the following incident, which occured on Limbaugh's television show: "Here is a Limbaugh joke: Everyone knows the Clintons have a cat. Socks is the White House cat. But did you know there is a White House dog?" He then puts up a picture of 13-year-old Chelsea Clinton. (*Arizona Republic*, 10/17/93)
* "If we're going to start rewarding no skills and stupid people—I'm serious . . . let stupid and unskilled Mexicans do that work." Quoted in *FRQ*, Fall, 1993.

GOOD OLD BOYS
Rush has long worked closely with Newt Gingrich. They

dismantled the Fairness Doctrine in the '80s, eliminating the federal requirement that the broadcast media present opposing sides of a given issue. That made fair discussion of public issues a rarity on the public's airwaves—a good deal for Rush.

ANAGRAMS

Rush Limbaugh
Sh, humbug liar

Rush Limbaugh
Big ham, U.S. hurl

Rush Don't Know Dittoheads
from *The American Prospect* (April 2002)
Chris Mooney

On a recent show, Rush Limbaugh once again swatted at *The American Prospect*. As he put it on his Web site, *TAP* had succumbed to something he termed "The Raspberry Effect":

For those of you who don't recall, the great columnist for the *Washington Post*, William Raspberry, wrote a 1993 column extremely critical of my program. He then heard from polite Dittohead readers disagreeing, and suggested he listen to my show, which he hadn't done.

Once Raspberry did spend some time listening, he wrote another column apologizing. So whenever a journalist writes something critical, then listens to the program and realizes the first effort was wrong, it's described as "the Raspberry Effect." It has now happened again with our friends over at *The American Prospect*, the people who first accused me of being deeply involved in a conspiracy to destroy Tom Daschle. Last week, Harold Meyerson ran a piece on the Bush White House political *strategery*.

I don't know that I praised it. I just cited it and agreed with Meyerson's analysis of the way the Bush White House is attempting to expand their circle of voters by going 75 percent of the way on liberal issues, rather than pushing our own. They're doing so, of course, in a way that doesn't necessarily broaden the base—and that's the whole point.

Well Chris Mooney, Online Editor at *The American Prospect*, wrote a piece illustrating a central element to the Raspberry Effect: the liberal in question panics at the very notion that I have agreed with them.

Huh. It's hard to decide what's more odd about this: Rush's notion that I panicked because he was agreeing with the *Prospect*—actually, I mostly found it funny—or the idea, mentioned in the first paragraph above, that Dittoheads are "polite."

But let's linger on the latter conceit, because as Rush seems to imply, I have indeed had an experience with Dittoheads that's relevant here. Last July I was sitting at my computer, doing God knows what, when I suddenly found myself witness to an incoming streak of angry white e-mails. "You are up there with the most hypocritical agenda-biased hate mongers on the planet," Thomas Dawsey wrote (presumably he excluded himself from the running). "Helen thomas, cokie roberts, maureen dowd, meg greenfield and chris mooney," Philip Ramsay wrote, "stinking cunts all."

Such was my cordial introduction to Rush's Dittoheads (and let us not forget that Meg Greenfield, former editorial page editor of *The Washington Post*, had been dead for two years when I received this e-mail). As I soon learned, that day Rush had spent more than 20 minutes of airtime reading aloud an article I'd written titled "The Secret War on Tom Daschle." Noting that the right's partisans were hungry for Daschle scandals, I simply catalogued some of the budding attack strategies. And with the help of the Web site Spinsanity.com, I traced many of them—like nick-naming the Senate's majority leader "Puff Daschle"—back to Limbaugh.

When I replayed the show from his Web site, it was clear to me that Rush enjoyed being credited with Daschle-bashing. But he was outraged that I had the nerve to complain when the left (he felt) had been doing the same to conservatives for years. "These people write in a vacuum," Limbaugh pronounced. "It's amazing to behold these liberals, ladies and gentlemen."

With these words, I became the latest incarnation of media bias to Rush's 19 to 20 million weekly listeners. An e-mail from "EbayElvis" put it nicely: "Thanks to Rush, you are probably more famous now than ever." The chief reminder of this, of course, was the barrage of vituperative e-mail. In total word count, the messages soon exceeded my original article's length by a factor of sixteen. "You're so full of 'Barbara Streissand,'" wrote one Dittohead. And they got much meaner. "I have never read more hogwash in my life," wrote Frank Guinley, devastatingly, "and I am 78 years old."

Shocked by the deluge of criticism, I quickly phoned Lee Vanden-Handel, the affiliate marketing director for the "Rush Limbaugh Show," demanding to know whether he was aware of what happens to people who get trashed by Rush. "Dittoheads are remarkable people," he responded cheerfully. "Some of them can be pretty vulgar, but they're just normal human beings." But I wasn't so sure that sending off e-mails with "brilliant article" in the subject field, and an invitation to fellate "puff daschle" in the body of the message, was normal behavior.

Granted, in some sense Vanden-Handel had been right. Indeed, I found that the more Rush's listeners berated me, the more the slanders and arguments melted into the background of an overarching aesthetic experience. I didn't find myself giving any ground about Limbaugh and Daschle, yet I became immersed in the language of the e-mails. Sometimes, I found, the most vulgar ones were also the richest. "[F**k] off into your homogenous vaccum of liberal Marxism," Peter Charow told me.

Polite this was not, and yet in spite of myself I began to empathize with the Dittoheads. Some of the nastier writers were deeply self-conscious about their descent into *ad hominem*. "P.S.," Mark wrote, "While it is quite easy to defeat liberal arguments, name-calling, while ineffective in debate, is rather fun at times." Others were acutely aware of their own personal inclination to vent. "I realize that I am whizzing in the wind to discuss this with you," Jon Brooks wrote. "But sometimes I need to tilt at windmills," he finished, metaphor by metaphor. "I needed something to laugh at today," Larry Gralewski added, "and you are it."

Only a few of the e-mails were from women. One came from Hong Kong. Tampas Sarma, from Kenner, Louisiana, via Bangladesh, sent me a huge book manuscript, promising that I could be co-author if I could help him edit and get it published. Tate Ulasker asked me: "If there is coordination from the Right, then why would I, living in Russia, working my own business, write to you?" (I'm still scratching my head about this one.) And on and on, the messages flooded in. Probably the most memorable one came from Michael Seitz, who wrote:

> Sir:
> Back in 1958 I served onboard the USS Hancock CV-19 with a guy from Lynn, Massachusetts named Chris Mooney. By chance are you related to that Chris Mooney and if so, I would be interested in contacting him.

This, I will readily admit, was indeed polite. It was also the exception.

As the above story shows, there's little doubt that Limbaugh has it within his power, via his army of Dittoheads, to give someone he discusses on the air quite a dramatic experience. He certainly did that to me. He can call it the "Raspberry Effect" if he wants to, and I imagine that William Raspberry's experience was not so very different from my own.

That's exactly why, despite what Rush says, I find myself doubting whether politeness was a very big part of it.

ANAGRAM

Rush Limbaugh
I gab, hurl mush

Rush to Judgment
from *The New Republic* (12/1/03)
The New Republic staff

Returning to his radio show this week after a month spent at a drug-treatment facility, Rush Limbaugh apologized to the drug addicts he has spent years vilifying, promised to be more compassionate in the future, and apologized for his own moral hypocrisy.

Just kidding. Rather, the Orotund One used his first show back to deny that he had ever been a hypocrite and wallow in newfound, New Age narcissism. "People are saying that I am a hypocrite, as I was using drugs. Yet I was telling people to lead a moral life," Limbaugh explained. "[But] my behavior doesn't change right and wrong. . . . There's no hypocrisy in this, because . . . it didn't change the value of right and wrong simply because I didn't abide by it at a particular time." Umm, exactly. No one is arguing that Limbaugh's transgressions made taking drugs "right," merely that, as he himself admits, he was saying one thing and doing another—in a word, a hypocrite.

To take just a couple examples from his past, Limbaugh once opined, "We have alcoholics and drug addicts in our society, don't we? And what do we say about them? Well, they can't help it. . . . [Y]eah, like that line of cocaine just happened to march into the hotel, go up to the athlete's room, and put itself right in front of him on his blotter." More to the point, he also once declared that "too many whites are getting away with drug use. . . . The answer is to go out and find the ones who are getting away with it, convict them, and send them up the river." Now that Limbaugh himself has been found, however, conviction and a trip up the river do not appear to be the next steps in his personal program. Instead, he wants to share with listeners his moving experience in rehab: "What I endured was a wonderful process. . . . I think what I went through in these last five weeks was as important as the first grade and maybe the second grade," he enthused. "And you can boil it down to one simple essence: I can't be responsible for anybody's happiness but my own. . . . It's wonderful. It actually is an amazing thing."

A new, more forgiving Rush? Sadly, it appears, only where Rush is concerned. Later, on the same show, he turned his MacLainesque balm of self-love into a vitriolic attack on liberals. "[T]he problem with liberals," he explained, "is that they don't like themselves. . . . All this phoniness, all this reaching out, all this: 'Please like me, please, we're not that bad, please, we don't want to hurt you, please get along with us.' It's not possible, my friends, because they don't like themselves. . . . We're not trying to establish intimacy with [liberals]. We want to crush them." Now that sounds more familiar. (Thanks to the *Chicago Tribune*'s Eric Zorn for capturing this nonsense.)

BY RUBEN BOLLING

Rush Limbaugh and the Hypocrisy Smokescreen

from CommonDreams.org (10/18/03)

Kimberle Williams Crenshaw

The Center for American Progress "Bill Bennett Hypocrisy" award went to a most deserving recipient this week, Rush Limbaugh. Until last week, Limbaugh was in the service of two masters, playing both the mighty trumpeter for the army of interests waging the costly and devastating war on drugs, and also apparently playing the junkie who scored black market drugs in the service of his need for a fix. The contradiction uncovered by the revelation of Limbaugh's addiction is breathtaking: perched safely away from the mass policing and incarceration of millions of Americans, Limbaugh sneered at the ruinous consequences of the war on drugs, particularly for people of color. Fairness, he blustered, did not require reductions in the incarceration of people of color, but rather an increase in the incarceration of whites who, all too often, get away with illegal drug use.

Of course no one should hold their breath waiting for Limbaugh or his supporters to submit to Limbaugh's edict. In fact, one can almost imagine Limbaugh morphing into that old "Saturday Night Live" character—Jon Lovitz's pathological liar: "Yeah, that's the ticket, I'm for incarcerating all white drug users too . . . No wait, forget about what I just said—that's not what I meant—what I meant to say was, uh."

Anyone expecting that Limbaugh or his apologists

would lay down their arms and take up Limbaugh's call for the incarceration of white drug abusers like himself, or better yet, call for a dramatic overhaul of American drug policy, is in for a rude awakening. Not only do his supporters refuse to confront the counterproductive consequences of this war and its obvious race- and class-based double standards, they've turned hypocrisy into their own rallying cry. With appalling chutzpa, the conservative choir has excused Limbaugh's hypocrisy while simultaneously accusing "liberals and the media" of either themselves doing drugs or defending those who do. Indeed, according to the warped logic of one of his most vocal supporters, Limbaugh's hypocrisy is acceptable in large part because of the media's hypocrisy. As conservative pundit Matt Drudge declared recently on MSNBC's "Buchanan and Press," "There's no law against being a hypocrite a few times in your life and this industry is built on hypocrisy. I'm challenging the media tonight to empty their pockets."

Drudge's defense of Limbaugh is taken directly out of the Right's playbook: "When caught red-handed living a lie, deflect attention from your personal responsibility and shoot one directly across the bow of those perpetual evildoers, 'the liberals and the media.'" This is classic misdirection, the key to the success of generations of politicians and charlatans for whom smoke and mirrors have always been a stock in trade. And it works. At best, the misdirection is entirely exculpatory; at minimum, the public is stymied and confused. When the public discussion over the "war on drugs" degenerates into a debate over who's the bigger hypocrite, Limbaugh and his apologists have effectively won.

Worst still is the effect that this paralyzing defense has

on the ability of those who want to use this moment to build momentum toward a saner drug policy. Unable to figure out how to slam this slow, fat pitch out of the park, critics of the current drug policies have resorted to articulating mushy calls for compassion for Limbaugh.

Limbaugh's camp has to be relieved—indeed ecstatic—that the so-called "liberals and media" are squandering this moment to voice support for what is essentially a foregone conclusion. The reality is that Limbaugh is unlikely to serve any jail time for his illegal drug use for reasons that everyone in the anti-incarceration movement knows.

Conservatives have little to worry about so long as their opponents can't make more hay out of moments like these. What needs to be captured is that this inhumane drug policy can be sustained only so long as it visits its most heinous consequences upon society's most disempowered. If political elites like the Limbaughs and Bushes of the world had to suffer the devastating penalties for drug use that hundreds of thousands of nameless others face on a daily basis, this drug war would come to a halt in short order. What is needed now, it seems, is less "and neither should you be incarcerated, Rush" and more hard-hitting analysis uncovering why the Limbaughs of the world are less likely to have their lives destroyed by draconian drug laws.

That analysis might begin in the conservative dug-out with their shockingly disparate sentiments of concern and support for the likes of Limbaugh, and their hardened, condemnatory attitudes toward the drug dependency of members of out-groups. Pat Buchanan and Matt Drudge's homage to Limbaugh's ability to triumph in the face of such a debilitating dependency typifies the tendency of people to "feel the pain" of those like them, while condemning those unlike them to the most punitive treatment conceivable. Perhaps this selectivity is typical for all groups, but it is especially pronounced when the in-group and out-groups are defined by race and class. When members of their own group falter, people tend to attribute the cause to circumstances largely beyond their control. In Limbaugh's case, the cause was debilitating back pain. But with regard to out-groups, their "criminal" behavior is read not as circumstantial, but as the product of inherent characteristics so deeply entrenched that they must be rooted out through unyieldingly punitive measures.

One needn't work hard to find the bias reflected in the wagon-circling around Limbaugh. Says Matt Drudge on MSNBC, "(it) makes me want to reach out to him and say we love you Rush, we know you are going through terrible hell." Of course, anyone going through drug addiction is going through terrible hell, but the magnitude of drug addiction faced by others is rarely if ever addressed by the likes of Buchanan or Drudge. To Pat Buchanan, the fact that Limbaugh would risk his entire career under the weight of this addiction simply reveals how devastating drug dependency can be. "He must have known these things were damaging his hearing his whole career. He's the king of talk radio, everything is on the line. (I)t suggests a really hellish addiction, does it not?"

Of course, the fact that millions of others face this addiction, and confront ever decreasing opportunities to rid themselves of it has not tempered the conservative support for the war on drugs. And if one wanted to press conservatives about their drumbeat of personal responsibility and choice, it's not too far off track to remind them that

Limbaugh, unlike millions of others, had resources and the opportunity to seek treatment for his addiction. If there is any culpability to go around, shouldn't it attach to those, like Limbaugh, who have been bested by their addiction despite treatment, yet who continue the drumbeat for mass incarceration for those who have had no such opportunity?

Given the ability of wealthy and well-connected people like Limbaugh to secure their own treatment and escape punishment, there will be little pressure to make treatment and other non-criminal interventions available for ordinary Americans most threatened by today's drug laws. In all likelihood, Rush will return, rehabilitated politically, if not physically, and this sorry chapter will fade into distant memory. Like the limited fall-out from his magnificent disintegration on ESPN, little structural or political change will come from the public's glimpse into the race and class disparities that prop up Limbaugh and the prevailing conventions around race, class and drugs. To engender this kind of change, we must use Limbaugh's story to expose the injustices and racist double standardsobfuscated by the hypocrisy smokescreen—that constitute the "war on drugs."

He Said It . . .

There's nothing good about drug use. We know it. It destroys individuals. It destroys families. Drug use destroys societies. Drug use, some might say, is destroying this country. And we have laws against selling drugs, pushing drugs, using drugs, importing drugs. And the laws are good because we know what happens to people in societies and neighborhoods, which become consumed by them. And so if people are violating the law by doing drugs, they ought to be accused and they ought to be convicted and they ought to be sent up.

What this says to me is that too many whites are getting away with drug use. Too many whites are getting away with drug sales. Too many whites are getting away with trafficking in this stuff. The answer to this disparity is not to start letting people out of jail because we're not putting others in jail who are breaking the law. The answer is to go out and find the ones who are getting away with it, convict them and send them up the river, too.

. . . We are becoming too tolerant as a society, folks, especially of crime, in too many parts of the country . . . . This country certainly appears to be tolerant, forgive and forget. I mean, you know as well as I do, you go out and commit the worst murder in the world and you just say you're sorry, people go, "Oh, OK. A little contrition." . . . People say, "I feel better. He said he's sorry for it." We're becoming too tolerant, folks.

—"Rush Limbaugh" TV show (10/5/95)

You want to see my Marion Barry impersonation? Do you want to see that? All right. I'll do the Marion Barry impersonation.

You put some stuff out here on the table and you go [pretends to snort cocaine]. "You tell Jesse to stay out of my town. This is my town, and Jesse—you tell him to stay out. [More snorting.] And I said no, no, no, no, I don't smoke it no more. Tired of ending up on the floor." [More snorting.]
—"Rush Limbaugh" TV show (12/8/92)

I want to let you read along with me a quote from Jerry Colangelo about substance abuse, and I think you'll find that he's very much right . . . "I know every expert in the world will disagree with me, but I don't buy into the disease part of it. The first time you reach for a substance you are making a choice. Every time you go back, you are making a personal choice. I feel very strongly about that." . . .

What he's saying is that if there's a line of cocaine here, I have to make the choice to go down and sniff it. . . . And his point is that we are rationalizing all this irresponsibility and all the choices people are making and we're blaming not them, but society for it. All these Hollywood celebrities say the reason they're weird and bizarre is because they were abused by their parents. So we're going to pay for that kind of rehab, too, and we shouldn't. It's not our responsibility. It's up to the people who are doing it. And Colangelo is right.
—"Rush Limbaugh" TV show (9/23/93)

The public is better served by treating addicts as patients rather than criminals.
—letter from Rush's lawyer to prosecutors, in which the attorney suggested dropping charges if Limbaugh entered rehab.

Animal House Meets Church Lady

from *The American Prospect* (March 1996)

Paul Safire

You have to wonder whether the apostles of the conservative movement, the self-anointed champions of public morality, read their own press. In May 1995, *The American Spectator* ran an article by senior editor P.J. O'Rourke entitled "Why the GOP Doesn't Suck," which defined the Republican Party as the natural home of the frat-boy mentality. "The thing I like about Republicans," he wrote, "is that they're no damn good at all. I know, I'm one of them. A Republican just wants to get rich, buy oceanfront property, dump the old wife and get a new blond one."

Meanwhile, the media organs of the right were busy heralding smoking—and all the defiant, Brando-esque images it conjures up—as the essence of the conservative personality. Even the unapologetically highbrow journal *Commentary* succumbed to Joe Camel posturing: In the same pages where Gertrude Himmelfarb argued that a restoration of Victorian-style social pressures is necessary to restore civic order, neocon Peter Berger celebrated smoking on the grounds that an antismoking New Class has bullied us into conformity at the expense of the rugged moral autonomy that once defined American society.

In the fall of 1995 the *National Review* advertised its 40th Anniversary Cruise, gleefully announcing that the cruise was "Ruled 'Politically Incorrect' by the FDA" and bragging about its "three cocktail bashes" and "two smokers" (cigar smoking fests). Then it pointed out that guests needn't worry about running into heathen like Arlen Specter, who presumably wouldn't feel comfortable among such pious guests as Ralph Reed and Judge Robert Bork. The cruise, the ad implied, would provide a welcome respite from both the left's repressive moralizing (represented here by the FDA) and its offensive amorality (here depicted by Arlen Specter, whose stubborn insistence on the separation of church and state places him solidly outside the pale).

This, say the good people at the *National Review*, is what a world without liberals would look like: spring break in Fort Lauderdale, only with church.

These are not isolated examples; indeed, they are indicative of an inconsistency at the heart of the modern conservative movement. With unwavering self-congratulation, conservatives increasingly present themselves as courageously puritanical *and* courageously antipuritanical—the answer both to the permissiveness of the "anything goes" left and to the prudishness of political correctness. Perhaps no one better embodies this pose than the brash Rush Limbaugh, who happens to be good pals with William Bennett, of the lofty *Book of Virtues.*

The same conservative intellectuals who bemoan our culture's general decline in manners and good taste embrace Limbaugh and even celebrate his crassness as the very essence of his charm. A 1993 *National Review* profile by James Bowman (now media critic for the *New Criterion*) unflinchingly anoints Limbaugh "The Leader of the Opposition," the natural heir to the Reagan legacy. Bowman even goes so far as to lament that Limbaugh's celebrity has forced him to tone down some of his "irreverence" and "spontaneity," causing him to abandon such antics as the "caller abortion"—the sound of a vacuum cleaner and woman's scream in lieu of a normal call termination—which, he says, "was in splendidly awful taste."

Limbaugh has made an entire career of having it both ways—and, for the most part, thriving as a result. On the one hand, he is always adding his voice to the familiar refrain about family values and the proper role of religion in public life, condemning liberals for losing touch with mainstream America. "Liberals excuse bad behavior. They rationalize it," he explains in his ghostwritten best-seller *See, I Told You So*. But Limbaugh is just as quick to portray himself as a victim of liberal prudishness, as yet another American who's had to suffer because some "femiNazi" just can't take a joke. The conflict becomes apparent every time he tells a dirty joke, then ducks sheepishly behind his hands as if deflecting blows, while the camera pans an audience full of men clapping excitedly and women shaking their heads in dutiful but halfhearted condemnation. (A typical example was his joke last year that Clinton's presidential motto should be "Speak softly and carry a big stiffie.")

These sudden shifts from boyish offensiveness to pious self-righteousness account for the almost exhilarating confusion Limbaugh's performances generate. The impropriety never quite becomes a threat to moral decency because everyone knows Limbaugh stands for moral decency; his sermonizing about moral decency never quite becomes heavy-handed moralizing because everyone knows he's all for having a good time. By never quite saying when he's kidding and when he's not, Limbaugh manages to sustain the "guilty pleasure" indefinitely. He gets to dangle courageously at both extremes, but with a built-in safety net—speaking passionately in the name of our shamed and forgotten moral truths (but without coming on too strong), while delighting in his own heresies (but without seeming like, well, a heretic).

For sure, Limbaugh is not the first public figure to embrace competing philosophical themes. But this stance hints at some of the hidden meanings of the right's culture wars. What conservatives demand, in point of fact, is not that so-called "traditional morality" always be strictly observed (although there are certainly a few within the movement who wish it were). They ask that the ultimate authority of those traditions not be called into question, that one's excursions from the moral center—while accepted, even celebrated—not be granted any final or lasting legitimacy.

That is why Rush Limbaugh is not on that infamous slippery slope from "Question Authority" to child-killer Susan Smith. That is why the jocular, politically incorrect amoralism of a P.J. O'Rourke is not a threat to "civic order," even though Hollywood sex and violence is. By virtue of its inevitable association with conservatism's more pious side, the right's bad-boy streak gets excused with a wink. The limits to the right's defiance are always implicitly understood, or at least supposed to be. When it gets out of hand—as, perhaps, it did around the Oklahoma City bombing—conservatives profess shock, apparently wondering how anybody could possibly have taken their words so seriously.

The fact of the matter is that, despite their posturing at either extreme, conservatives have no real interest in being serious about their traditionalism or their iconoclasm.

Both poses, if genuine, would get in the way of the easy complacency of the frat-boy way of life. In their hands, traditional piety is turned into simple recitation, a merely perfunctory nod to conventional wisdom, while going against the grain becomes nothing more than harmless childishness. Instead of a sincere and committed conversation about values, they want a public square filled with *Book of Virtues*-style platitudes, pithy moralisms that are shielded both from debate and from any contact with actual life. In a public square like this, there is no difference between a Mother Theresa and a William Bennett or between the genuine transgressing of social norms and the madcap antics of the guys over at the Chi Psi lodge.

Conservatives claim that they stand for an ethic of freedom wedded to responsibility. But what they're really asking for is a perpetual moral adolescence—a world in which, no matter how hungover you are on Sunday morning, there's still someone around to make you go to church.

RIDDLE

What's the difference between Rush Limbaugh and the Hindenberg?
One's a flaming Nazi gasbag; the other's a dirigible.

BILL O'REILLY

with quotes by Bill O'Reilly;
a short take by The Beast *staff;*
a cartoon by Daryl Cagle;
and an anagram

Bill O'Reilly paints himself as a friend of the common man. That's his niche in the marketplace of radical right-wing ideas, and it's a good one. O'Reilly—otherwise known as "Oh, Really?"—earns an estimated $4 million a year for pretending that he cares about working people even as he shamelessly shills for the powers-that-be who exploit them. He also works hard to perfect the politics of bullying and personal attack, picking easy targets—the entertainment industry is a favorite—and honing his techniques on the occasional guest who dares to disagree with him. Al Franken offers the perfect description of O'Reilly: lying, splotchy bully.

Bill O'Reilly

from deal-with-it.org

Gus DiZerega

According to the Drudge Report, Fox News star Bill O'Reilly lobbied his network to file suit against author Al Franken and book *Lies and the Lying Liars Who Tell Them: A Fair and Balanced Look at the Right.*[1]

Bill O'Reilly's amazing defense of Fox's suit certainly supports Drudge's claim. First he bragged about Fox's success, and denied that Fox is conservative (!), points utterly irrelevant to the issue. O'Reilly then claimed that Al Franken was part of a liberal effort to destroy the company through character assassination. In a very strange statement, given the history of Fox News, O'Reilly writes "It makes me sick to see intellectually dishonest individuals hide behind the first amendment to spread propaganda, libel, and slander." (*Walla Walla Union Bulletin*, 8/17/03).

Really? In a Florida court case in which a reporter brought charges against Fox Television because they demanded she broadcast false information, and fired her when she wouldn't, Fox argued to have the case tossed out on the grounds *there is no hard, fast, and written rule against deliberate distortion of the news*. A breathtaking argument, to say the least. They argued the First Amendment gives broadcasters the right to lie or deliberately distort news reports on the public airwaves. After three rejections of this ploy, Fox finally found a court that agreed, and their argument was upheld in a strange opinion by a Florida Court of Appeals. After the ruling, the FOX station aired a report saying it was "totally vindicated" by the verdict.[2]

It is strange that a news network would trademark the common English term "fair and balanced." It's even stranger that a broadcasting company could then use its alleged ownership of part of our language to seek to halt printing of a critical book. It's stranger yet that a man who makes his living in broadcasting, and has no compunction about shouting down those who disagree with him, would be behind the suit.

Bill O'Reilly appears to have difficulties with the truth. In Los Angeles, on May 31, at the Book Expo America 2003, Al Franken skewered O'Reilly, catching him in two back-to-back lies. O'Reilly said he was awarded a prestigious Peabody award for working on "Inside Edition." No such award was ever given. He then changed his story: he received a Polk award. But the Polk award was earned AFTER he left the show.[3] This embarrassing exposure is probably why he went after Al Franken.

For another example of O'Reilly's lies, we refer to *Slate*'s Whopper of the Week for February 14, 2003.[4] *Slate* quoted Lise Rousseau as saying: "Mr. O'Reilly, imagine my confusion as I watched you criticize the protester for organizing the Limbaugh boycott. Last August, I heard you tacitly call for a boycott against Pepsi for hiring [the rap singer] Ludacris. There is a lack of consistency in your rhetoric."

O'Reilly answered, "No, there isn't. . . . I simply said I wasn't going to drink Pepsi while that guy was on their payroll. No boycott was ever mentioned by me. "

But this is what he really said:

"So I'm calling for all responsible Americans to fight back and punish Pepsi for using a man who degrades women, who encourages substance abuse, and does all the things that hurt particularly the poor in our society.

"I'm calling for all Americans to say, Hey, Pepsi, I'm not drinking your stuff. You want to hang around with Ludacris, you do that, I'm not hanging around with you."

—Bill O'Reilly, Aug. 27, 2002

"Because of pressure by Factor viewers, Pepsi-Cola late today capitulated. Ludacris has been fired."

—Bill O'Reilly, Aug. 28, 2002.

You can go to http://www.fair.org/extra/0205/oh_ really.html to discover more about O'Reilly's falsehoods.

O'Reilly is at least as much a populist as a conservative, and one healthy dimension of populism is a general disrespect for authority. O'Reilly has given a hard time to some conservatives on his show, including George W. Bush when he was running for President.

Populists are an interesting crowd. Some are personally anti-authoritarian. Other populists question authority not because they distrust it but because they don't have it. O'Reilly seems to be the latter kind of populist—a frustrated authoritarian. His distrust of government is a bit like John Ashcroft's.

O'Reilly's bullying style and his refusal to acknowledge opposing viewpoints result in his unthinking acceptance of most of the Radical Right's policies—and equally unthinking dismissal of any critics.

For example, a reliable blog reports that in March,

2003, O'Reilly "interviewed" Steve Rendall, the Senior Analyst at FAIR (http://www.fair.org), a media watch group. Rendall was on the show to talk about FAIR's documenting a near absence of critics of government policies during the Iraq crisis on network newscasts. Rendall named Fox as the most hawkish of the networks.[5]

When O'Reilly challenged him for an example, Rendall described a Fox report in March, 2003, of a 'huge chemical weapons factory' discovered by coalition forces. The Pentagon later clammed up about the supposed "discovery." As usuall, the "discovery" was no discovery at all. But Fox was not forthcoming with a retraction. O'Reilly tried to use Rendall's example to attack his patriotism. He suggested Rendall didn't want chemical weapons to be found because he was "against America." Rendall replied that all he wants is truth in journalism.[6]

Rendall is hardly the only guest who has been treated rudely and unfairly by O'Reilly. Using Microsoft's word count, the *Progressive Review* did a statistical study of an O'Reilly "interview." They discovered that the interviewee, Jacob Sullum, got in a scant 35 more words than O'Reilly over the course of their conversation. O'Reilly's method was personal attack, using terms such as "pinheads like you" and "irresponsible libertines." And O'Reilly tells us he opposes character assassination![7]

O'Reilly's behavior entertains some viewers. But he is not reporting the news, or educating the public, or serving citizens. People who take O'Reilly seriously are less able to evaluate what government is doing, less able to think independently, and less likely to respect others with whom they disagree. O'Reilly helps to discourage decent people from taking part in political discourse.

As a country, we become poorer even as Bill O'Reilly grows richer.

1. See: http://www.drudgereport.com/bof.htm
2. See: http://www.fromthewilderness.com/free/ww3/022703_fox.html
http://www.populist.com/01.1.krebs.html
3. See: For more on this series of lies by O'Reilly go to: www.oregonlive.com
4. See: http://slate.msn.com/id/2078577/
5. For the study go to: http://www.fair.org/reports/iraq-sources.html
6. See: http://princeroy.blogspot.com/2003_03_23_princeroy_archive.html
7. For that report go to: http://prorev.com/oreilly.htm

Bill O'Reilly
The Beast staff
from BuffaloBeast.com (2002)

Misdeeds
At least Rush Limbaugh is funny every now and then. This new monster deals in untrammeled viciousness and invective, and his "Talking Points" help the Great Beast out there to reduce the entire world to six-word bulletins. He does a lot of waving and snorting at his guests whenever they disagree with him. To watch him is to be inspired to thrilling hatred, which may explain his ratings success, beyond the fact that 90 percent of the public buys him as real journalism.

Aggravating Factor
Claimed on the air that his former show, "Inside Edition," won a Peabody award when it didn't; assailed Tom Arnold for allowing highly entertaining former criminal Michael Irvin on "The Best Damn Sports Show, Period."

Aesthetic
Brothel customer who won't pay a dollar over the list price, occasionally gets rough and takes a long time.

He Said It . . .

"I don't know what this serves to take a look at our enemy's religion. See? I mean, I wouldn't give people a book during World War II on the emperor is God in Japan, would you?... I wouldn't read the book. And I'll tell you why: I wouldn't have read Mein Kampf either. If I were going to UNC in 1941, and you, Professor, said, 'Read Mein Kampf,' I would have said, 'Hey, Professor, with all due respect, shove it. I ain't reading it.'"

—Bill O'Reilly, 7/7/02, on a University of North Carolina requirement that freshmen read a book called *Approaching the Q'ran*. (O'Reilly later denied that he had compared the Q'ran to *Mein Kampf*.)

ANAGRAM

Bill O'Reilly
Bile or Lilly

Word of Oaf

from Soundbitten.com (February 2004)
Greg Beato

"I was single for a long time. I was all over the world covering
wars and met thousands of women."
—*Bill O'Reilly,* Playboy *interview, May 2002*

"I've got hos in different area codes."
—*Ludacris, "Area Codes"*

While Bill O'Reilly's mother Angela explained to the
Washington Post that her son "grew up in Westbury,
Long Island, a middle-class suburb," Bill O'Reilly used to
claim that he grew up in a more proletarian locale, the
nearby suburb of Levittown. In the first chapter of his
book *The O'Reilly Factor,* he writes of his "working-class"
background, and suggests that his family was "pretty far
down the social totem pole." And it's true that the
O'Reillys could only afford to go on Florida vacations
once a year, and that his dad did hard, grimy, back-
breaking labor as an accountant.

But the family also had enough money to send O'Reilly

to private school, and then college (with a year abroad in England), and then college again. "You don't come from any lower than I came from on an economic scale," O'Reilly once told the *New York Observer*. "I fully realize that blacks in the ghetto, and all that, had a much rougher life than I had. But I started from ground zero. When I got out of B.U., I had not a nickel."

Here, you have to give O'Reilly his due: if you ask the average employer, "Hey, who are you most likely to hire— a black from the ghetto, or a white guy with a master's degree from Boston University, the employer will reply, 'Whoever's got the nickel!'"

But is O'Reilly really the salt-of-the-earth type he plays on his very popular, very entertaining TV series? O'Reilly says his show on Fox News looks at "things from a blue-collar, workingman's point of view." To convey that view, O'Reilly says things like "corporate America, in my opinion, needs to rethink their responsibility to their country" and "I'm in the vanguard on television of our search-and-destroy mission about the elite media . . . They don't want to hear from [regular people]. They don't want to address our concerns . . . "

Interestingly enough, Bill O'Reilly is married to a woman named Maureen McPhilmy, vice president of DWJ Television, a company that specializes in producing commercials for big, rich, powerful corporate clients like Sun Microsystems and Kellogg's, and then passing these commercials off as genuine news stories on channels like Fox News. And, of course, O'Reilly makes a lot of money from one of the world's biggest media conglomerates to portray a regular guy—$4 million a year, according to the *Boston Globe*.

So given the shaky foundation on which Bill O'Reilly's blue-collar, workingman's persona rests, his recent vendetta against 24-year-old Chris Bridges, aka Ludacris, is surprising. After all, Bridges appears to hail from relatively modest origins himself: he grew up in College Park, Georgia, a town of 20,000 near the Atlanta airport, where the median household income is $38,558. (O'Reilly famously exclaimed that his father, who retired in 1978, never made more than $35,000 a year. What he didn't acknowledge was that $35,000 went a lot further in the 1970s than it does today.)

Bridges attended Banneker High School, a public institution where the student body is 97 percent black. At the age of 8, he exclaimed to his mother, "Mom, I love music and whether I am in front of a microphone or behind it, I will be in the music industry." In pursuit of this dream, his mother recounted, he obtained "internships in radio and entertainment law."

Eventually, he turned an internship at an Atlanta radio station into a job as a producer there. At the age of 21, he bought his first house. At the age of 23, he created his own record label and produced his first album. Now, at 25, he's a platinum-selling artist.

I'm not sure if Ludacris ever had to suffer the indignity of having only two sports coats to wear to school—according to the *Washington Post*, O'Reilly frequently cites his own memories of such hardship—but I'd say that he certainly qualifies as a hard-working, self-made man.

On a certain level, then, you'd think Bill O'Reilly would recognize Chris Bridges, aka Ludacris, as a kindred soul. But apparently that's not the case: on August 27th, during the "Talking Points" portion of his TV show, O'Reilly described

Ludacris as "a man who is demeaning just about everybody, and is peddling antisocial behavior." O'Reilly then blasted Pepsi for using Ludacris as a commercial pitchman: "I'm calling for all responsible Americans to fight back and punish Pepsi for using a man who degrades women, who encourages substance abuse, and does all the things that hurt particularly the poor in our society." A day later, Pepsi announced that it was discontinuing its ad campaign with Ludacris.

It's true that Ludacris is probably not the best choice to serve as spokesperson for a large corporation that wants to convey hipness in a completely safe, antiseptic, non-controversial way. In addition to penning some funny, clever rhymes, he writes lyrics like "Move bitch, get out the way/Get out the way bitch, get out the way/OH NO! The fight's out/I'ma 'bout to punch yo . . . lights out." And: "I gotta big weed stash, pocket full of cash/Just seen a big ol' ass, it's Saturday/Sticky, icky, icky, icky/Sticky, icky, icky, icky."

But of course it seems fairly unlikely that Pepsi planned to use any lyrics like that in its commercials featuring Ludacris. And while O'Reilly argued that Pepsi was "rewarding" Ludacris for rapping about "anti-social behavior," the truth is that it was rewarding him for being popular with the demographic it wants to reach.

So why focus on Ludacris? If O'Reilly truly believes that celebrities shouldn't be rewarded for their anti-social behavior, why not target someone whose commercial appearances actually celebrate his real-life misdeeds? One good candidate: temperamental basketball coach Bobby Knight, who was fired from Indiana University for habitually assaulting folding chairs and players, then hired by Clorox to smash dishes against a wall in a Glad trashbag commercial.

Or how about Tonya Harding? After she approved of her boyfriend's plan to cripple Nancy Kerrigan, O'Reilly's then-employer *Inside Edition* reportedly paid her $375,000 to appear on O'Reilly's show. Back then, he was so enamored of the concept of rewarding anti-social behavior with big money—aka "checkbook journalism," the practice of paying people like Joey Buttafuoco to share their sins with the news media—that he wrote a glowing op-ed piece about it for the *New York Times*.

And then of course there's Britney Spears, whom Pepsi has employed for some time now as a spokes-dancer, most memorably in that creepy spot where Bob Dole barked at his cock ("Down, boy!") while Spears did her standard Tribute-To-The-Ladies-Of-Hooters crotch-grinding. But even though Spears is an icon to millions of children, O'Reilly thinks her call-girl-next-door persona is just "immature and silly."

"I don't feel Britney Spears is a threat to the nation," he said on his TV show. "She may not be a good role model, but I don't think she's going to do any permanent damage to anybody, whereas [Ludacris] is."

So what is it, exactly, about Ludacris that makes O'Reilly think such dark, dark thoughts?

While O'Reilly acknowledges that the 25-year-old rapper is "not as bad as [genocidal dictator] Pol Pot," he does believe that Ludacris is pretty darn bad. According to O'Reilly, Ludacris is:

- a "dangerous" man whose message is "Look, be an outlaw. Take narcotics. Abuse people. Punch people. Hurt people."

- "a dumb idiot who got lucky and exploits the system."

- "subverting the values of the United States."

Plus he "hurts children." Given Ludacris' status as O'Reilly Enemy #1, I expected to find quite a bit of information detailing his arrest record, his criminal past, and his nefarious plot to subvert American values by turning schoolchildren into violent Communist junkies. So far, however, I haven't found anything like that—except perhaps for one or two mentions of a mysterious institution known as the Ludacris Foundation. Allegedly created to "provide gifts, grants, and scholarships to Foster Care Shelters, Stay-in-School and High School athletics programs, Book Drives/Reading and Art Appreciation programs and many other initiatives," it sounds a hell of a lot like a drug-and-prostitution ring to me.

But other than that, what?

Given that O'Reilly heads up the most popular series on the most popular cable news network, he must have plenty of investigative resources at his disposal. And given that the Fox News corporate slogan is "We report, you decide," I can only conclude that O'Reilly and his reporters did the in-depth background check that one would expect any responsible news organization to do if it were planning to describe someone as a dangerous, subversive individual who hurts children. And since O'Reilly has made no mention of Ludacris' criminal record or anything like that, I can only conclude that his investigation didn't actually turn up anything too damning.

Except for Ludacris' aforementioned lyrics, that is.

But even there, O'Reilly sees things that don't really exist. Indeed, O'Reilly repeatedly characterizes Ludacris as an emphatic prosyletizer: "Take narcotics. Abuse people. Punch people. Hurt people." But I couldn't find any lyrics where he explicitly encourages people to do any of these things. He talks about his *own* drug and alcohol use, his *own* violent exploits, and his *own* misogynistic treatment of women, yes, but such blustery boasting isn't the same thing as insisting to others that they should do the same.

More importantly, O'Reilly seems to betray no suspicions whatsoever that (a) Ludacris' lyrics aren't necessarily based in fact, and (b) Ludacris' lexicon isn't necessarily literal.

When a guest on O'Reilly's show asked him if any hip-hop figure might make an acceptable Pepsi spokesperson, O'Reilly replied "Chubby Checker." Surprisingly enough, Chubby Checker is still alive and still performing regularly, but he's not a hip-hop figure by any stretch of the imagination, unless that imagination simplistically equates black skin with hip-hop. So what does O'Reilly's answer say? That he has either a deep ignorance or a deep contempt for the genre, or possibly both.

Because of his apparent ignorance and contempt, perhaps O'Reilly doesn't realize that a hip-hop lyric shouldn't be automatically interpreted as a deposition: it can be fictional, hyperbolic, metaphorical. Ludacris is a character that Chris Bridges invented. Like many rappers, he rhymes in a deliberately over-the-top, hyper-aggressive way. And for the record, he's actually mostly known as a comic presence—more crazy, bugged-out prankster than thugged-out gangster. "I grew up watching Richard Pryor, The Three Stooges and Dolemite," he told one interviewer.

"I've always been the funny dude in my crew, so I wanted to put that humor into my lyrics."

(Memo to O'Reilly: has anyone taught more children to be violent than the Three Stooges? You need to stop those guys!)

Now, O'Reilly might not think that lyrics like "Just keep on pissin me off, like a weak kidney/And you will find your family reading your obituary" are particularly funny. But does he really think Ludacris murders anyone who gets on his nerves?

To promote his own show, O'Reilly uses similar (albeit not as clever) vocabulary. One of his favorite adjectives to describe his work is "hard-hitting." He talks about "hammering" Alan Iverson and other public figures. In a *Playboy* interview, he says he "slapped around" Jerry Falwell on his show. In the same interview, he says he "smashed" Michael Kinsley when Kinsley visited *The O'Reilly Factor*, and follows up with this anecdote: "When I went home to the neighborhood, people who saw the show came up to me and asked, 'How come you didn't punch him?' I had to explain that he was in Washington and I was in New York and I couldn't go through the camera. They said, 'We would have fucking killed him.'"

Clearly a double standard is at work here. When Bill O'Reilly uses violent imagery to promote his persona, it's marketing. And when Ludacris does it, it's a subversive threat to American values.

Similarly, when Bill O'Reilly writes a novel that includes plenty of sex and violence, it's harmless entertainment. But when Ludacris writes a rap lyric that includes plenty of sex and violence, it's "dangerous" advocacy of a destructive lifestyle. In 1998, O'Reilly published

Those Who Trespass, a novel that stars, in the words of its back-jacket promo copy, "a low-profile killer, brutally sadistic and maddeningly professional." The story is further enlivened by a "triangle of erotic suspense." In truth, there is little eroticism and little suspense in this brutally generic and maddeningly delusional book. But there are passages like these ones:

> "Goddamn bitch. She'll be sorry. Goddamn Clinton and his stupid family. What the fuck am I doing here?"

> "Costello tasted the salty flavor of blood running in his throat . . . The assailant's right hand, now holding the oval base of the spoon, rocketed upward, jamming the stainless stem through the roof of Ron Costello's mouth. The soft tissue gave way quickly and the steel penetrated the correspondent's brain stem."

> "She tried not to stare at his crotch, even though she saw movement there."

> "Then he slipped her panties down her legs and, within seconds, his tongue was inside her, moving rapidly."

> "He was speaking hushed tones, telling her how much he enjoyed her body, using words that in polite conversation would have been vulgar, but in this context were extremely erotic. His hands firmly gripped her buttocks."

"Silence circled the room like a starving turkey buzzard."

"These TV guys really are pricks . . . "

How does *Those Who Trespass* stack up against Ludacris' *Word of Mouf* album as a whole? Consider the following statistics:

Number of Murders Depicted
Those Who Trespass: 6
Word of Mouf: 4

Teen Crack Slut Oral Sex Scenes
Those Who Trespass: 1
Word of Mouf: 0

Total "Fucks" or Variants Thereof
Those Who Trespass: 39
Word of Mouf: 68

Total "Bitches" or Variants Thereof
Those Who Trespass: 12
Word of Mouf: 41

Tedious Digressions re: Media Corruption
Those Who Trespass: Many
Word of Mouf: None

If O'Reilly's novel actually features more murders than Ludacris' CD, why isn't he boycotting himself? My guess is that O'Reilly would probably defend his novel in the same way that he defends *The Sopranos*: "Is the program a corrupting influence on America? The answer is no, because the terrible acts that Tony and his thugs commit are not condoned or encouraged on the show . . ."

And it's true that in *Those Who Trespass*, after depicting numerous sadistic murders, and explaining how the victims did kind of deserve it (because they were mean!), O'Reilly is careful to dramatize the fact that Crime Doesn't Pay.

Nonetheless, his comments about his book's success clearly suggest that he knows it's not the triumph of law and order that his readers are buying: "[My publisher is] telling me to write another one quick. Kill more people!" he exclaimed to the *Dallas Morning News* with apparent glee. So far, killing people in print has been a profitable undertaking for him: *Those Who Trespass* has had several printings to date, and Mel Gibson is planning to turn it into a feature film.

Which is great for O'Reilly: people should be allowed to pursue all kinds of different projects, for different audiences and different venues, and with different standards of decorum informing them. O'Reilly has proven that he can do a Fox News broadcast without blurting out sentiments like "His hands firmly gripped her buttocks," so I think he should be allowed to write erotic murder fantasies about killing his peers in the media world if that's what makes him happy. And since Ludacris has on occasion demonstrated that he can write a rap song without using the words "bitch," "ho," or "motherfucker," then I think he actually can function as a commercial spokesperson.

But I know there are a lot of people out there who

aren't as open-minded as I am. And those people are probably wondering why it's OK for Fox News to employ a man who brags about "slapping" and "slamming" his adversaries, and also enjoys day-dreaming about ways to murder characters based on real-life people he has known, while it's wrong for Pepsi to employ a man who engages in similar literary transgressions. The answer is simple, however: in America, we expect far more moral accountability from our soft drink manufacturers than we do from the news media.

FORTY YEARS OF PROGRESS.

Scold Move

from *The American Prospect* (April 2002)

Noy Thrupkaew

Culture has been corroding young minds and horrifying parents ever since Mozart wrote *Le Nozze di Figaro*, complete with a randy count and a who's-yo-mama subplot. More recent examples might include Elvis and his hips, or Madonna and, well, herself.

It's an old, old story. But some people can't seem to stop telling it.

A case in point is news commentator/professional old coot Bill O'Reilly's interview of shock rocker Marilyn Manson for the recent O'Reilly special, "The Corruption of the American Child." Marilyn Manson is *so* 1999. Yawn.

The show on the evils of pop culture ran on Fox, the same network that has brought viewers such wholesome classics as *Celebrity Boxing, Glutton Bowl*, and *Temptation Island*. I first saw a commercial for O'Reilly's special while watching *Greg the Bunny*, a Fox show that features adorable, fuzzy puppets swearing, farting in their bathwater, and staggering around drunk.

The irony of airing his moralistic special on dirty ol' Fox was clearly lost upon O'Reilly, who only made one mention of the network's egregious, if entertaining, ways: "All the networks, including Fox, present adult situations to children."

Change "including" to "especially" and you might have something closer to the truth.

You might call this Fox-O'Reilly conundrum the

"devil-divine dialectic": Hysteria about nonexistent Satan worshippers often occurs in very Christian towns. So perhaps it's only appropriate that the Sodom and Gomorrah that are Fox should have its own preacher of cultural fire-and-brimstone. It's even more perfect that O'Reilly's special displayed scads of the offending heaving bosoms, bloody gore, and booty shots that he claimed to be protesting. He was truly preaching against sin, Fox-style.

"This special is not designed for preteens, so if they're in the room, you might want to ask them to leave," O'Reilly intoned.

If there were any unsupervised preteens in the house, they definitely stuck around to watch O'Reilly's smorgasbord, including "rage rockers" the Insane Clown Posse (ICP), naughty footage from *American Pie 2*, and images from Internet porn sites.

The opening interview with the ICP yielded few memorable moments, other than when O'Reilly displayed some choice ICP lyrics, including: "I stabbed a fat guy in the butt."

"These songs . . . they're strictly entertainment," said Violent J, a largish man dolled up in clown makeup. "I'm guaranteeing you whatever you listen to, I don't find entertaining."

Things heated up when O'Reilly donned a hideous, offensive accent to announce the segment on rap music: "Inner-city rap and kids: What's up with that?"

Rap and its glorification of drugs, guns, and the pimpin' lifestyle, O'Reilly charged, are "not exactly a recipe for success for children trapped in poverty." "Sixty-three percent of black fourth-graders cannot read," he said to Russell Simmons, founder and chairman of Def Jam Records. "Rap won't help them lift themselves out of poverty."

I slipped into a reverie about O'Reilly giving Guns 'n' Roses, the musical juggernauts of my Midwestern youth, a talking-to. "Many of your fans are glue-sniffing white teens who have no future outside of minimum-wage jobs," he said. "Your immigrant- and gay-hating music won't make them stop hating, won't give them decent jobs outside of McDonald's. They're spending their money on incredibly ugly acid-washed jeans and bandannas instead."

Whoops, my bad. It's only black musicians who have an obligation to be uplifting.

I snapped out of my daydream to hear Russell Simmons deliver one of the hour's rare words of wisdom: "The war on poverty is a much greater war than the war on music."

But O'Reilly, unfazed, continued to harp on gangsta rap, labeling a whole genre of music by one of its subsets. Rock music happily escaped this treatment—when he was trashing ICP and Marilyn Manson, he had the courtesy to label their music "shock rock." He also neglected to mention that with rap and hip hop's booming popularity, most of their audiences are not "these people," but white teens.

Whoops, his bad.

O'Reilly did score some points between the blunders, like comparing Hollywood tactics to market R-rated films to those under 17 with tobacco company ploys to hook the next generation of smokers. He summoned up viewers' gag reflex by discussing the online North American Man/Boy Love Association. And he even targeted bad parents by focusing on the rabid screaming and assaults that have marred the idyllic childhood joys of Little League.

But then "cringe radio" personalities Opie & Anthony, who had the temerity to call themselves "artists," sank O'Reilly's credibility completely when they asked, "Do you have any proof that we're corrupting society?" O'Reilly admitted, "I have no proof."

He did, however, have lots of waggling butts, potty mouths, and World Wrestling Federation scenes to go along with his hair-raising, alarmist, and conspiracy-laden (Hollywood! The music industry! The Internet! Are out to get our children!) harangue. Whatever else you might say about his moralism, on O'Reilly's segment there could be no doubt that the two sides of Fox—the sex and violence part, and the lurid *X-Files* part—had at last been reunited.

He Said It . . .

"Get out of my studio before I tear you to fucking pieces."
—Bill O'Reilly, 2/4/02, as quoted by the victim of his threat, Port Authority worker Jeremy Glick. Glick, whose father had died in the 9/11 attacks, criticized O'Reilly on his program, saying, "you evoke 9/11 to rationalize every-thing from domestic plunder to imperialist aggression."

PSEUDO-INTELLECTUALS

*Every political movement needs its eggheads—
the academics and other brainy types whose
research and analysis eventually lead to party
platforms and policy. The Republicans and the
Radical Right nurture a cadre of reactionary
pseudo-intellectuals who do their thinking for
them. These so-called experts envision a world
run by rich Americans for rich Americans; a
world order where might makes right. Their
vision of a world devoid of community or toler-
ance leads to a politics of fear and violence: Bill
Kristol is Ann Coulter in drag.*

Bill Kristol

from deal-with-it.org
Gus DiZerega

Bill Kristol, editor of *The Weekly Standard*, is perhaps the most influential conservative journalist in the United States today. Unlike the Coulters, O'Reillys, Limbaughs, and similar bloviating blowhards, Kristol does not write for readers who need "red meat," no matter how rancid, to read a sentence longer than a Coca Cola ad. Kristol writes for the most sophisticated members of the Radical Right, particularly neoconservatives.

"Neocons" focus mostly on foreign policy, and appear willing to ally themselves to anyone willing to embrace their views. This in itself is not surprising. But the views Kristol promotes are deeply subversive to American institutions, especially our Constitution.

In the July/August 1996 issue of *Foreign Affairs*, perhaps the most important American foreign policy journal, Kristol, along with Robert Kagan, advocated a new international role for the United States: "Benevolent global hegemony."

Kristol and Kagan continued: "In a world in which peace and American security depend on American power and the will to use it, the main threat the United States faces now and in the future is its own weakness. American hegemony is the only reliable defense against a breakdown of peace and international order. The appropriate goal of American foreign policy, therefore, is to preserve that hegemony as far into the future as possible."

George Szamuely perceptively suggests "When you

come across a passage like this, substitute the words 'German' and 'Germany' for 'American' and the 'United States,' and then see how it sounds."[1]

Hegemony is never benevolent, although some kinds are more brutal than others.

If anything distinguishes nearly all our Radical Right advocates of "hegemony," it is their utter lack of service in the military. Indeed, far more Democratic leaders than Republican ones have served in our armed forces. War is fun for the neoconservatives because they always avoid it when their turn to serve comes up. The wars they advocate are fought by other people.

Kristol's dream of global hegemony for the U.S. threatens American security. The 9-11 terrorists were armed with airline tickets and box cutters. All our tanks, submarines, aircraft carriers, and nuclear weapons did nothing to preserve the World Trade Center and the Pentagon. The FBI and CIA had the evidence they needed to prevent 9/11. But the Bush administration had other priorities. A bigger military budget would not have helped. Bigger people in offices of public trust would.

Other Al Qaeda attacks have involved small boats and trucks laden with explosives, driven by people willing to die for their beliefs. The best defense against such people requires international cooperation. Thanks to Kristol and his allies, we are now pleading for help in Iraq from countries whose opinions we ignored. Hegemony is expensive in blood and treasure. It is also unnecessary.[2]

But Kristol's vision isn't just stupid. It is deeply un-American. He should be ashamed of himself. This nation is based on the principle that citizens are superior to government, and that, as Jefferson put it "the mass of mankind has not been born with saddles on their backs, nor a favored few booted and spurred, ready to ride them. . ."

There will always be Americans who oppose attacking other nations simply because the President's ego compels it, as was the case with Iraq. Such Americans will take America's founding principles seriously. They will use our constitutional government and their rights as citizens to fight the new imperialists and would-be Caesars.

A United States such as the one Kristol advocates cannot afford this kind of opposition. Teddy Roosevelt argued that "To announce that there must be no criticism of the president, or that we are to stand by the president, right or wrong, is not only unpatriotic and servile, but is morally treasonable to the American public." Such a view now sounds vaguely un-American to the citizens who have listened to the rhetoric of neoconservatives such as Kristol who advocate American hegemony.

Bill Kristol, the so-called intellectual, had the temerity to accuse Senator Chuck Hagel (R: NB) of being part of the "axis of appeasement" for questioning Bush's reasons for war with Saddam. Interestingly, Hagel is almost alone among Republican political leaders in actually having served in the military. He earned two purple hearts in Vietnam.[3]

In July Dick Gephardt criticized Bush's inept foreign policy, arguing that it "has left us less safe and secure than we were four years ago." Kristol responded that Gephardt "stand[s] in fundamental opposition" to Bush's struggle with terrorists and "rogue regimes . . . But the American people, whatever their doubts about aspects of Bush's foreign policy, know that Bush is serious about fighting terrorists and terrorist states that mean America harm. About Bush's Democratic critics, they know no such thing."[4]

David Kusnet reported that Kristol had largely repeated his father Irving Kristol's words in praise of Joe McCarthy, simply substituting Bush for the Wisconsin demagogue. In 1952 Irving Kristol wrote "There is one thing that the American people know about Sen. McCarthy. He, like them, is unequivocally anti-Communist. About the spokesmen for American liberalism, they feel they know no such thing." (*Commentary*, 1952)[5]

McCarthy ruined lives, lied about his military record, defended Nazi murderers of American troops, and ultimately attacked the liberals who were the architects of our Cold War policy, which led to Communism's defeat without the catastrophe of a nuclear war. Finally, disgusted Republicans, including President Eisenhower, put McCarthy in his place.

Kristol's attack on the patriotism of Bush's critics harkens back to those dark days. Gephardt helped draft the bipartisan resolution authorizing military action against Iraq, and strongly supported our war on the Taliban and Al Qaeda. Kristol neglected to mention this in his attack on the congressman.

Gephardt served in the Missouri National Guard, where, unlike Bush, he did not go AWOL. Bill Kristol, like Dick Cheney, had other priorities during the Vietnam War. His is a cheap sort of patriotism, long on words and short on deeds.

1. See: www.antiwar.com/szamuely/pf/p-sz022200.html

2. See: http://www.hawaii.edu/powerkills/welcome.html
3. See: http://www.awolbush.com/whoserved.html
4. See: http://www.washingtonpost.com/wp-dyn/
articles/A38029-2003Jul23.html
5. See: http://www.prospect.org/webfeatures/2003/07/
kusnet-d-07-24.html

Breaking Kristol
from *The American Prospect* (April 2003)
Michael Tomasky

As a single cloud at sea can augur a typhoon, so can a short and superficially amiable piece by conservative intellectual godhead William Kristol in *The Weekly Standard* describe a coming right-wing line of attack against liberals that will thunder across the airwaves and op-ed pages for months, probably right up through November 2004. So buckle up, folks, because Kristol, for the April 7 *Standard*, has just written such a piece.

It is a house—no, a skyscraper—of propaganda and lies.

American liberalism faces a crisis, according to Kristol, because it sits on the cusp of one of its historic schisms, this time between "the Dick Gephardt liberals and the Dominique de Villepin left." The Gephardt liberals are the good guys here; they are pro-war, they understand the nefarious nature of the dragons out there that must be slain and they even earn the appellation "patriots." The Villepinistes—well, you can imagine.

There is, obviously, objective truth in the fact that the

party is split on the war. And there is a deeper problem than even Kristol describes, which is that the Democratic Party has no foreign policy (more on this later). But his firm command of the obvious is not what makes his column worth noting. It's the propagandistic ends to which the observation will be put.

Because, you see, opponents of the war—all opponents of the war, no matter their reasoning or motivation—are Villepinistes. And something worse: They are Wallaceites, as in Henry Wallace, the 1948 Progressive Labor Party presidential candidate, who was naive in the extreme about Joseph Stalin and whose campaign was rife with fellow travelers. Democrats and liberals who oppose the war in Iraq, Kristol suggests, are inheritors of this ignoble mantle, while those who back the war are the right and proper children of Harry Truman and the Democratic Cold Warriors of the late 1940s.

A seductive line of reasoning. Like much of what the right puts out, it sort of sounds logical—logical enough not to be challenged by either timorous Democrats (is there any other kind now?) or mainstream journalists who don't know any better. And—like much of what the right puts out—it is Orwellian duplicity, straight out of the Oceania Ministry of Truth, known these days as the Murdoch Empire, in whose very fertile soil Kristol digs his spade.

It would certainly be news, for example, to George Kennan, arguably the most important and influential of the Cold Warriors. How do I know this? Because Kennan is still alive and kicking, nearing 100, and he gave an interview to *The Hill* last Sept. 25 in which he savaged the Bush administration and its perversion of his famous doctrines. Kennan told that newspaper's Albert Eisele the following: that an attack on Iraq would amount to a second war that "bears no relation to the first war against terrorism"; that the administration's attempts to link Saddam Hussein to al-Qaeda were "pathetically unsupportive and unreliable"; that the United States can't "confront all the painful and dangerous situations that exist in the world"; and that the Democratic congressional acquiescence to Bush's war resolution, then fresh, was "a shabby and shameful reaction."

So if we are to believe Bill Kristol, Dick Gephardt is a Kennanite, but even George Kennan is not a Kennanite.

Kristol's take would be news, too, to Arthur Schlesinger Jr. No shrinking violet on Cold War matters, he helped found Americans for Democratic Action specifically to marginalize fellow travelers and soft-headed Stalin apologists from mainstream liberalism. But Schlesinger wrote in the *Los Angeles Times* on March 23: "The president has adopted a policy of 'anticipatory self-defense' that is alarmingly similar to the policy that imperial Japan employed at Pearl Harbor on a date which, as an earlier American president said it would, lives in infamy. Franklin D. Roosevelt was right, but today it is we Americans who live in infamy."

Is Schlesinger, then, a latter-day Wallaceite? No one was a more articulate critic of Wallace-like Soviet apologism in its day than Schlesinger. Pick up your copy of *The Vital Center*, Bill. Read Schlesinger's depiction of the Doughfaces, as he called the PLPers and their kin. It's between pages 42 and 48, depending on your edition. It rings with contempt—and it is, incidentally, a spot-on description of today's Naderites, whom I assure you the vast majority of liberal opponents of the war apprehend with equal disrespect.

Propagandizing about the present cannot work without first lying about the past, and Kristol and others on the right accomplish this with an easy cynicism. They know that the very moniker "Cold Warrior" sounds hawkish, no-nonsense, America-first-like. This, too, is false. Cold Warriors were hawks, but of a self-questioning and deliberative sort. They were multilateralists who built the very organizations today's hawks are out to tear apart. Further, they understood that authority and power were two different things and that the former did not issue solely from the barrel of a gun. They knew that, just as in the old Westerns, unless the circumstance is absolutely dire and no alternative for survival exists, the good guy never shoots first. Richard Perle and Paul Wolfowitz—and Kristol—have nothing whatsoever to do with the old Cold Warriors. And while some opponents of this war are anti-American—and, sure, silly in their arguments—far, far more of us have legitimate concerns about the precedent this sets for other nations and the coming boomerang effect the administration's intentionally failed diplomacy (you read that right) will produce.

But legitimate debate means nothing to these people. Only partisan advantage does. The point is to scare the other side, club it into submission, and you do that by setting up a phony argument and repeating it over and over. And, tragically, it works. That's the fun thing about being in the Ministry of Truth: If you say it, it's true.

That's the propaganda part. Now for the lie.

In his last paragraph, Kristol writes that today's alleged Doughfaces are motivated chiefly by their hatred of

George W. Bush. He writes that it is with sorrow that he recognizes the condition (oh, please!) because in the 1990s, "parts of the Republican Party, and of the conservative movement," were driven by hatred of Bill Clinton. Then we come to this sentence, and it is choice: "But this wing of the GOP and conservatism lost in an intra-party and intra-movement struggle, and has now been marginalized—Pat Buchanan is no longer a Republican, and his magazine these days makes common cause with Norman Mailer and Gore Vidal."

First of all, what "intra-party and intra-movement struggle"? There may have been a few minor reassessments of the party's 1990s posture by a handful of people (let us hope by Kristol himself, who wrote in May of 1998 that Clinton "is doomed" and that Republicans would sweep the midterm elections by focusing on nothing but the president's louche ways). But mainly what happened is that their guy won—hijacked—the White House, so they didn't have anyone in power to hate anymore. Suppose that President Gore were in the White House, and suppose that his military had not captured Osama bin Laden after 18 months; or that anthrax had been mailed to Trent Lott and Jesse Helms' offices, and Gore's Justice Department, 17 months later, didn't even have a *suspect*! It's obvious to anyone with a mind that the Republicans, and Kristol, would be doing to Gore exactly what they did to Clinton in 1998.

But the most dishonest part of the paragraph comes after the dash. So Pat Buchanan led the crusades against Clinton, did he? Granted, Buchanan was no wallflower. But led the opposition? Hardly. Among pols the leader was Tom DeLay, who is still going strong and showing no visible signs of having reassessed anything. And who led the frantic Clinton-hating among writers? At this point, I turn to another for a contemporaneous account:

> No conservative thinker has done more to advance this new moralism than William Kristol. . . . And no journal has done more to propagate, defend, and advance this version of conservatism than the magazine Kristol edits, *The Weekly Standard*. . . . Most of the year, Kristol and *The Standard* have gleefully egged on Republicans in their moral crusade. . . . (P)erhaps no edition of *The Standard* captured the current state of American conservatism better than the one that came out immediately after the Starr report was made public. Its cover portrayed Starr as Mark McGwire, with the headline: 'Starr's Home Run.' Inside, page after page of anti-Clinton coverage, anchored by an essay by Kristol advocating a full House vote for impeachment of the President within a month. . . .

Paul Krugman? Joe Conason? Guess again. That was Andrew Sullivan, in one of his rare lucid moments, in *The New York Times Magazine* for Oct. 11, 1998.

The import of the lie is not merely that Kristol today purports to disdain a posture he in fact endorsed full throttle when it mattered, dishonest though that is. Rather, the importance is the implication that, now that conservatives have thrown Pat overboard, they're sensible, reasonable people.

This much I concede: The Democrats need a foreign policy. They need one that opposes the ultra-hawks and their designs for empire but that also discards Vietnam-era distrust of American power as a potential instrument for good. They need one, in other words, that owes a greater intellectual debt to the likes of Kennan and Schlesinger than to Gene McCarthy; they should be making those historical links explicit in their rhetoric, and they should have been doing so for at least the past year. That they haven't shows not that they are all closet McGovernicks—after all, even the Democratic hawks don't really have a foreign-policy vision, they just think it's a safer position from which to seek the presidency—but that they lack imagination and are captive to poll-sters who tell them no one even knows who Dean Acheson is anymore so why bother?

So, yes, that's a problem for liberalism. But it hardly means that anyone who questions the wisdom of this war is in league with the French and a hellspawn of Henry Wallace. (And speaking of Wallaces, is Lt. Gen. William Wallace, the commander of the ground forces in Iraq who earned conservative ire last week with candid remarks about the war strategy, part of this anti-American cabal as well? A conspiracy so immense . . .) But something tells me that won't prevent Kristol and his comrades from saying it, and saying it again, right up to election day 2004. Until Democrats learn how to define themselves, there will be nothing to prevent the Bill Kristols of the world from doing so for them.

A Dying Breed
from Salon.com (10/03/02)

Louis Bayard

A nd so we beat on," F. Scott Fitzgerald famously wrote, "boats against the current, borne back ceaselessly into the past."

Leading with a quote is surely the appropriate thing to do when reviewing the notoriously allusive George F. Will. But this quote seems particularly relevant to defining the oddly poignant figure that Will cuts at this stage in his career. Two decades ago, he was secretly prepping Ronald Reagan for debates (albeit with briefing papers swiped from the Carter White House), lunching with Nancy Reagan, and guarding the right wing's intellectual flank like a one-headed, four-eyed Cerberus. With his starched shirts and bow ties, with his impassive demeanor and ecclesiastical gestures and the ever-ready epigram squeezing through his pursed lips, he had the feel of his very own establishment—permanent and immovable.

And in fact, he hasn't moved much in the past two decades; it's just the rest of the establishment that has. Conservative policy is no longer hashed out in the gray pages of the *National Review* but in the fractious, jangling confines of talk radio and the Fox News Network. The genteel harrumphs of William F. Buckley and James J. Kilpatrick have given way to the braying outrage of Rush Limbaugh and Brit Hume, and in this new higher-decibel culture, Will, always a throwback, has been thrown so far back as to seem irrelevant.

The White House is no longer requesting talking

points, Laura Bush is *not* calling for lunch, beloved mentors like Meg Greenfield have passed on, nimbler colleagues like Bill Kristol are dancing rings around him on TV, and shriller colleagues like Charles Krauthammer and Michael Kelly are drowning him out on the Op-Ed pages. It's a Roger Ailes world we live in, and the pundits who ascend most rapidly are the ones who most closely resemble psychotic toddlers. (Oh, let's just use Ann Coulter as an example.)

All of which raises an interesting question: Is there any longer a place for George F. Will and what he represents in the Republican republic?

For answer, we have the partial, occluded evidence of his columns, highly burnished artifacts that reflect their creator more vividly than he knows. The last five years' worth have now been gathered into a volume awkwardly titled "With a Happy Eye But . . . " and subtitled "America and the World (1997-2002)," which pretty much covers it all, as far as I can see. Before we address what the author has to say, however, let us see how he is holding up.

The cover photograph finds him in the expected Brooks Brothers suit—navy-blue pinstripes—the once-ubiquitous bow tie now exchanged for a less eccentric rep tie. Arms folded, he poses against an ecru pilaster and paisley-patterned ecru wallpaper, leaning (ever so slightly) on a buffed wooden stair rail. The setting is archetypal gentry, but Will's body language is unique to him and unmistakable. In his own wry, ascetic fashion, he is trying to hold the barbarians at the gate.

But what is this castle he is defending? That takes actually plowing through the columns, and the plowing is, for the most part, easy work. Will may be too arch by half—his favored adjective for Bill Clinton is "glandular"—and years of writing for deadline have imparted their tics, but the prose continually refreshes with its grace and nimbleness and its easy range of reference. Blowhards like William Bennett make lots of noise on behalf of the Western canon without actually imparting very much of it. I can't think of any other mass-media columnist who can so readily avail himself of civilization's contents as Will does.

This is not simply a matter of quoting famous dead people (G.K. Chesterton is a favorite), but of building synthetic bridges between past and present. Will can discourse knowledgeably on everything from the Hegelian theory of history to the rape of Nanking and make it all seem uniquely relevant. He can, with no apparent strain, extrapolate lessons from John Adams, William Tecumseh Sherman and Hannah Arendt. He can produce an assessment of the controversial modern ethicist Peter Singer (then a new hire at Princeton) that is a small masterpiece of intellectual exposition, locating Singer in a utilitarian line that extends back to Jeremy Bentham and coming to a surprisingly equivocal conclusion: "[Singer] will do more to stimulate serious reflection—and more to stimulate opposition to his (literally) homicidal ideas—than he will to make his ideas acceptable. Which is to say, Princeton can justify his appointment by utilitarian arithmetic."

This is as thoughtful as it is elegantly turned, and it is of no small significance that Princeton is the occasion for it, this being the institution that sanctified Will's vocation by awarding him a doctorate in politics. Little wonder, then, that Princeton should be the citadel from which he surveys the enemy position and that his most definitive declaration of war should come in an address commemorating Old Nassau's 250th anniversary.

"Vulgarians are thick on the ground in the nation's capital," he announces. Not a new development, he quickly concedes, but he nevertheless speaks darkly of "the thinning of the common culture" and harks back to the days when "The Old Curiosity Shop" and "Uncle Tom's Cabin" (rather bad books, but never mind) were "part of the shared vocabulary, the casual discourse" of family life, when everyday people could make allusions to the Bible and the classics with the full expectation that they would be understood by other people.

Those days are not quite gone, he acknowledges—civilized people still recognize Dickensian allusions like "Barkis is willin'" and "Something will turn up"—but our fund of reference, he thinks, is being vitiated by the inroads of popular culture. "Contemporary America can still work itself into something of a swivet over the question of 'Who shot J.R.?'" he huffs. "A century and a half on, Micawber and Little Nell, Pickwick and Mr. Bumble, and a host of other Dickensian figures are still part, if a steadily diminishing part, of our common conversation. Who really thinks that even just ten years from now such 'Seinfeld' characters as George Costanza or Kramer will remain fixtures in the public mind?"

To which one might say: Well, if that's the case, what is he whingeing about? It sounds to my ear like whistling in the dark, the positing of a future that is by no means certain, even to Will. This is the man, after all, who believes that "classic" is "a designation usually reserved in America for a variant of Coca-Cola." In his heart of hearts, he must know that, with the benefit of reruns and reunion specials, the characters of "Seinfeld" will still be fixtures in the public mind a decade, three decades hence (just as Lucy Ricardo and Ralph Kramden are still with us half a century later).

What he doesn't seem to recognize is the wobbly line he has drawn in the sand. Even if he hadn't chosen as his whipping boy "Seinfeld," one of the smarter entertainments TV has given us in recent years, even if he had dragged into the equation "American Idol" or "The Osbournes" or "Touched by an Angel," he would still have to acknowledge that high and low can co-exist, that people can read Dickens *and* watch "American Idol." Surely one kind of familiarity does not preclude the other.

But television is, of course, one of modernity's tools, and Will is modernity's sworn enemy. "Schools, including universities, must insist upon the prestige of reading," he writes, "and especially of reading old books." Without contesting the point, we may still glimpse here the defining quality of Will's ideal society: a village of anti-quarians. A populace that still weeps at the deaths of Little Nell and Little Eva. A populace that, in short, no longer exists.

This reactionary, almost necrophiliac esthetic is best observed when Will dips his toes into the currents of popular culture. We get crumpet-laden pleasantries with over-rated mystery writer P.D. James ("Baroness James of Holland Park," he instructs us). A head bowed over the grave of overrated historical novelist Patrick O'Brien ("proof of Chesterton's axiom that great men take up great space even when gone"). A swift boot to the keister of Salinger's Holden Caulfield ("as limited and tiresome as his vocabulary") and a warm bath in the apologetics of

C.S. Lewis, hailed for his "adversarial stance toward life in our time."

Even from this small sampling, a pattern emerges, yes? Anglophiliac. (It is surely no accident that Will's daughter is named Victoria.) Deeply at variance with the present day. And firmly, if unconsciously, rooted in the strictures of class.

To the casual eye, of course, Will's ramrod WASP posture has always looked like blue blood in its most extruded form. You would have to know a little bit about his history to know that he hailed from Champaign, Ill., that his father taught at a public university and that he got his undergraduate degree at Hartford's non-Ivy Trinity College. It hardly matters. Will's Gatsbyite self-reinvention as East Coast Brahmin has been so persuasive that he himself is the most persuaded of all, and his columns are an increasingly desperate search for the right kind of people—the ones who have read the right books, absorbed the right etiquette and have *le mot juste* for every occasion. (In this context, Will's obsessive love for baseball and its practitioners is a bit like the 19th century fondness for the "noble savage.")

Will's treatment of Bill Clinton is instructive in this regard. As *l'affaire Lewinsky* heats up, the columnist's rhetoric rises to higher and higher dudgeon: "A liar . . . a narcissist's delight . . . unserious . . . the worst person ever to have been president" . . . a sower of "moral chaos." But is that the problem with Bill Clinton? Or is it that he misattributed Lincoln's "of the people, by the people, for the people"? Or is it, more likely, the assertion of an Oxford newsletter that Clinton "followed the B.Phil. course." "'Followed'?" sniffs Will, a genuine Oxford grad. "What a delicate way of saying he failed to get a degree." There you have it. Not only a sower of moral chaos but a pretender . . . a social-climbing hick from Arkansas.

It takes some doing to paint a Rhodes scholar as intellectually backward, and one would think that a bar raised so high would effectively decapitate Clinton's successor, who, despite his Ivy pedigree, has been found guilty of such locutions as "Build the pie higher" and "Is our children learning?" Perhaps the challenge of defending Ronald Reagan's intellect during the 1980s proved too taxing in the end, for Will is strangely silent on the whole subject of George W. An approving nod for Bush's post-Sept. 11 orations, a dollop of praise for his position on stem cell research, scattered digs at his positions on education and campaign finance reform . . . little else.

He is silent, too—has always been silent—about the carny barkers of the religious right who have spent the last three decades wrestling Will's Brahmins for control of the Republican Party. A glancing reference to the Rev. Jerry Falwell (defending him from Hillary), no mention at all of Pat Robertson or Ralph Reed or Gary Bauer or any of their yahoo brethren. So much silence from such a ready tongue, and herein lies the irony of George Will's situation. To maintain the aristocratic *ton* that forms the basis of his personality and his credo and his life's work, he must exclude from his field of vision large precincts of his own party, up to and including the president of the United States.

So where does that leave our doughty intellectual? Delivering his tart rejoinders to an increasingly empty chamber, like the professor of an under-subscribed course. God knows, the man still has his viewership and readership— ABC Sunday mornings, *Newsweek*, the *Washington Post*—

but how many followers? How many hungry young Republicans will sit on their hands and listen to him hold forth one more time on Stonewall Jackson (what if he *hadn't* died at Chancellorsville?) or call up the ghost of Henry Adams or recount that awfully interesting lunch he had last week with Avery Dulles? How many of these Young Turks would do anything but gaze in bafflement at the tasks Will calls central to conservatism: "keeping government where it belongs, which is on a short constitutional leash, and politics in its place, which is at the margins of life." Politics at the margins of life? You might as well say *life* is at the margins of life.

Perhaps this feeling of being out of step with his audience accounts for the flagging one detects in Will's writing now. The high notes are still there: missile defense, school choice and school prayer, the natural aristocracy of baseball, the inanity of the NEA, the perils of political correctness and activist judges and the "therapeutic ethos." Will's pleasing vein of self-deprecation is still intact: "My friends, happily rooting for Stan Musial, Red Schoendienst, and other great Redbirds, grew up cheerfully convinced that the world is a benign place. So, of course, they became liberals. Rooting for the Cubs in the late 1940s and early 1950s, I became gloomy, pessimistic, morose, dyspeptic— in a word, conservative." But everything is shot through with elegiac threads: the remains of the columnist's day.

"Being sixty in Washington sometimes feels like having had one year's experience sixty times," he writes. "However, age can confer a certain calm about the passing circus, a preference for understatement and for people with low emotional metabolisms." One of those people, by implication, was Meg Greenfield, the *Washington Post*

eminence who first launched Will into the national mainstream. Will's remembrance of her is warmer than anything else in this volume (warmer even than his memorial
for his father), and while this partiality leads him, I think,
to overvalue Greenfield's writing, it also inspires in him
some of the most explicit renderings of his *beau idéal*:

"For years Meg and I and columnist Charles
Krauthammer regularly met on Saturdays for lunch and
conversation with a guest, usually someone newsworthy.
We met at a greasy spoon on upper Connecticut Avenue in
Washington. The name, Chevy Chase Lounge, was decidedly more upscale than the place. Meg's favorite
moment—how she savored such scenes from Washington's version of the human comedy—was when a
guest, a senator once considered a presidential prospect,
asked the waitress if the tuna was fresh. The waitress said,
sure it was. She meant the can had just been opened."

On one level, this is classic WASP reportage. Note how
that musical line of privilege is ever so delicately sustained: the "greasy spoon" in an otherwise unimpeachable
part of the District, Will and Greenfield and Krauthammer
posed against it like slumming royalty, sniggering in each
other's ear while Washington's elite ("usually someone
newsworthy") stoops to kiss their collective ass. *Asks if the
tuna's fresh! What can the fellow be thinking?*

We can do our own share of sniggering at this self-
important triumvirate, but there is something quite
touching about the tableau they form. Will seems to be
openly hankering for a time—before Bill O'Reilly,
before "The McLaughlin Report"—when people on both
sides of the aisle could be counted on to set the right tone.
When no one raised his voice or sawed his sentences down

to a sound bite (the poor man's epigram) or did anything that could earn eviction from either a Georgetown salon or a Chevy Chase greasy spoon. "A little academe," to quote Shakespeare, "still and contemplative in living art." This is the past into which George Will is ceaselessly borne. May he find rest there.

George Will's Ethics: None of Our Business?

from www.counterpunch.org (1/2/04)

Norman Solomon

We can argue about George Will's political views. But there's no need to debate his professional ethics.

Late December brought to light a pair of self-inflicted wounds to the famous columnist's ethical pretensions. He broke an elementary rule of journalism—and then, when the *New York Times* called him on it, proclaimed the transgression to be no one's business but his own.

It turns out that George Will was among a number of prominent individuals to receive $25,000 per day of conversation on a board of advisers for Hollinger International, a newspaper firm controlled by magnate Conrad Black. Although Will has often scorned the convenient forgetfulness of others, the *Times* reported that "Mr. Will could not recall how many meetings he attended." But an aide confirmed the annual $25,000 fee.

Even for a wealthy commentator, that's a hefty pay-
check for one day of talk. But it didn't stop Will from lav-
ishing praise on Black in print—without a word about
their financial tie.

In early March, Will wrote a syndicated piece that
blasted critics of President Bush's plans to launch an all-
out war on Iraq. Several paragraphs of the column featured quotations from a speech by Black. The laudatory
treatment began high in the column as Will referred to
some criticisms of Bush policies and then wrote: "Into this
welter of foolishness has waded Conrad Black."

The column did not contain the slightest hint that this
wonderful foe of "foolishness" had provided checks to
fatten the columnist's assets at $25,000 a pop.

But Will claimed in a December interview that nothing
was amiss. "Asked in the interview if he should have told
his readers of the payments he had received from
Hollinger," a *New York Times* article reported on Dec. 22,
"Mr. Will said he saw no reason to do so."

The *Times* quoted Will as saying: "My business is my
business. Got it?"

Yeah. We get it, George. The only question is whether
the editors who keep printing your stuff will get it, too.

After three decades as a superstar pundit, Will continues to flourish. Several hundred newspapers publish
his syndicated column, Newsweek prints two-dozen essays
per year, and he appears each Sunday on ABC's "This
Week" television show.

The syndicate with a very big stake in George Will
cannot be indifferent to the latest flap, but there's obvious
reticence to singe the right-winged golden goose. The man
who's the Washington Post Writers Group editorial

director and general manager, Alan Shearer, said: "I think I would have liked to have known."

A week later, via a letter in the *New York Times*, a more forthright response came from Gilbert Cranberg, former chairman of the professional standards committee of the National Conference of Editorial Writers: "When a syndicated journalist writes favorably about a benefactor, that is very much the business of Mr. Will's editors and readers."

Cranberg quoted from the National Conference of Editorial Writers code of ethics, which includes provisions that "the writer should be constantly alert to conflicts of interest, real or apparent"—including "those that may arise from financial holdings" and "secondary employment." Noting that "timely public disclosure can minimize suspicion," the code adds: "Editors should seek to hold syndicates to these standards."

But will they? George Will is a syndicated powerhouse. And he has gotten away with hiding other big conflicts of interest over the last quarter-century.

In October 1980, Will appeared on the ABC television program "Nightline" to praise Ronald Reagan's "thoroughbred performance" in a debate with incumbent President Jimmy Carter. But Will did not disclose to viewers that he'd helped coach Reagan for the debate—and, in the process, had read Carter briefing materials stolen from the White House.

When, much later, Will's "debategate" duplicity came to light, his media colleagues let him off with a polite scolding. The incident faded from media memory. Thus, in autumn 1992, when Will reminisced on ABC's "This Week" about the 1980 Carter-Reagan debate, he didn't mention his own devious role, and none of his journalistic buddies in the studio were impolite enough to say anything about it.

Will has also played fast and loose with ethics in the midst of other contests for the presidency. At the media watch group FAIR (where I'm an associate), senior analyst Steve Rendall pointed out: "During the 1996 campaign, Will caught some criticism for commenting on the presidential race while his second wife, Mari Maseng Will, was a senior staffer for the Dole presidential campaign. Defending a Dole speech on ABC News (1/28/96), Will, according to *Washingtonian* magazine (3/96), 'failed to mention . . . that his wife not only counseled Dole to give the speech but also helped write it.'"

In 2000, Will "suffered another ethical lapse," Rendall recounts in *Extra!*, FAIR's magazine. The renowned columnist "met with George W. Bush just before the Republican candidate was to appear on ABC's 'This Week.' Later, in a column (3/4/01), Will admitted that he'd met with Bush to preview questions, not wanting to 'ambush him with unfamiliar material.' In the meeting, Will provided Bush with a 3-by-5 card containing a crucial question he would later ask the candidate on the air."

George Will has long been fond of denouncing moral deficiencies. Typical was this fulmination in a March 1994 column: "Taught that their sincerity legitimized their intentions, the children of the 1960s grew up convinced they could not do wrong. Hence the Clinton administration's genuine bewilderment when accused of ethical lapses."

In what can be understood as a case of psychological projection, Will derisively added: "It is a theoretical impossibility for people in 'the party of compassion' to behave badly because good behavior is whatever they do."

During the past three decades, Will—who chose to become a syndicated *Washington Post* columnist in the early 1970s rather than continue as a speech writer for Sen. Jesse Helms—has been fond of commenting on the moral failures of black people while depicting programs for equity as ripoff artistry. In February 1991, for instance, he wrote: "The rickety structure of affirmative action, quotas and the rest of the racial spoils system depends on victimology—winning for certain groups the lucrative status of victim."

In subsequent years, not satisfied with his own very lucrative status, Will made a quiet pact with corporate wheeler-dealer Conrad Black. When exposed, Will compounded his malfeasance by declaring that it was only "my business."

Words that George Will wrote 10 years ago now aptly describe his own stance: "It is a theoretical impossibility" that he behaved badly. "Good behavior" is whatever he does.

Nice work if he can get it. And he can.

Got it?

White Whine

from Slate (3/29/01)

William Saletan

A few weeks ago, conservative activist David Horowitz asked college newspapers to print an ad titled "Ten Reasons Why Reparations for Blacks is a Bad Idea *for Blacks*—and Racist Too." The ad provoked a few campus uprisings and a national uproar over race relations and political correctness. The 10 points stated in the ad can be boiled down to four principles about racial generalizations, divisiveness, gratitude, and victimization. Whether reparations advocates, blacks, college students, or liberals should heed the four principles can be debated. What is certain is that these principles are being ignored by David Horowitz.

1. DON'T LUMP PEOPLE INTO GROUPS.

The ad points out that the coarse idea of transferring money from all whites to all blacks overlooks distinctions within these groups. "Black Africans and Arabs were responsible for enslaving the ancestors of African-Americans," says the ad. "There were 3,000 black slave-owners in the antebellum United States," and "many blacks were free men." Moreover, "Only a tiny minority of Americans ever owned slaves," and many people who would be asked to pay reparations are "descendants of the 350,000 Union soldiers who died to free the slaves."

In debating his critics, however, Horowitz casts aside such distinctions. "America has given black America a great gift of freedom and prosperity and opportunity. But the black leadership just wants to shake down . . . the rest of America," Horowitz charged on Fox News' *The Edge* two weeks ago. On *The O'Reilly Factor*, he deplored "the very sad state to which the black movement, political movement, has come." And while protesting that blacks shouldn't be lumped together when discussing what some of them are owed, Horowitz casually lumps them together when discussing what some of them have been paid. "Forty percent of all the welfare moneys went to black people, who only paid 13 percent of the taxes," he argued on *Hannity & Colmes* this week. "So there has been a net transfer of wealth through welfare to black America, from all the rest of America, of trillions of dollars."

Similarly, Horowitz dismisses all critics of his egotism, tastelessness, casual exaggeration, petty belligerence, and/or political views as "the left." "Every American is suspect in the eyes of the left—and this is about the left—as somebody harboring racist ideas," Horowitz complained on *Hannity & Colmes*. "Leftists have contempt for America," he declared at Berkeley two weeks ago. "What the left is about is a species of civil war." To *Newsweek*, he complained, "The left boycotts my events and burns down my posters." From whom has Horowitz extrapolated this monolithic picture? Himself. "I adopted the tone and the style of the left, and they can't handle it," he says.

2. Don't foment ethnic conflict.

"The African-American community has had a long-running flirtation with separatists, nationalists and the political left, who want African-Americans to be no part of America's social contract. African Americans should reject this temptation," Horowitz writes in his ad. "The reparations claim is

one more assault on America, conducted by racial separatists and the political left. . . . The American idea needs the
support of its African-American citizens."

To illustrate his concern that reparations might stir up
racial conflict, Horowitz uses the example of an immigrant from Mexico. "How could you tell Jose Martinez,
who may have come to this country 10 years ago and is
struggling to put bread on the table for his family, to pay
reparations to Johnnie Cochran and Jesse Jackson, who
are multimillionaires? This is a very divisive campaign,"
Horowitz protested on CNN's *The Point* March 27. The
warning might have seemed more sincere if it hadn't been
at least the 11th time Horowitz had delivered exactly the
same sound bite—Jose Martinez, bread on the table,
Johnnie Cochran, Jesse Jackson, multimillionaires—over
the course of three weeks. When Horowitz repeatedly goes
on television to predict that the black leadership's "constant shakedown of the rest of America" will "alienate the
black America from Hispanic America, Asian America,
and European America" (Fox News, March 12) and will
"pit Hispanic-Americans, Asian-Americans, as well as
European-Americans, and all other Americans against the
African-American community" (CNN, March 26), he has
crossed the line from forecasting a backlash to inviting it.

Horowitz also complains that three college newspapers
that rejected his reparations ad "printed an ad denying the
Holocaust a few years ago." This complaint clearly isn't
about consistent censorship of views that might be
deemed offensive to minorities. It appears to be about dif-
ferential treatment of views pertaining to two different
minorities. What exactly is Horowitz's point?

3. ALL'S WELL THAT ENDS WELL.
According to Horowitz, "African-Americans have benefited from slavery." In the ad, he dissolves past wrongs
with a utilitarian shrug, arguing that blacks have gained
more from the United States in the long run than they
lost in the short run. "The claim for reparations is
premised on the false assumption that only whites have
benefited from slavery. If slave labor created wealth for
Americans, then obviously it has created wealth for black
Americans as well," he writes. "American blacks on
average enjoy per capita incomes in the range of twenty
to fifty times that of blacks living in any of the African
nations from which they were kidnapped. . . . If not for
the dedication of Americans of all ethnicities and colors
to a society based on the principle that all men are created equal, blacks in America would not enjoy the
highest standard of living of blacks anywhere in the
world. . . . Where is the gratitude of black America and
its leaders for those gifts?"

The same question could be asked of Horowitz. By a
similarly utilitarian calculus, he has profited from his persecution. Thanks to radical students at three campuses
who tried to punish editors for running his ad—and who
took copies of the Brown University newspaper to prevent
the ad's dissemination—Horowitz has now reaped, by his
own admission, "the most publicity I've ever got." He fills
college lecture halls and appears on national TV virtually
every day. His run-ins with hecklers and protesters at campuses a few weeks ago have given way to well-attended
speeches and orderly question-and-answer sessions. But
that hasn't stopped him from harping on his persecution,
which evidently includes the public regrets of editors who

printed his ad. Such apologies are "a way of stigmatizing me and my views," Horowitz told *Newsweek*.

4. GET OVER IT.

Even if slavery's injustice hasn't been canceled out by subsequent progress, Horowitz argues in his ad that it was a long time ago and that it's unhealthy for blacks to dwell on it. The hardships created by slavery "were hardships that individuals could and did overcome," he writes. "The renewed sense of grievance—which is what the claim for reparations will inevitably create—is neither a constructive nor a helpful message for black leaders to be sending to their communities and to others. To focus the social passions of African-Americans on what some Americans may have done to their ancestors fifty or a hundred and fifty years ago is to burden them with a crippling sense of victimhood." Extending this anti-whining argument to critics of his ad, Horowitz told the *New York Times*, "These black students come in and say, 'This hurts our feelings.' Come on, an argument hurts your feelings? Fight back."

But when it comes to wallowing in grievances, victimization, and hurt feelings, nobody can match Horowitz. For weeks, he has fled from one media venue to another, claiming to be oppressed by "fascists" and "witch hunters" who are subjecting universities to a "dictatorship of the politically correct" and an oxymoronic reign of "intellectual terror." Today's accusations of racism against campus conservatives are "much worse than the McCarthy era ever was," Horowitz declared a week ago. This week he proclaimed, "There is no editor of a campus paper who does not have to live in some kind of fear of vigilante action if he should print something that deeply offends the far political left."

Horowitz says that Harvard and Columbia "banned" his ad. "When the University of Wisconsin *Badger-Herald* ran the ad, its editorial offices were visited by 150 angry protesters. Campus police instructed the editors to take refuge in their dorms and lock the doors to ensure their safety," he reports. "At Brown the entire print of the *Daily Herald* was stolen and trashed. At UC Berkeley and UC Davis, the campus papers printed the ad, but after being visited by angry protesters in their offices, the editors of both papers performed public acts of contrition—one for 'inadvertently' becoming a 'vehicle for bigotry' and the other for printing 'discriminatory statements(!)' "

Actually, not a single act of violence has been reported. Harvard and Columbia didn't ban the ad. Their principal student newspapers declined to take the ad, leaving Horowitz the option of submitting his message as an op-ed or delivering it through other outlets on those campuses. Student protesters tried to pressure or punish editors at Wisconsin and Brown who ran the ad, but the editors stood up to them and kept their jobs. Campus police, as the Wisconsin case illustrates, protected the editors. Brown reprinted 1,000 copies of its newspaper, and campus police guarded the newsstands where they were delivered. The editor at Berkeley who apologized for running the ad has been derided in the national media for doing so—and what's important for the exchange of ideas is that he ran the ad, not what he said afterward. "I had 30 armed guards at Berkeley. And there seem to be some here today," Horowitz complained at the University of Texas. "This is an outrage on a college campus." An outrage?

Imagine what Horowitz would have said if he *hadn't* been protected. Finding a grievance either way is the highest art of the professional martyr.

Horowitz's most ludicrous complaint is that his oppression is even worse because his views are overwhelmingly popular. "I cannot go and speak on the University of California campus without being concerned about my security," despite the fact that "70 percent of the American people support the anti-reparations view," he protested on Fox News. On CNN, Horowitz said of a leftist professor, "This is the way he intimidates his campus community, by calling perfectly reasonable arguments—shared by 70 percent of the American people—calling them racist." To *Newsweek*, Horowitz flatly declared, "The issue of reparations isn't going anywhere." So where's the crisis? Horowitz isn't the isolated minority. His "intimidators" are.

Absent any violence or successful attempt at suppression, what crime has been committed against Horowitz? He says campus leftists have "censored" him and other conservatives through "bullying" and "moral intimidation." He defines moral intimidation as "a species of racial McCarthyism—wild accusations of racism and bigotry, and indiscriminate use of guilt by association." How exactly do nasty accusations violate free speech? "There's a very important issue at stake here," Horowitz explained on CNN. "And that is not only my right to say what I want to say . . . but to say it without coming under attack with a smear campaign." On Fox News, he demanded the "right . . . to be able to express reasonable views without being accused of racism or bigotry." At Berkeley, he faults "an assistant chancellor who sat with the bullies in the back and refused, as I had asked them to do, to introduce me and to insist on order and decorum." The result was that students "organized" and "chanted" at Horowitz. At the University of Texas, Horowitz criticized administrators for failing to ensure that "views like mine can be heard regularly without it being a big controversy."

To rectify the left's crimes against Horowitz, in short, colleges would have to stop tolerating so much controversy, protest, and talk of bigotry. And to think the descendants of slaves are only asking for money.

Right Reverent
from *The New Republic* (3/25/02)
Jonathan Chait

It was during the summer of 2000 that Peggy Noonan's adoration of George W. Bush began in earnest. The GOP candidate, she wrote in her *Wall Street Journal* column, "seems transparently a good person, a genuine fellow who isn't hidden or crafty or sneaky or mean, a person of appropriate modesty." Over the next year or so, she went on to call him "respectful, moderate, commonsensical, courteous," and "a modest man of faith." She has seen in him "dignity" and "a kind of joshy gravitas." And this was before September 11. Since then, he has risen in her estimation. The president has "a new weight, a new gravity, a new physical and moral comfort." He possesses "a sharp and intelligent instinct, an inner shrewdness." He is "emotionally and intellectually mature."

The interesting thing here isn't Noonan's devotion to the president—most conservatives praise Bush, just as most liberals criticize him—but rather the personal nature of that devotion. She exhibits little interest in the president's policies except as windows into the greatness of his character. And Noonan is not alone in this politics of hero worship. She shares a sensibility with pundits like Mark Helprin, a fellow *Journal* contributor who penned speeches for Bob Dole in 1996, and Noemie Emery, a contributor to *The Weekly Standard* and *National Review*. In fact, the genre seems to be in vogue on the right.

The hallmarks of the hero-worship style are a Manichaean moral sensibility, eloquent prose, and assertion rather than argument. This might seem like a harmless, even refreshing, counterpoint to the politics of personal destruction, which both parties now disdain as mindlessly partisan and corrosive to civic health. But Peggy Noonan's glorification of George W. Bush isn't a departure from the politics of personal destruction at all. It's the very same thing.

Noonan, like Bush himself, invests considerable meaning in the phrase "good man." ("Good man" is also the president's favorite tribute when announcing a nominee.) The term suggests an all-encompassing personal uprightness that trumps any particular questions about professional qualifications or issue positions. The good man can be trusted to do the honorable thing.

For conservatives, of course, the modern model of the good man in politics is Ronald Reagan. And Noonan, his former speechwriter, has carved out a role for herself as the Gipper's swooning head cheerleader. Her most recent book, *When Character Was King: A Story of Ronald Reagan*, casts the former president in almost mythical terms. "It was [Reagan's] character—his courage, his kindness, his persistence, his honesty, and his almost heroic patience in the face of setbacks," her book claims, summarizing its central contention, "that was the most important element of his success."

Indeed, Noonan sees character as virtually the *only* element of Reagan's success. To the minimal extent that she addresses Reagan's policies, she considers them outgrowths of his personal integrity. She writes, for instance, that Reagan "was by nature a conservationist because he believed what [his mother] told him: Man was made in God's image and given dominion over natural things." What about his environmental policies and his fiercely pro-development Interior Secretary James Watt? Noonan does not even mention them. She glides over Reagan's divorce and indifferent parenting; instead she lavishes attention upon his poor, character-building childhood, his kindness to underlings, and other personal virtues. Her biography has all the moral nuance of a fairy tale.

If Reagan helped establish the good-man theory of politics among conservatives, Bill Clinton confirmed it—by serving as the quintessential bad man. Just as Reagan's policies were seen as an extension of his inner goodness, Clinton's policies were deemed an extension of his inner evil. Clinton, in Noonan's columns, does not just pursue misguided policies; he pursues them with malicious intent. "They are atheists. They don't believe in God," she quotes the Miami mayor as saying of the Clintonites in a column on the Elián Gonzalez affair. She dismisses the possibility that Clinton believed he was acting in Elián's best interests and speculates that Castro blackmailed him, sexually or otherwise. ("Is it irresponsible to speculate? It is irresponsible not to," she explains.) She ends the column by wondering "what Ronald Reagan, our last great president, would have done." One answer is that her hero "would not have dismissed the story of the dolphins [sent by God to rescue Elián] as Christian kitsch, but seen it as possible evidence of the reasonable assumption that God's creatures had been commanded to protect one of God's children." She concludes, "But then he was a man."

Given the popularity of Clinton's policies and the unpopularity of his personal behavior, Noonan's characterological analysis dovetailed neatly with the political interests of the Republican Party. But it is striking how easily Noonan and her associates have transposed it onto the post-Clinton era. Even Al Gore's fiercest conservative detractors did not, during the Clinton years, put him on the same moral plane as Clinton. In fact, for most of his political career, Gore had the reputation of something of a Boy Scout. But when he won the nomination, Gore quickly came to embody the moral depravity of liberalism. Noonan, in fact, worked herself into such a moralistic lather that by mid-fall she considered Gore "not fully stable" and "altogether as strange and disturbing as Bill Clinton." For her part, Emery wrote a cover story for *National Review* after Gore sewed up the nomination, tabbing him "WORSE THAN CLINTON," and by fall he was worse than that: "self-obsessed, conniving, dangerous," "a monster willing to trash the whole country." (The tactic was handy with other threats as well: When John McCain became a danger to Bush, conservative hero-worshipers attacked even him. Helprin, who has spent his career writing about martial valor—and who wrote poetically in 1996 of Bob Dole's wartime bravery—attacked the Republican apostate as "not honorable" and committing "betrayals.")

The problem with Noonan's brand of hero-worship isn't that character doesn't matter. Reasonable people can disagree about the proper weight to place on personal virtue versus ideology in evaluating a politician. But for Noonan and her ilk, conservative ideology and personal virtue are so deeply intertwined that it is virtually impossible for a good person to pursue liberal policies or for a conservative politician to be morally flawed. And this allows Noonan to view similar sets of facts in wildly inconsistent ways. Earlier this year Noonan wrote an entire column praising Bush for prohibiting his staff from leaking to the press. One year before, she denounced Clinton for the same thing. "The code of omerta," she thundered, "ran strong and was obviously enforced." Noonan defended Bush's vicious attacks on McCain in the South Carolina primary, which included racial innuendo and disparagement of his military record. "You make the best case possible for yourself and what you stand for, and you paint your opponent in less attractive light," she lectures. "That's what politics is." Unless, of course, a Democrat is practicing politics. "Al Gore is surrounded by tough mean operatives whose sole political instinct is to rip out the other guy's guts and dance in the blood," she later raged.

Noonan's unstated assumption is that Democratic politicians do not have the moral right to, well, do what politicians do. She attacks Clinton for "unleashing the fierce energy of your hatred into the national bloodstream, and getting all your people out there on television every day to hate for you," as if Clinton loyalists ruled the airwaves unopposed for eight years. She sneers that "the endlessly calculating Tom Daschle"—in Noonan's world, only Democrats have pollsters—"did his hair up and got made up" to do a speech. Vanity is another telltale liberal trait. Emery approvingly cites Bush's observation about Gore— "The man dyes his hair. What does that tell you about him? He doesn't know who he is."—as evidence of his sound judgment. But wait: Reagan dyed his hair, too! Somebody needs to get the catechism straight on this point.

In one preelection column, Noonan went so far as to assert that Gore doesn't actually believe his political positions, but hews to them out of expediency. On partial-birth abortion, she writes, Gore "supports something he knows to be sick and wrong." On education, he "knows the most hopeful proposal of our time to make government schools better is the school liberation movement— including scholarship vouchers . . ." but because teachers unions oppose them, "Al Gore lies and says vouchers are bad." "Al Gore knows that it is responsible and constructive to allow greater freedom and choice in Social Security," she continues. "But he lies and says it's bad." Noonan presents no evidence of the bad faith she attributes to Gore. She simply assumes that no one who holds his policies can be well-meaning.

In other words, the seemingly sweet hero-worship in Noonan's writing is merely the flip side of all the traits that have made politics a death struggle—think impeachment and Florida—in recent years. If politics is a struggle between good ideas and bad ideas, a compromise can be found. If it is a struggle between good people and bad people, then absolute victory and absolute defeat are the only options.

"JOURNALISTS" AND OTHER SCOUNDRELS

with quotes by Tucker Carlson;
a cartoon by Daryl Cagle;
and an anagram

*The media is not liberal. True, some journalists—
the best of them—are. Good journalists, like
good liberals, are intellectually curious people
who know how the world works. A good journalist can't help but recognize that the Radical
Right is morally and intellectually bankrupt and
thus unfit to set our nation's policy. But big
media is a for-profit enterprise, and its owners
tend to be conservatives—some are card-
carrying members of the Radical Right. That's
why the media savaged Al Gore during the
2000 election campaign, while his sock-puppet
opponent got a free ride.*

The media should do a better job of defending itself from the lies of its right-wing critics. Eric Alterman offers plenty of ammunition in this article, and in his 2003 book of the same title.

What Liberal Media?

from *The Nation* (2/24/03)

Eric Alterman

Social scientists talk about "useful myths," stories we all know aren't necessarily true, but that we choose to believe anyway because they seem to offer confirmation of what we already know (which raises the question, If we already know it, why the story?). Think of the wholly fictitious but illustrative story about little George Washington and his inability to lie about that cherry tree. For conservatives, and even many journalists, the "liberal media" is just that—a myth, to be sure, but a useful one.

Republicans of all stripes have done quite well for themselves during the past five decades fulminating about the liberal cabal/progressive thought police who spin, supplant and sometimes suppress the news we all consume. (Indeed, it's not only conservatives who find this whipping boy to be an irresistible target. In late 1993 Bill Clinton whined to *Rolling Stone* that he did not get "one damn bit of credit from the knee-jerk liberal press.") But while some conservatives actually believe their own grumbles, the smart ones don't. They know mau-mauing the other side is just a good way to get their own ideas across—or perhaps prevent the other side from getting a fair hearing for theirs. On occasion, honest conservatives admit this. Rich Bond, then chair of the Republican Party, complained during the 1992 election, "I think we know who the media want to win this election—and I don't think it's George Bush." The very same Rich Bond, however, also noted during the very same election, "There is some strategy to it [bashing the 'liberal' media] . . . . If you watch any great coach, what they try to do is 'work the refs.' Maybe the ref will cut you a little slack on the next one."

Bond is hardly alone. That the media were biased against the Reagan Administration is an article of faith among Republicans. Yet James Baker, perhaps the most media-savvy of them, owned up to the fact that any such complaint was decidedly misplaced. "There were days and times and events we might have had some complaints [but] on balance I don't think we had anything to complain about," he explained to one writer. Patrick Buchanan, among the most conservative pundits and presidential candidates in Republican history, found that he could not identify any allegedly liberal bias against him during his presidential candidacies. "I've gotten balanced coverage, and broad coverage—all we could have asked. For heaven sakes, we kid about the 'liberal media,' but every Republican on earth does that," the aspiring American ayatollah cheerfully confessed during the 1996 campaign. And even William Kristol, without a doubt the most influential Republican/neoconservative publicist in America today, has come clean on this issue. "I admit it," he told a reporter. "The liberal media were never that powerful, and the whole thing was often used as an excuse by conservatives for conservative failures." Nevertheless, Kristol apparently feels no compunction about exploiting and reinforcing the ignorant prejudices of his own constituency. In a 2001 pitch to conservative potential subscribers to his Rupert Murdoch-funded magazine, Kristol complained, "The trouble with politics and political coverage today is that there's too much liberal bias . . . . There's too much tilt toward the left-wing agenda. Too much apology for liberal policy failures. Too much pandering to liberal candidates and causes." (It's a wonder he left out "Too much hypocrisy.")

In recent times, the right has ginned up its "liberal media" propaganda machine. Books by both Ann Coulter and Bernard Goldberg have topped the bestseller lists, stringing together a series of charges so extreme that, well, it's amazing neither one thought to accuse "liberals" of using the blood of conservatives' children for extra flavor in their soy-milk decaf lattes.

Given the success of Fox News, the *Wall Street Journal* editorial pages, the *Washington Times*, the *New York Post*, *The American Spectator*, *The Weekly Standard*, the *New York Sun*, *National Review*, *Commentary*, Limbaugh, Drudge, etc., no sensible person can dispute the existence of a "conservative media." The reader might be surprised to learn that neither do I quarrel with the notion of a "liberal media." It is tiny and profoundly underfunded compared with its conservative counterpart, but it does exist. As a columnist for *The Nation* and an independent weblogger for MSNBC.com, I work in the middle of it, and so do many of my friends. And guess what? It's filled with right-wingers.

Unlike most of the publications named above, liberals, for some reason, feel compelled to include the views of the other guy on a regular basis in just the fashion that conservatives abhor. Take a tour from a native: *New York* magazine, in the heart of liberal country, chose as its sole national correspondent the right-wing talk-show host Tucker Carlson. During the 1990s, *The New Yorker*—the bible of sophisticated urban liberalism—chose as its Washington correspondents the belligerent right-winger Michael Kelly and the soft, DLC neoconservative Joe Klein. At least half of the "liberal *New Republic*" is actually a rabidly neoconservative magazine and has been edited in recent years by the very same Michael Kelly, as well as by the conservative liberal-hater Andrew Sullivan. *The Nation* has often opened its pages to liberal-haters, even among its columnists. *The Atlantic Monthly*—a mainstay of Boston liberalism—even chose the apoplectic Kelly as its editor, who then proceeded to add a bunch of *Weekly Standard* writers to its antiliberal stable. What is "liberal" *Vanity Fair* doing publishing a special hagiographic Annie Leibovitz portfolio of Bush Administration officials that appears, at first glance, to be designed (with the help of a Republican political consultant) to invoke notions of Greek and Roman gods? Why does the liberal *New York Observer* alternate *National Review*'s Richard Brookhiser with the Joe McCarthy-admiring columnist Nicholas von Hoffman— both of whom appear alongside editorials that occasionally mimic the same positions taken downtown by the editors of the *Wall Street Journal*? On the web, the tabloid-style liberal website *Salon* gives free rein to the McCarthyite impulses of both Sullivan and David Horowitz. The neoliberal *Slate* also regularly publishes both Sullivan and Christopher Caldwell of *The Weekly Standard*, and has even opened its "pages" to such conservative evildoers as Charles Murray and Elliott Abrams.

Move over to the mainstream publications and broadcasts often labeled "liberal," and you see how ridiculous the notion of liberal dominance becomes. The liberal *New York Times* Op-Ed page features the work of the unreconstructed Nixonite William Safire, and for years accompanied him with the firebreathing-if-difficult-to-understand neocon A.M. Rosenthal. Current denizen Bill Keller also writes regularly from a DLC neocon perspective. The *Washington Post* is just swarming with conservatives, from Michael Kelly to George Will to Robert Novak to Charles Krauthammer. If you wish to include CNN on your list of liberal media—I don't, but many conservatives do—then you had better find a way to explain the near-ubiquitous presence of the attack dog Robert Novak, along with that of neocon virtuecrat William Bennett, *National Review*'s Kate O'Beirne, *National Review*'s Jonah Goldberg, *The Weekly Standard*'s David Brooks and Tucker Carlson. This is to say nothing of the fact that among its most frequent guests are Coulter and the anti-American telepreacher Pat Robertson. Care to include ABC News? Again, I don't, but if you wish, how to deal with the fact that the only ideological commentator on its Sunday show is the hard-line conservative George Will? Or how about the fact that its only explicitly ideological reporter is the journalistically challenged conservative crusader John Stossel? How to explain the entire career there and on NPR of Cokie Roberts, who never met a liberal to whom she could not condescend? What about *Time* and *Newsweek*? In the former, we have Krauthammer holding forth, and in the latter, Will.

I could go on, but the point is clear: Conservatives are extremely well represented in every facet of the media. The correlative point is that even the genuine liberal media are not so liberal. And they are no match—either in

size, ferocity or commitment—for the massive conservative media structure that, more than ever, determines the
shape and scope of our political agenda.

In a careful 1999 study published in the academic
journal *Communications Research*, four scholars examined
the use of the "liberal media" argument and discovered a
fourfold increase in the number of Americans telling poll-
sters that they discerned a liberal bias in their news. But a
review of the media's actual ideological content, collected
and coded over a twelve-year period, offered no corrobo-
ration whatever for this view. The obvious conclusion:
News consumers were responding to "increasing news
coverage of liberal bias media claims, which have been
increasingly emanating from Republican Party candidates
and officials."

The right is working the refs. And it's working. Much of
the public believes a useful but unsupportable myth about
the so-called liberal media, and the media themselves
have been cowed by conservatives into repeating their
nonsensical nostrums virtually nonstop. As the economist/
pundit Paul Krugman observes of Republican efforts to
bully the media into accepting the party's Orwellian arguments about Social Security privatization: "The next time
the administration insists that chocolate is vanilla, much
of the media—fearing accusations of liberal bias, trying to
create the appearance of 'balance'—won't report that the
stuff is actually brown; at best they'll report that some
Democrats claim that it's brown."

In the real world of the right-wing media, the pundits
are the conservatives' shock troops. Even the ones who
constantly complain about alleged liberal control of the
media cannot ignore the vast advantage their side enjoys

when it comes to airing their views on television, in the opinion pages, on the radio and the Internet.

Take a look at the Sunday talk shows, the cable chat fests, the op-ed pages and opinion magazines, and the radio talk shows. It can be painful, I know, but try it. Across virtually the entire television punditocracy, unabashed conservatives dominate, leaving lone liberals to be beaten up by gangs of marauding right-wingers, most of whom voice views much further toward their end of the spectrum than any regularly televised liberals do toward the left. Grover Norquist, the right's brilliant political organizer, explains his team's advantage by virtue of the mindset of modern conservatism. "The conservative press is self-consciously conservative and self-consciously part of the team," he notes. "The liberal press is much larger, but at the same time it sees itself as the establishment press. So it's conflicted. Sometimes it thinks it needs to be critical of both sides." Think about it. Who among the liberals can be counted upon to be as ideological, as relentless and as nakedly partisan as George Will, Robert Novak, Pat Buchanan, Bay Buchanan, William Bennett, William Kristol, Fred Barnes, John McLaughlin, Charles Krauthammer, Paul Gigot, Oliver North, Kate O'Beirne, Tony Blankley, Ann Coulter, Sean Hannity, Tony Snow, Laura Ingraham, Jonah Goldberg, William F. Buckley Jr., Bill O'Reilly, Alan Keyes, Tucker Carlson, Brit Hume, the self-described "wild men" of the *Wall Street Journal* editorial page, etc., etc.? In fact, it's hard to come up with a single journalist/pundit appearing on television who is even remotely as far to the left of the mainstream spectrum as most of these conservatives are to the right.

Liberals are not as rare in the print punditocracy as in

television, but their modest numbers nevertheless give the lie to any accusations of liberal domination. Of the most prominent liberals writing in the nation's newspapers and opinion magazines—Garry Wills, E.J. Dionne, Richard Cohen, Robert Kuttner, Robert Scheer, Paul Krugman, Bob Herbert, Mary McGrory, Hendrik Hertzberg, Nicholas Kristof, Molly Ivins—not one enjoys or has ever enjoyed a prominent perch on television. Michael Kinsley did for a while, but only as the liberal half of *Crossfire*'s tag team, and Kinsley, by his own admission, is not all that liberal. The *Weekly Standard* and *National Review* editors enjoy myriad regular television gigs of their own, and are particularly popular as guests on the allegedly liberal CNN. Columnists Mark Shields and Al Hunt also play liberals on television, but always in opposition to conservatives and almost always on the other team's ideological field, given the conservatives' ability to dominate television's "he said, she said" style of argument virtually across the board.

As a result of their domination of the terms of political discourse, conservative assumptions have come to rule the roost of insider debate. And they do so not only because of conservative domination of the punditocracy but also because of conservative colonization of the so-called center—where all action in American politics is deemed to take place.

Consider the case of Howard Kurtz. By virtue of his responsibilities at CNN as host of *Reliable Sources* and at the *Washington Post* as its media reporter and columnist, Kurtz is widely recognized as the most influential media reporter in America, akin to the top cop on the beat. There is no question that Kurtz is a terrifically energetic reporter.

But all media writers, including myself, walk a difficult line with regard to conflicts of interest. As a reporter and a wide-ranging talk-show host, Kurtz, unlike a columnist, cannot choose simply to ignore news. What's more, the newspaper for which he writes cannot help but cover CNN, the network on which he appears, and vice versa, as they both constitute 800-pound gorillas in the media jungle. *Post* executive editor Len Downie Jr. says he thinks "the problem is endemic to all media reporters. Everyone in the media universe is a competitor of the *Washington Post*, and so it's impossible to avoid conflicts of interest. Either we tell him the only people he can cover is *The Nation* or we set up this unique rule for him that he has to identify his relationship with whomever he writes about." Downie may be right. But the system didn't work perfectly when Kurtz covered Walter Isaacson's resignation from CNN recently. He wrote a tougher piece on Isaacson than most, which is fine, and noted that he worked for CNN at the end, but did not note that the network brass— meaning, presumably, Isaacson—had just cut his airtime in half. (Kurtz later explained this in an online chat.)

Regarding the political coloration of his work, it is no secret to anyone in the industry that CNN has sought to ingratiate itself with conservatives in recent years as it has lost viewers to Fox. Shortly after taking the reins, in the summer of 2001, Isaacson initiated a number of moves designed to enhance the station's appeal to conservatives, including a high-profile meeting with the Congressional Republican leadership to listen to their concerns. The bias reflected in Kurtz's work at the *Post* and CNN would be consistent with that of a media critic who had read the proverbial writing on the wall.

Whatever his personal ideology may be, it is hard to avoid the conclusion, based on an examination of his work, that Kurtz loves conservatives but has little time for liberals. His overt sympathy for conservatives and their critique of the media is, given the power and influence of his position, not unlike having the police chief in the hands of a single faction of the mob. To take just one tiny example of many in my book *What Liberal Media?*, Kurtz seemed to be working as a summer replacement for Ari Fleischer when Bush's Harken oil shenanigans briefly captured the imagination of the Washington press corps, owing to the perception of a nationwide corporate meltdown during the summer of 2002. Over and over Kurtz demanded of his guests:

> "Why is the press resurrecting, like that 7-million-year-old human skull, this thirteen-year-old incident, in which Bush sold some stock in his company Harken Energy?"

> "Laura Ingraham, is this the liberal press, in your view, trying to prove that Bush is soft on corporate crime because he once cut corners himself?"

> "Regulators concluded he did nothing improper. Now, there may be some new details, granted, but this is—is this important enough to suggest, imply or otherwise infer, as the press might be doing, Molly Ivins, that this is somehow in a league with Tyco or WorldCom or Enron?"

> "Is there a media stereotype Bush and Cheney,

ex-oilmen, ex-CEOs in bed with big business that
they can't shake?"

"Are the media unfairly blaming President Bush for
sinking stock prices? Are journalists obsessed with
Bush and Cheney's business dealings in the oil
industry, and is the press turning CEOs into black-
hatted villains?"

"If you look at all the negative media coverage, Rich
Lowry, you'd think that Bush's stock has crashed
along with the market. Is he hurting, or is this some
kind of nefarious media creation?"

"And why is that the President's fault? Is it his job
to keep stock prices up?"

Kurtz even went so far as to give credence to the ludicrous, Limbaugh-like insistence that somehow Bill
Clinton caused the corporate meltdown of the summer of
2002. Kurtz quoted these arguments, noting, "They say,
well, he set a bad example for the country. He showed he
could lie and get away with it, so is that a reverse kind of
'Let's drag in the political figure we don't like and pin the
tail on him?'" It was, as his guest Martha Brant had to
inform him, "a ridiculous argument," surprising Kurtz,
who asked again, "You're saying there's no parallel?"
Recall that this is the premier program of media criticism
hosted by the most influential media reporter in America.
It did not occur to Kurtz to note, for instance, as Peter
Beinart did, that Clinton vetoed the 1995 bill that
shielded corporate executives from shareholder lawsuits

(when every single Republican voted to override him), or that Clinton's Securities and Exchange Commission chief wanted to ban accounting firms from having consulting contracts with the firms they were also auditing. Thirty-three of thirty-seven members of Congress who signed their names to protests against the Clinton SEC were also Republican. The man who led the effort was then-lobbyist Harvey Pitt, whom George W. Bush chose to head the SEC and who was later forced to resign. But to Kurtz it is somehow a legitimate, intelligent question whether Clinton's lying about getting blowjobs in the Oval Office was somehow responsible for the multibillion-dollar corporate accounting scandal his Administration sought to prevent.

The current historical moment in journalism is hardly a happy one. Journalists trying to do honest work find themselves under siege from several sides simultaneously. Corporate conglomerates increasingly view journalism as "software," valuable only insofar as it contributes to the bottom line. In the mad pursuit for audience and advertisers, the quality of the news itself becomes degraded, leading journalists to alternating fits of self-loathing and self-pity. Meanwhile, they face an Administration with a commitment to secrecy unmatched in modern US history. And to top it all off, conservative organizations and media outlets lie in wait, eager to pounce on any journalist who tries to give voice to almost any uncomfortable truth about influential American institutions—in other words, to behave as an honest reporter—throwing up the discredited but nevertheless effective accusation of "liberal bias" in order to protect the powerful from scrutiny.

If September 11 taught the nation anything at all, it

should have taught us to value the work that honest journalists do for the sake of a better-informed society. But for all the alleged public-spiritedness evoked by September 11, the mass public proved no more interested in serious news—much less international news—on September 10, 2002, than it had been a year earlier. This came as a grievous shock and disappointment to many journalists, who interpreted the events of September 11 as an endorsement of the importance of their work to their compatriots. And indeed, from September 11 through October, according to the Pew Research Center for the People and the Press, 78 percent of Americans followed news of the attacks closely. But according to a wide-ranging study by Peyton Craighill and Michael Dimock, interest in terrorism and fear of future terrorist attacks have "not necessarily translated into broader public interest in news about local, national, or international events. . . . Reported levels of reading, watching and listening to the news are not markedly different than in the spring of 2000," the report found. "At best, a slightly larger percentage of the public is expressing general interest in international and national news, but there is no evidence its appetite for international news extends much beyond terrorism and the Middle East." In fact, 61 percent of Americans admitted to tuning out foreign news unless a "major development" occurs.

The most basic problem faced by American journalists, both in war and peace, is that much of our society remains ignorant, and therefore unappreciative of the value of the profession's contribution to the quality and practice of our democracy. Powerful people and institutions have strong, self-interested reasons to resist the media's inspection and the public accountability it can inspire. The net effect of their efforts to deflect scrutiny is to weaken the democratic bond between the powerful and the powerless that can, alone, prevent the emergence of unchecked corruption. The phony "liberal media" accusation is just one of many tools in the conservative and corporate arsenal to reorder American society and the US economy to their liking. But as they've proven over and over, "working the refs" works. It results in a cowed media willing to give right-wing partisans a pass on many of their most egregious actions and ideologically inspired assertions. As such it needs to be resisted by liberals and centrists every bit as much as Bush's latest tax cut for the wealthy or his efforts to despoil the environment on behalf of the oil and gas industries.

The decades-long conservative ideological offensive constitutes a significant threat to journalism's ability to help us protect our families and insure our freedoms. Tough-minded reporting, as the legendary *Washington Post* editor Ben Bradlee explains, "is not for everybody." It is not "for those who feel that all's right with the world, not for those whose cows are sacred, and surely not for those who fear the violent contradictions of our time." But it is surely necessary for those of us who wish to answer to the historically honorable title of "democrat," "republican" or even that wonderfully old-fashioned title, "citizen."

Matt Drudge et al.
from *What Liberal Media?* (2003)
Eric Alterman

The explosion of the use of the Web may prove to be one of the great technological transformations in the history of human communications. By the end of 2001, a single site, www.yahoo.com, boasted more than 70 million users, with an annual increase rate of 18 percent. While the Internet has enormous value for more reasons and purposes than can be profitably counted, for scholars, for communities, for journalists, and for just goofing off, for political purposes it turns out to have a great deal in common with radio. Not unlike the way in which the irresponsible right-wing talk-show network forms its own self-referential information circuit, "news" on the Net is passed along from one site to another with little concern for its credibility. Also like radio, this tactic of combining the unverifiable with a metaphorical microphone has been perfected by the far right to create a doubly deceitful dynamic of ideological extremism, false information, and accusation against which truth—and liberalism—have little chance to compete. Rush Limbaugh, meet Matt Drudge.

While the Net is economically dominated by a tiny number of large corporations, just like television and radio, the information that appears on it is not. Standards for established news services with a net presence have by and large been maintained; however, the true story of political news on the Net is with the small, right-wing sites that use the Web almost as effectively as they use talk radio. Web sites like the Drudge Report, NewsMax.com, WorldNetDaily.com, FreeRepublic.com, Townhall.com, Lucianne.com, JewishWorldReview.com, and National Review Online boast regular readers in the millions. What's more, they are dedicated readers and in many cases, like the Limbaugh audience, so far to the right as to tend toward outer space. For instance, Joseph Farah, a columnist for Worldnet, warned his readers in October 2002, "The Democrats—far too many of them—are evil, pure and simple. They have no redeeming social value. They are outright traitors themselves or apologists for treasonous behavior. They are enemies of the American people and the American way of life." On Lucianne.com, a number of posters celebrated the plane crash that killed Paul Wellstone, his wife, and daughter, in late October 2002 and expressed the hope that Ted Kennedy would meet a similar fate. Even further out in the right wing ozonosphere, is the site FreeRepublic.com. While posts terming Gore a "traitor" are commonplace, alongside the addresses and phone numbers of allegedly liberal politicians and judges, a UPI story unearthed one user who sympathized with Timothy McVeigh and another who called him a "modern-day Paul Revere." According to figures published in the *New York Times*, the average "Freeper" Web visit lasts an amazing five hours and fourteen minutes. It's not a hobby for these people, it's a life.

During the election crisis in Florida, these sites demonstrated their political value to the Republican side. As the Web site funded by Richard Mellon Scaife, frontpage.com, reported, conservative "community news sites like Free Republic.com and conservative news sites like News Max.com and WorldNetDaily.com, which earned their chops during the impeachment imbroglio" were, during the Florida crisis, "once again galvanizing the political right in support of George W. Bush's claim that he won the election." Weeks before President Clinton's impeachment by the House, FreeRepublic sponsored a rally that drew an estimated 5,000 to 6,000 pro-impeachment protestors to the Washington Monument. One user posted the e-mail addresses and work phone numbers of the seven justices of the Florida Supreme Court. If it is possible, as I'll discuss, to trace the ultimate determination of the 2000 Florida fracas to what the conservative pundit Paul Gigot approvingly termed a "bourgeois riot" outside the Miami-Dade County board of elections office, then the activists inspired by these sites and organized within them can take credit for helping Republican Party officials make history—and undermine democracy.

Liberals, of course, have their own sites, and some generate a great deal of traffic. But the best known, Salon.com and Slate.com, are run by journalists, not activists. And both make it a point of regularly publishing the views of the other side, including even the right's most extreme expressions, including Andrew Sullivan and David Horowitz in Salon's case, and Sullivan, Christopher Caldwell, and even Charles Murray in Slate's. (Many liberals also believe that Slate's official Weblogger, Mickey Kaus, is playing for the conservative team as well. Though he terms himself a "neoliberal," Kaus happily admits to being "a Dem who likes trashing Dems.") Those liberal sites that are devoted to activism, such as Media Whores Online, BartCop, and Buzzflash, process a miniscule amount of traffic (and vitriol, for that matter) compared to, say, the folks at FreeRepublic.com and Lucianne.com.

In the relatively new phenomenon of Weblogging—or "blogging"—the biggest names are also conservatives. Perhaps the best known of all non-professional Webloggers is Glenn Reynolds of "Instapundit," whose open-minded politics lean libertarian, but who is definitely in the conservative camp. The rest of the "Blogosphere" is also more conservative than liberal, but when speaking exclusively of the elite media, does not have much relevance beyond the Web sites of those journalists who have established their names elsewhere, such as Mickey Kaus or Josh Marshall.*

Undoubtedly the biggest star of Net journalism—its Rush Limbaugh if you will—is the self-styled Walter Winchell-in-a-fedora, Matt Drudge, who claims more than 100 million visits a month to his bare-bones, next-to-no-graphics site. Like Limbaugh, Drudge professes nothing but contempt for the mainstream news establishment. Viewed, he crows, "daily not only by presidents and world leaders, CEOs, anchormen and top media editors," Drudge claims to be "powered" only by endless curiosity and a love of freedom. Of course with numbers like his, the media he disdains cannot help but celebrate him. Drudge was named one of *Newsweek*'s new media stars and *People*'s Twenty-Five Most Intriguing People. The *American Journalism Review* ran a cover story entitled, "Journalism in the Era of Drudge and Flynt," and the *Columbia Journalism Review* cited his outing of the Monica Lewinsky affair in 1998 as one of the ten key dates in the media history of the twentieth century.

---

* I suppose I am one of these, as I write a daily Weblog at www. altercation.msnbc.com. Check it out.

Originally an amateur Hollywood gossip who picked through garbage cans to get his goods, Drudge became an overnight phenomenon as a kind of bulletin board for unsubstantiated political rumor and right-wing character attacks. Drudge describes his work habit as sitting in his apartment "petting the cat and watching the wires—that's all I do." But he also receives a great deal of e-mail. One of his favorite tactics is to steal a working journalist's story—leaked to him internally—and post its still-in-the-works details on his Web site before the author can publish them. His big moment in media history consisted of little more than posting the purloined work of *Newsweek*'s Michael Isikoff, while the magazine's editors sought further confirmation before publishing it. Drudge did it again when NBC News was trying to decide how to handle an unsubstantiated twenty-one-year-old accusation of sexual assault against President Clinton. Drudge rarely bothers to independently verify his stories, so he often appears prescient—when, in fact, he is simply overlooking what is widely understood to be the essence of journalism. Tim Russert learned this to his chagrin when Drudge posted three stories on his site about the Buffalo-born newsman's considering a run for governor of New York. "All three stories—they are just plain dead wrong," Russert complained. "And he never called me about them, never." The only surprising thing here is Russert's surprise.

Drudge is a self-described misfit with few social graces, and modesty is certainly not one of them. Drudge calls his apartment "the most dangerous newsroom in America." "If I'm not interesting, the world's not interesting," he writes. "And if I'm boring, you're boring." Despite his disdain for traditional news ethics, and a lack of any discernible effort in the areas of reporting or punditry, Drudge's impact is huge. He counts his hits in the millions and can single-handedly drive hundreds of thousands—sometimes millions—of readers to any story he posts on the Web. When he purloined and posted Isikoff's Lewinsky scoop, he jump-started a political meltdown that led to the only impeachment of an elected president in American history. When he then went on to post the story of Clinton's alleged mulatto "love child," he made a national fool of himself, but hurt no one, save those gullible and irresponsible media outlets— most notably Rupert Murdoch's *New York Post* and Sun Myung Moon's *Washington Times*—who trusted him and reprinted it. But when he posted a malicious lie about Clinton adviser and ex-journalist Sidney Blumenthal having "a spousal abuse past that has been effectively covered up," replete with "court records of Blumenthal's violence against his wife," Drudge attacked an innocent man. But even this did not seem to hurt Drudge's reputation. Much of the media preferred Drudge to Blumenthal, whom many reporters resented for personal and professional reasons. In none of these cases did Drudge profess regret, though he did retract his false accusation against Blumenthal before the latter launched a libel suit against him. As for the Clinton "love child" concoction, Drudge bragged, "I'd do it again."

During the Lewinsky crisis, Drudge became so big the Internet could no longer contain him. He was given his own television program on Fox, where he was free to spout unconfirmed rumors with fellow conservative conspiracy nuts until he was informed by management that he would not be allowed to show a *National Enquirer* photo of a tiny hand emerging from the womb during a spina bifida operation on the fetus. Drudge wanted to use the photo as part of his campaign against legal abortion. When even the Fox executives found this idea not only repulsive but misleading, Drudge quit the show. Roger Ailes, whose brilliant idea it had been to hire Drudge after watching him spout baseless conspiracy theories on Russert's program, complained, "He wants to apply Internet standards, which are nonexistent, to journalism, and journalism has real standards. It can't work that way." It should come as no surprise to anyone that Drudge is also a successful force in radio, with a two-hour Sunday evening show hosted by ABC that is heard in all fifty states and literally hundreds of major markets.

Drudge also published a book—well, sort of a book. The tome was "written" with the assistance of the late Julia Phillips. Of the 247 pages contained in *The Drudge Manifesto*, the reader is treated to forty blank pages; thirty-one pages filled with fan mail; twenty-four pages of old Drudge Reports; a thirteen-page Q & A from Drudge's National Press Club speech; ten pages of titles and the like; six pages of quotes from various personalities like Ms. Lewinsky and Madonna; four pages of a chat transcript; and, well, a great deal more filler. That leaves the reader with just 112 pages or barely 45 percent of actual book. (And even nine of these are Drudge poetry.)

But even with all the strikes any journalist could imagine and then some against him, Drudge still gets results for his combination of nasty innuendo and right-wing politics, often by planting items that would be picked up by allegedly respectable journalists in national newspapers. In the Arkansas Senate race of 2002, the Associated Press reported that Democrat Mark Pryor found himself forced to respond "to an item on the Drudge Report Web site of Internet gossip Matt Drudge" in a lightly sourced story that alleged the hiring of an illegal immigrant for housekeeping duties. (In fact the woman in question later signed a sworn affidavit testifying to the fact that she was a legal U.S. resident and had been paid to lie.) In May of the same year, for example, Drudge carried a report that ex-conservative journalist David Brock, whose *Blinded by the Right* embarrassed virtually the entire movement, had suffered a "breakdown" while writing the book and had to be hospitalized—something Brock reluctantly confirmed when contacted. Drudge did not mention on his site that he had considerable reason to hold a grudge against Brock, who had published in his book that he received an e-mail from the Internet snoop that said he wished the two could be "fuck buddies." (Brock is an open homosexual. Drudge is not.) As the gay journalist Michelangelo Signorile wrote, "You'd think that no respectable journalist would further the new Drudge sludge on Brock, at least not without a fuller explanation that included Drudge's possible motives." But in fact the *Washington Post* did publish it—or at least the parts Drudge wanted published, leaving out any discussion of his motives—and adding quotes from three conservatives who continued the character assassination of Brock that Drudge initiated. Nowhere in the *Post* item did the newspaper attempt to establish any journalistic relevance to the item, which is rather amazing when you consider the fact that its former publisher, the late Philip Graham, father of the current head of the Post Company, Donald Graham, was himself hospitalized for mental illness, before taking his own life. (Making this story even stranger, the *Post*'s Howard

Kurtz reported in 1999 that Drudge's own mother had been hospitalized for schizophrenia.)

Just before Election Day 2002, Drudge and Limbaugh combined, together with Brit Hume of Fox News and the *Wall Street Journal* editorial page, to effect a smear against the Democratic Socialists of America (DSA) and, by extension, the late Senator Wellstone's re-election campaign. This episode too had all the trademarks of the conservative echo-chamber effect, including unproven innuendo, inaccuracy, repeated cavalier use of unchecked facts, all in the service of a clear political/ideological goal. As reported by Brian Keefer of Spinsanity, DSA posted a pop-up advertisement on its site on October 9 seeking contributions to pay the cost of bringing young people to Minnesota, where same-day registration is legal, to help register Wellstone voters in what was certain to be a close race. Shortly after the advertisement appeared, however, a local conservative organization sent out a press release in which it manipulated the original text to make it appear that DSA was planning to transport people not to register Minnesotans to vote, but to vote themselves, with the hopes of stealing the election.

Drudge saw the story in a local paper and headlined his site's line: "Socialists Sending People to MN to Illegally Vote for Wellstone." This apparently sent Limbaugh into action, as the radio host melodramatically informed his listeners, "DSA has been caught." With his typical respect for *accuracy*, Rush added, "You can go in there and register and vote and split the same day, you can go home, you don't even have to spend the night in Minnesota and freeze if you don't want to, you can go in there and vote and leave." Next up was Fox News's Brit Hume, who announced to that network's viewers, "The Democratic Socialists of America, which bill themselves as the largest socialist organization in the country, is raising tax-deductible money to send you people to the state of Minnesota, where they can take advantage of same-day registration to vote for the liberal incumbent Paul Wellstone." These reports apparently inspired the *Journal* editors who—again, contrary to all available evidence—insisted, "The Democratic Socialists of America recently posted an ad on their Web site inviting tax-deductible contributions to 'bring young people to Minnesota' to vote in the close U.S. Senate race there." As Keefer noted, while the loosely worded ad did originally raise questions about whether tax-deductible funds were being properly used for issue advocacy—and hence was rewritten for clarifying purposes—never in any of its texts did it even imply, much less encourage, anyone but Minnesotans to pick their own senator. It is perfectly legal in that state to encourage people to vote and even to take them to the polls.

Of course, Wellstone's death made the effects of this story moot, but cases like the above demonstrate just how profoundly journalistic times are a-changing. And the result of these changes is yet another victory for conservatives and scandal-mongers—and in Drudge and Limbaugh's cases, both at once—who seek to poison our political discourse with a combination of character assassination, ideological invective, and unverified misinformation. The resulting loss of credibility for phantom SCLM bespeaks not only the profession's misfortune, but democracy's as well.

Fox News, media flagship of the Radical Right, has become a byword for biased reporting, a disgrace to its industry. Fox sank to new lows during the run-up to the U.S. invasion of Iraq.

The Fox of War

from Salon.com (3/30/04)

David J. Sirota

Before the Iraq invasion, the Bush administration made many declarations to build its case for war: There was "no doubt," as the president said, Iraq had weapons of mass destruction, including nuclear weapons, making it an imminent threat to America; Saddam Hussein was working closely with Osama bin Laden and al-Qaida; and the invasion would minimize civilian casualties.

While many intelligence and military experts knew how hollow these claims were, there was one place where the Bush administration was given an open microphone: Fox News. By the time U.S. soldiers were headed across the desert to Baghdad, the "fair and balanced" network, owned by media mogul Rupert Murdoch, looked like a caricature of state-run television, parroting the White House's daily talking points, no matter how unsubstantiated.

Of course, Fox and the White House had forged their nexus well before Iraq. Immediately after 9/11, for instance, Fox chief Roger Ailes (a former Republican Party media consultant) wrote a confidential memo to President Bush saying that America wanted him to "use the harshest measures possible" in the war on terrorism. On the eve of the Iraq invasion, the *Washington Post* reported that neoconservative Fox contributors, such as

Murdoch-owned *Weekly Standard* editor William Kristol,
were "well wired" into the White House, meeting peri-
odically with top administration national security officials and "huddling privately" every three months with
Karl Rove, who was urging Republicans to seek maximum
political advantage from a war in Iraq. Fox News became
the White House's most reliable amplifier—claims went
from the podium, into the news scripts, and out to the
American public as fact.

Fox News began by broadcasting the Bush administration's line that there was "no doubt" Iraq had WMD,
despite repeated warnings by the intelligence community
that the WMD case for war was weak and dubious. As
early as August 2002, Fox News contributor Fred Barnes
said, "We know beyond a shadow of a doubt that
[Saddam Hussein] has been pursuing aggressively
weapons of mass destruction, including nuclear
weapons." He was refuted a month later by UPI, which
reported that "a growing number of experts say that the
administration has not presented convincing evidence"
that Iraq was pursuing WMD or nuclear weapons. (UPI
is owned by the Rev. Sun Myung Moon, who also publishes the conservative *Washington Times*.)

But that did not stop the drumbeat. By spring, Fox was
rolling full steam ahead. On March 23, 2003, Fox headline
banners blared "Huge Chemical Weapons Factory Found
in Southern Iraq"—a claim that never panned out. On
April 11, a Fox News report announced: "Weapons-Grade
Plutonium Possibly Found at Iraqi Nuke Complex."
Sourced to an embedded reporter from the right-wing
Richard Mellon Scaife-owned *Pittsburgh Tribune-Review*,
the story was soon debunked by U.S. officials.

Bill O'Reilly, host of the most popular Fox News show, "The O'Reilly Factor," took to the airwaves on March 4, 2003, to ramp up the claim that not only did Iraq have WMD, but nuclear weapons. He stated definitively that "a load of weapons-grade plutonium has disappeared from Nigeria" and that the theft "should send a signal to all Americans that a nuclear device could be planted here." When he was challenged on his assertion, he insisted, "You cannot refute, and neither can anyone else, that we have plutonium missing in Nigeria, we have two rogue governments, North Korea and Iraq, who are certainly capable of aiding and abetting people who will plant an atomic device, a nuclear device in a city in this country."

O'Reilly was referring to a story that week about radioactive material missing in Nigeria. But it was not plutonium, as he claimed, or anything nearly as lethal as plutonium. It was a compound called Americium 241, wholly unsuitable for the creation of the imaginary "atomic device" O'Reilly referred to. The compound is commonly used for industrial purposes, as opposed to plutonium, which is used primarily for weapons and nuclear reactors. The compound, in fact, was misplaced by Vice President Cheney's old oil firm, Halliburton. (The Nigerian operation under Cheney has sparked an international bribery investigation by the Justice Department.)

On the Saddam-al-Qaida connection, Fox never considered that the connection was nonexistent. Barnes declared on Oct. 9, 2002, that "the CIA now believes there's a real connection between Saddam Hussein and al Qaeda, the terrorist group that attacked the United States." He provided no evidence. For years, in fact, the CIA was reporting the opposite.

"JOURNALISTS" AND OTHER SCOUNDRELS

Sean Hannity, host of the Fox talk show "Hannity and Colmes," claimed with no proof on Dec. 9, 2002, that al-Qaida "obviously has the support of Saddam." He specifically ignored a *Los Angeles Times* report of a month earlier that found "U.S. allies have found no links between Iraq and al Qaeda." Hannity later announced on April 30, 2003, that he possessed documents proving a "direct link between Osama bin Laden's al Qaeda network" and the Iraqi regime, and disparaged critics of the war, saying, "If you listen to the people on the left, they're not fazed by this evidence." They may not have been fazed because earlier that month the *Miami Herald* reported that senior U.S. officials confirmed they had found "no provable connection between Saddam and al Qaeda."

In June, the chairman of the U.N.'s terrorist monitoring group reiterated that there was "no evidence linking al Qaeda to Saddam Hussein." A month later the *L.A. Times* reported that declassified documents from the 9/11 commission had "undercut Bush administration claims before the war that Hussein had links to al Qaeda." That was of no concern to Fox News contributor Ann Coulter, who went on the air in September to proclaim: "Saddam Hussein has harbored, promoted, helped, sheltered al Qaeda members. We know that."

Before the war began, Fox tried to minimize the inevitable human cost. Hannity echoed the administration line, claiming in January of 2003 that "Iraqis are not going to be bombed by the United States. The United States will use pinpoint accuracy, like we always do." Within the first few days of the invasion, the *New York Times* noted that aid groups estimated "thousands of civilian casualties, many more than in the recent conflict in Afghanistan or the Persian Gulf War of 1991."

Before the war, O'Reilly issued a promise. "If the Americans go in and overthrow Saddam Hussein and it's clean, he has nothing, I will apologize to the nation, and I will not trust the Bush Administration again, all right?" This February, on ABC's "Good Morning America," he offered an apology. "My analysis was wrong and I'm sorry. What do you want me to do? Go over and kiss the camera?" But he explained that his lack of skepticism wasn't his fault. "All Americans should be concerned about this, for their families and themselves, that our intelligence isn't as good as it should be." The next day, back on Fox, O'Reilly claimed the controversy over his apology was a plot by the "left wing press" who "used my words to hammer the President." Then he introduced his next guest on what he called "the no spin zone."

But Fox didn't reflect when the network's talking heads were proved wrong. Instead the talkers blamed others. Hannity said on Aug. 20, 2003, that "all the predictions of liberals and Democrats in this country were wrong about thousands of people [being] dead, innocent civilians murdered, and we'd anger the Arab world." Yet, the U.S. military reports that it "has received more than 15,000 claims" for compensation for noncombatant Iraqi deaths, with Amnesty International reporting at least 10,000 civilian Iraqi casualties. Meanwhile, the latest Pew Poll shows burgeoning anti-Americanism, not only throughout the Arab world, but worldwide after the Iraq war.

The Fox-Bush alliance was summed up, apparently without irony, by Bill O'Reilly himself. In his column this week, O'Reilly observed, "There is nothing wrong with news organizations endorsing a candidate or a columnist writing about his or her political preferences. But actively participating in political campaigns . . . is absolutely against every journalistic standard, and it is happening—usually under the radar."

After a review of the record, however, it is clear that Fox was an enthusiastic participant in the White House's campaign of disinformation leading the country into war. And it was not under the radar—it happened in our living rooms every night.

A Pox on Fox:
Latest Lies From Fox News

from www.antiwar.com (12/29/03)

Dale Steinreich

> [I]t disturbs me because I think a lot of nasty stuff went on
> behind the scenes [during Hussein's rule] that people don't
> know about and they should.
> —*Bill O'Reilly, Dec. 16, 2003*

While the capture of Saddam Hussein has so far meant little in terms of stemming the violence in Iraq, it has certainly emboldened the Fox News Channel (FNC) to curiously trumpet the capture as *ex post* validation of the coalition's invasion. Since Sunday December 14, FNC has been almost one continuous Saddamathon with the now-famous footage of the latex-gloved frisker searching Saddam triumphantly showing on the channel almost every hour on the hour. The following is a chronicle of recent war and other lies and spin from Fox. As with my earlier report in June, my comments are in brackets.

SUNDAY DECEMBER 14:
The Saddamathon begins. A David Lee Miller report runs several times throughout the day purporting to be a history of Saddam's rise and rule over Iraq. It's as if Hussein came out of nowhere to brutalize Iraqis. [The effective lies by omission make the "report" surreal. On the "Fair and Balanced" Fox, Miller inexplicably forgets to mention the extensive U.S. involvement in effectively creating and

sustaining the Hussein monster: no mention of the U.S.-aided assassination of Abdul Karem Kassim and rise of the Baathists in March 1963 (also the U.S.-aided putsch of '68—a great help to Saddam), no mention of Reagan-administration support for Hussein (including ingredients for biological and chemical weapons) during the 1980-88 Iran-Iraq war, no mention of former Hussein buddy Don Rumsfeld's December 19, 1983 and March 24, 1984 visits to Baghdad (the latter visit being on the very same day as press reports that a U.N. team found that Iraqi forces had used mustard gas laced with a nerve agent on Iranian soldiers).

There are constant references on Fox to Hussein "gassing his own people" but no mention of Stephen Pelletiere's gutting of that tale. Also no mention of Assistant Secretary of State John Kelly and U.S. ambassador April Glaspie effectively giving Saddam the green light (as Saddam apparently saw it) for his August 1990 invasion of Kuwait. No mention of the slaughter of more than 100,000 Shiites that occurred when the U.S. encouraged their rebellion and then failed to support it. No mention of the estimated half million deaths from U.S.-supported sanctions. All these topics are of course *verboten* on "Fair and Balanced" Fox.]

The O'Reilly Factor (7:00 p.m. CT). O'Reilly's first guest is Marc Ginsburg, presented not only on O'Reilly's show but numerous times on Fox's *Special Report with Brit Hume* as an objective Middle-East analyst. [Ginsburg—like the "impartial" Dennis Ross, Frank Gaffney, and Cliff May—is of course a neocon shill every bit as much as Fox contributors Kristol, Barnes, and Krauthammer. Sometimes *Special Report*'s All-Star panel is a stomach-retching neocon sandwich: Krauthammer, Barnes, and Kristol bread with quasi-neocon Kondracke or Sammon baloney filler laughably included for "balance."]

Next is O'Reilly's in-your-face trumpeting of a weekend report by the appropriately named Con Coughlin of the London *Telegraph* supposedly uncovering a direct link between Saddam and Osama bin Laden. The report centers around a "top-secret memo" found by the U.S.-appointed government of Iraq asserting that Mohammed Atta was trained in Baghdad by Abu Nidal in the summer of 2001 just before the September 11 attacks.

Convenient for the Bush administration is that the memo was allegedly written by the former head of Iraqi intelligence to Saddam, however the memo suggests that there really was a shipment of uranium from Niger to Iraq after all. Further, the Niger shipment would never have been accomplished without a "secret meeting" between Saddam and (how convenient!!) current neocon bogeyman Syrian president Bashar al-Assad. (You can almost hear Perle cursing in the background about the "stupid ragheads" on Washington's payroll who manufactured the memo but forgot that the White House conceded there was no shipment!)

[Update 12/17/03: *Newsweek*'s Isikoff and Hosenball have labeled the memo a probable fake, and report that the memo is "contradicted by a wealth of information that has been collected about Atta's movements." Despite this news, Bill O'Reilly tonight once again refers to the Coughlin report on his show.]

[Update 12/18/03: California Republican Congressman David Drier on *Hannity and Colmes* twice cites the *Telegraph* article based on the fraudulent memo as evidence for a

Saddam-al Qaeda link. Hannity also briefly adduced the fraud toward the beginning of his show.]

[Recall Con artist Coughlin's visit to Fox in late April to trumpet the *Telegraph*'s Inigo Gilmore report claiming to find "the first proof of direct links" between Saddam and bin Laden. We were to believe that Gilmore just "sweet talked" his way past the 3rd Infantry into the Mukbaharat to somehow find documents sitting out in the open that the CIA just happened to miss. Because it followed so closely on the heels of other false reports, few gave any credence to the article. Interesting also for Con Man has been his recent work attempting to bolster Tony "Bliar's" notorious and laughable 45-minute claim.

With regard to the neocon obsession with finding a link between Saddam and 9-11/al Qaeda, recall also Fox's role in mid-November of playing up Stephen Hayes' article in the *Weekly Standard* "Case Closed," which supposedly provided proof of not just a link but a longstanding "operational relationship" between Saddam and bin Laden. The article wasn't much more than a collection of assertions from raw intelligence data. Fox presented the article's contents as fact all day on November 15, the same day as a DOD statement which labeled such reporting "inaccurate." Fox still presented the article's assertions as fact for another two days!]

MONDAY DECEMBER 15:
Fox and Friends. Fox Business analyst Neil Cavuto predicts a market rally from the Saddam capture. [The know-nothing Cavuto, who sometimes seems like he can't tell preferred stock from livestock, is wrong as securities markets from NYSE (down 0.39 percent) to AMEX (down 0.59 percent)

to NASDAQ (down 1.58 percent) all close down for the day. Even the Wilshire 5000 is down 0.76 percent. Yeah, I'd say the markets were impressed with the capture, Neil.]

It's Joe Lieberman Day at Fox, as footage of his comment that if Howard Dean had his way, Saddam would still be in power is running almost as much as the footage (running practically every ten minutes) of the latex-gloved guy searching Saddam's hair and mouth for insurgent cooties. [Fox really has their sites set on Dean. The constant playing and replaying of the latex-gloved guy frisking the mangy Saddam becomes so annoying I have to turn off Fox for the day. Judging by reports about Fox e-mail, even many of the network's fans are annoyed.]

TUESDAY DECEMBER 16:
Your World with Neil Cavuto. Midway through the show (3:31 p.m. CT) Cavuto refers to the day's stock-market performance as the Saddam Rally. [I guess the Saddam Rally could have come next February if the market's next rise hadn't been until then.]

Cavuto (3:49 p.m. CT) gives the frothing pro-war president of the Catholic League, William Donohue, a platform to bash Cardinal Renato Martino. Donohue says Martino only represents "the total fringe" in the Catholic church. He claims that Catholics the world over were in favor of the war. [Anti-war Catholics?! Why there's almost no such thing!]

Special Report with Brit Hume (5:00 p.m. CT). A report by Bret Baier on how the capture of Saddam with documents has yielded all sorts of supposed benefits in terms of fighting the insurgency network. [Fox journalists appear bent on showing immediate benefits, no matter how

vague or assertive, of Saddam's capture.] Reporter Mike
Emanuel repeats the tired lie that the U.S. killed 54 guer-
rillas in Samarra. [Nine dead civilians is apparently the
real story.] Footage is aired of Don Rumsfeld claiming that
Saddam's spider hole could hold WMD that could kill
scores of people. [Maybe true, but the misleading implication Rumsfeld and (at times) Fox are trying to advance is
that the WMD jackpot, like Saddam, can be found with
enough searching.]

The O'Reilly Factor (7:00 p.m. CT). [This was the most
unbelievable episode I've ever seen, and I've seen a lot.] In
his opening monologue O'Reilly rips into Cardinal Martino, but (unlike Hannity later in the night) charitably
quotes him: "I felt pity to see this man destroyed. The military looking at his teeth, as if he were a beast. They could
have spared us these pictures. Seeing him like this, a man
in his tragedy, *despite all the heavy blame he bears,* I had a
sense of compassion for him." [Hannity removed the
words in italics.]

O'REILLY [Talking Points Memo]: The problem with the
Vatican and the UN and others who have no solution to
fascism, terror, atrocities, and mass murder is that they live
in a dream world and they are afforded that luxury by
America, Britain, and other free nations who stood up to
the Nazis, communists, Japanese imperialists, and now
the terrorists. Cardinal Martino and Kofi Annan may be
well intentioned but they are not looking out for us. And
we are the only thing standing between them and a bullet
to the head.

[The Vatican has no solution, lives in a dream world,
and would get a bullet to the head without the U.S.A.?
O'Reilly next debates Father Ryscavage, a Jesuit priest

over the appropriateness of the humiliating footage of Hussein.]

O'REILLY: Father, I don't get it here. I think that God actually orchestrated this [the capture of Hussein], this is how religious I am . . . you would censor that image?

RYSCAVAGE: I would censor the image of him being humiliated in public.

O'REILLY: I would have no problem brutalizing this man to protect others, to find out what he knows. I would not believe that would be sinful, Father.

RYSCAVAGE: The Church provides a moral framework for decisions, it doesn't tell you what you have to decide.

O'REILLY: Martino has been rabidly anti-American in this whole campaign, in the beginning the Pontiff and this cardinal declared the war immoral. I thought that declaration was immoral because of all the people who have been killed by Saddam.

[Update 12/23 Recent reports have the Kurds orchestrating the capture of Hussein. Fox has yet to mention these even to deny them.]

[Next came one of the most shocking exchanges, marking a new level of overt depravity even for Fox.]

O'REILLY: Let me ask you about Jesus in the temple, driving the money changers out with a whip. Was he affording those people dignity, Father?

RYSCAVAGE: He was protecting the dignity of the temple, the people who prayed in it and the merchants who worked in it.

O'REILLY: That's exactly what President Bush and the

U.S.A. was [sic] doing when they went in to remove Saddam. They were protecting the dignity of the Iraqi people and they were protecting the dignity of the world so we wouldn't have to deal with a guy who clearly was out to hurt people . . . So we were doing exactly what Jesus did in the temple, weren't we?

FATHER RYSCAVAGE: No, I don't think so.

[There you have it! George W. Bush and the U.S.A. "exactly" as Jesus in the temple. This from the No Spin Zone.]

Hannity and Colmes (8:00 p.m. CT). Torture Saddam Day on *H&C*, with Bill Bennett and Sean Hannity enthusiastic interlocutors on the subject.

BENNETT: . . . if it's the only means necessary to get information out of him which will save other people . . . then yes I would do it . . . I would not be reluctant to use fairly strong pressure.

COLMES: What do you mean?

BENNETT: The standard things people do. Sodium pentathol, needles under the finger nails . . . I would do it publicly, admit I was doing it, and say why I was doing it.

Hannity quotes Cardinal Martino, careful to doctor the quote (especially on screen) to remove Martino's statement about Hussein bearing blame for his predicament:

HANNITY [verbatim as if quoting Martino]: "I feel pity at seeing this destroyed man treated like a cow, having his teeth checked. I have seen this man in his tragedy. I have a sense of compassion." That's fine but where has he [Martino] been for the compassion [sic] of all the people that have been murdered all these years? I find this embarrassing as a Catholic.

BENNETT: . . . the Vatican has missed some things in the last couple years, they've missed the moral significance of some things going on in their own church and they've missed the moral significance of this war.

[Of course there's no moral significance in a *soi disant* virtue czar gambling away half a million dollars at the Bellagio in one weekend while there are children starving in Iraq. Oh, that's right, Bennett quit his lavish gambling for some reason.]

WEDNESDAY DECEMBER 17

Fox and Friends (5:00 a.m. CT). More denouncing of the Pope for being anti-war. Host Brian Kilmeade celebrates the U.S.-appointed Iraq foreign minister's condemnation of the UN for hindering the U.S.-led invasion of Iraq. [As if there's any significance to what a U.S. puppet minister thinks.] Then (7:10 CT) Kilmeade tells the Fox audience that what's so neat about Hussein being handed over to the CIA is that although they can't torture him, they can deprive him of sleep, food, and light as well as blast him with unpleasant music. [Kilmeade is a hilarious and psittacine disaster who shows what happens when a sports reporter crosses over to serious news analysis.]

Host Steve Doocy proudly shows the audience photos of his family socially cavorting with Don Rumsfeld and White House staff member Bradley Blakeman. [Now try to imagine how conservatives, Republicans, and latex-gloved friskers would have greeted say, CNN, for having a morning show with hosts that cheered the Clintons, openly showed themselves socially cavorting with their staff, while CNN claimed to be "Fair and Balanced."]

O'Reilly Factor (7:00 p.m. CT). O'Reilly's opening monologue is entitled "The Death of Shame in America." He cites "dishonest news analysis" as a symptom of the death of shame. [No irony there! His first guest is this odd ex-CIA guy who keeps referring to Hussein over and over as "the hard drive": "We will not take a sledge hammer to the hard drive."]

O'REILLY: What about sodium pentathol, mind altering drugs, chemicals, things like that?
SIMMONS: Fair game, absolutely fair game.

[There are U.S. officials—especially ex-CIA types like the guest—who have almost, if not as much, information as Hussein has, since he was their on-again, off-again employee. Will they be tortured as well?]

(7:15 p.m. CT) O'Reilly tells Jessica Stern from Harvard's Kennedy School that Syria and Iran should be nervous if they've hidden Saddam's WMD. [Fox bashes Madeleine Albright for her nutty conspiracy theory that Bush has bin Laden hidden away, yet they employ a grown man who thinks it plausible that Syria or Iran has Saddam's non-existent WMD.]

O'Reilly (7:38 p.m. CT) is enraged that Drudge exposed his *Today* show lie that his new book is rivaling Hillary Clinton's in sales. [O'Reilly's book sales aren't even half of Clinton's and are quite a bit below those of his arch-enemy Al Franken. By the way, Matt, O'Reilly repeated the same lie on his own show on Monday.] O'Reilly states that "you can't believe a thing Matt Drudge says" yet doesn't correct Drudge and calls Internet journalism "a threat to democracy."

[Recall O'Reilly suggesting on June 16 of this year that the Internet should be federally regulated to prevent false-hoods from being told! Apparently the big government-media establishment is the only entity that should be able to lie with impunity. O'Reilly's two guests, Liz Trotta and Quentin Hardy of *Forbes*, start fighting over whether Internet free speech should be shut down because, God forbid, it's allowing citizen journalists to have their say and that, according to Trotta, has made the Internet "a garbage dump."]

HARDY: Are you telling me you want to shut down the Internet and keep people from finding out information?
TROTTA: No, I want to keep it responsible and safe for democracy instead of a garbage can for people's ridiculous fantasies.
O'REILLY: Shouldn't there be some standards of behavior, some kind of standard?
TROTTA: Exactly.
HARDY: I believe the viewers can judge for themselves.
O'REILLY: Do you?

Hannity and Colmes (8:40 p.m. CT). When Hannity brings up the subject of 270 mass graves under Hussein, actor Mike Farrell fights constant interruptions from Hannity to point out that the mass graves were mainly filled in during the Reagan and Bush I administrations. [Hannity's brilliant rebuttal: "Oh, it's Reagan's fault!"]

Okay, enough of Fox. The last four days have been quite

a re-education for me. Here's what I learned: that the history of Hussein's rule of Iraq is relevant, but only selectively. The dirty business that France, Russia, and Germany did with Hussein is an endless outrage but when it comes to the U.S., no discussion is allowed with offenders interrupted, shouted down, and called names. I learned that the Internet needs federal regulation ("standards") because the bad, bad people who write on it spin, distort, and propagandize. "We Report, You Decide" is appropriate for Fox, but for some reason I missed, not for the Internet.

I also learned that it's a respectable view (with no evidence provided) that Saddam's WMD could be hidden in Iran or Syria and that it couldn't possibly be a coincidence that those are the two nations that our beloved neocons want to invade next. Most important of all, I learned that George W. Bush and the U.S.A. are now Jesus, roaming the world with a whip to root out sin and iniquity. Poor Jesus. I guess He should feel so lucky to be compared to George W. Bush.

The success of Fox's "fair and balanced" approach has inspired imitators at CNN and MSNBC, proving once again that big media will gladly drift to the far right if there's a buck to be made by doing so.

Ten Great Moments in Jingoism

from Salon.com (4/18/03)

Ben Fritz

As the war in Iraq raged overseas, a battle also broke out between the rival cable news networks that might best be described as: Who can make White House press secretary Ari Fleischer happiest?

CNN, MSNBC and Fox News duked it out for the attention of a concerned public that, by and large, could get the same press conferences, attack footage and falling statues from every outlet. The competitive credo all three networks seem to have followed from the very beginning — when in doubt, wave a flag — was largely a reaction to Fox, which vaulted past CNN in the past year by embracing a conservative coloring of all news. CNN rallied with some shameless patriotism of its own, as did the major networks. But before long it was the struggling MSNBC that may have wrested from Fox the mantle of most blatant, schmaltzily jingoistic network in the land. MSNBC is still a distant third in the ratings race, but it tightened the slack between it and second-place CNN.

Ah, but why give MSNBC all the glory? All the networks have had their moments in the past month. It's time for the highlight reel. So pin that flag on your lapel, and let's survey the top 10 moments in jingoistic war coverage.

10. THE "SURGICAL STRIKE"

A favored military term picked up by the most credulous media is the use of "precision" or "surgical" bombings. While bombs in the Iraq war are undoubtedly much more accurate than those used in the past, there were still reports of inevitable missed targets and civilian casualties in the current conflict, a number that might not be determined for some time. But the Pentagon fed that terminology to a willing media, and the more clueless reporters eagerly gobbled it up.

As the liberal media watchdog group FAIR reported, the term popped up frequently on NBC. Reporter Bob Faw described "a community which very much endorses that surgical strike against Saddam Hussein," and "Today" co-host Matt Lauer, in reference to Baghdad, said, "The people in that city have endured two nights of surgical airstrikes." The terms were also casually used on other networks, including CNN, Fox News and CBS.

9. PUBLIC ENEMY NO. 2: THE FRENCH!

"What do you think of the French in general?" Fox News anchor Neil Cavuto asked Rep. Dan Burton, R-Ind., while interviewing him about how the U.S. should now deal with nations that opposed the war. "They're not a power that I know of . . . Why do we even bother with them?"

Joe Scarborough, former Republican congressman and host of the nightly "MSNBC Reports" (now called "Scarborough Country"), took a similarly gratuitous swipe at our erstwhile allies who opposed our war with Iraq. Introducing a news segment about U.S. victories over Iraqi troops, Scarborough intoned, "But first, Saddam's French advisors taught him how to do one thing right: surrender."

8. PUBLIC ENEMY NO. 3: ENTERTAINERS!

The worst in this department was most certainly Scarborough, who devoted regular segments on his show to mocking celebrities after it became clear the war was nearly over. He showed a clip of Jessica Lange saying, "The path this administration is on is wrong, and we object. We object in our hearts, in our minds. It is an immoral war." Similarly, he showed Ed Asner saying, "I would never give this administration any sign of approval, because I think that they've ripped up this war to satisfy their own needs, not the nation's needs."

Neither of these actors, of course, predicted the U.S. would lose the war. The fact that the U.S. won doesn't make their arguments that the war was immoral or that President Bush is not to be trusted more or less arguable. But Scarborough was undeterred. "I've always found it so remarkable that these leftist stooges, for anti-American causes, are always given a free pass," he said April 10.

7. PUBLIC ENEMY NO. 4: THE MEDIA!

Among the favorite targets: the New York Times, and especially its elder news analyst R.W. "Johnny" Apple. Criticism of Apple has become so constant as to become a cliché, one often unexamined. As the Web site Daily Howler pointed out, for example, Fox News' Brit Hume complained on April 10, saying, "Let me mention one other person who deserves special mention. And it's R.W. 'Johnny' Apple, legendary reporter of the *New York Times*. This is what he wrote today. 'News of fierce fighting in Hilla, 50 miles south of Baghdad, and on the eastern and southern sides of the capital belies talk of collapse.'"

The headline of Apple's piece? "Bush's War Message:

Strong and Clear." And it featured such fiercely antiwar statements as "Bush has carried the country with him, and most of the second-guessers among Washington's policy experts are keeping their voices down these days."

Fox's Sean Hannity busily trashed the media with statements like, "If you read the *New York Times* [or] the *Washington Post* at any point during that three-week period [since the war began], you would think we were losing this war." Of course, when it suited his needs, Hannity was happy to turn tail. While arguing with Rep. Charles Rangel, D-N.Y., about whether Iraqi citizens were welcoming U.S. troops, Hannity chided the congressman, "You're not reading the *New York Times*."

6. "Coalition of the willing"
Another Bush administration catchphrase, it is, understandably, a hotly contested term. But that didn't bother several cable news anchors. "Some world leaders, even close allies, criticized the U.S. and its coalition of the willing prior to the war in Iraq," said CNN's Paula Zahn. "When we come back, we'll hear and see some of the other reaction in the world to what has been happening in the last several days, including the reaction in the coalition of the willing," previewed Peter Jennings on ABC. And Fox's Sean Hannity was more than happy to make statements like, "Look at the coalition of the willing."

5. When "war" just doesn't do the trick
Ever forget the name the government has given to the war? Not if you watched Fox News or MSNBC. Unlike CNN, which used a more neutral "War in Iraq" graphic, the two networks seemed locked in a tight competition over who

could show the phrase "Operation Iraqi Freedom" more often and more prominently.

Fox News won the contest for quantity, with the words on the screen nearly 24/7. MSNBC, however, scores points for size, with huge hanging signs and wall graphics screaming "Operation Iraqi Freedom" emblazoned throughout its warehouse-like studio.

4. THAT BIG CLOCK

MSNBC placed a "deadline" clock on its graphics-heavy screen, counting down, second by second, President Bush's 48-hour deadline for Saddam Hussein and his sons to leave Iraq. Perhaps the network missed the president's statement that war would be "commenced at a time of our choosing"? The clock ultimately ran out, disappearing before any significant invasion news.

3. AND NOW, A WORD FROM OUR SPONSOR …

Rather than stick to its version of "fair and balanced" news coverage, Fox News often opted for a much simpler, direct route: looping gratuitous speech excerpts by President Bush, including agitprop like, "The vise is closing, and the days of a brutal regime are coming to an end" and "Against this enemy we will accept no outcome except complete victory." The clips were not related to any story or feature, they were usually just used to lead into or out of commercial breaks, to make sure they maintained a pro-war state of mind, we guess.

2. THE WAR PROMO

House ads MSNBC ran between programs and during commercial breaks functioned like movie trailers, both promoting the war and touting its heroes in such heart-tugging cinematic style they could have been produced by the Defense Department's Tori Clarke. MSNBC ran one promo, scored with "The Star-Spangled Banner," that flashed phrases like "land of the free" and "home of the brave" over shots of soldiers, tanks and Iraqi children. The Microsoft-NBC joint venture also ran promos using similar footage over the sound of patriotic speeches, such as John F. Kennedy's "pay any price" inaugural address, and others by President Bush.

1. The Osama-Saddam connection

Ultimately, Fox wins the top prize not for its relentlessly pro-war anchors and news angles, but for the simple graphic that so often brought viewers back from commercials. "War on Terror" the intro began, before whooshing off the screen as a new phrase jumped on and took its place: "Target: Iraq."

Enough said.

Fox News: The Inside Story

from Salon.com (10/31/03)

Tim Grieve

When veteran television journalist Chris Wallace announced this week that he was leaving ABC for Fox News, reporters asked him whether he was concerned about trading in his objectivity for Fox's rightward slant. "I had the same conception a lot of people did about Fox News, that they have a right-wing agenda," Wallace told *The Washington Post*. But after watching Fox closely, Wallace said, he had decided that the network suffered from an "unfair rap," and that its reporting is, in fact, "serious, thoughtful and even-handed."

It was all too much for Charlie Reina to take. Reina, 55, spent six years at Fox as a producer, copy editor and writer, working both on hard news stories and on feature programs like "News Watch" and "After Hours." He quit in April, he says, in a fit of frustration over salary, job assignments and respect. Since that time, he has watched the debate over whether Fox is really "fair and balanced." He held his fire, bit his tongue. But then he heard Chris Wallace—an outsider to Fox, for now—proclaim the network fair. Reina couldn't remain silent any longer, and so he fired off a long post to Jim Romenesko's message board at the Poynter Institute. In his view, he was setting the Fox record straight.

"The fact is," Reina wrote, "daily life at FNC is all about management politics." Reina said that Fox's daily news coverage—and its daily news bias—is driven by an "editorial note" sent to the newsroom every morning by John

Moody, a Fox senior vice president. The editorial note—a memo posted on Fox's computer system—tells the staff which correspondents are working on which stories. But frequently, Reina says, it also contains hints, suggestions and directives on how to slant the day's news—invariably, he says, in a way that's consistent with the politics and desires of the Bush administration.

Before starting work at Fox in 1997, Reina had a long career in broadcast journalism. He worked on the broadcast wire at the Associated Press, wrote copy for CBS radio news and worked on ABC's "Good Morning America." Along the way, he says, no one ever told him how to slant a story—until he started working at Fox. At the "fair and balanced" network, Reina says, he and his colleagues were frequently told—sometimes directly, usually more subtly—to toe the Republican Party line.

Reina is out of journalism for the moment—he's running his own woodworking business in suburban New York—and he realizes that going public about his experience at Fox won't improve his career prospects. He says he doesn't care.

Fox did not respond to calls or a faxed letter from Salon seeking comment on Reina's tenure at the network or his comments about news values there. But Reina has plainly hit a nerve. Late Thursday, Romenesko posted a response to Reina's note that appeared to be from Sharri Berg, a vice president for news operations at Fox. The response called Reina a "disgruntled employee" with "an ax to grind." And Berg included comments she attributed to an unnamed Fox staffer who described Reina as one "any number of clueless feature producers" who made inane calls to the news desk, "the kind of calls where after you hung up you say to the phone, 'go f?k yourself.'" Berg quoted the newsroom employee as saying, "[I]t's not editorial policy that pisses off newsroom grunts—it's people like Charlie."

Reina said he wouldn't dignify Berg's note with a response. He spoke with Salon by phone from his home in New York.

Is there an ideological agenda at work in the newsroom at Fox?

All I can say is, everybody there knows what the politics of the bosses are. You feel it every day, and in good part because of this daily editorial note that comes out. I suppose there are similar things [at other networks] which say who's stationed where that day, where the correspondents are, what we'll be covering and so on. But [in the Fox memo], oftentimes when there are issues that involve political controversy and debate or what have you, there are also these admonitions, these subtle things like, "There is something utterly incomprehensible about Kofi Annan's remarks in which he allows that his thoughts are 'with the Iraqi people.' One could ask where those thoughts were during the 23 years Saddam Hussein was brutalizing those same Iraqis. Food for thought."

That's something you just don't see in a traditional newsroom. You see a news budget going around, but they'd be a lot like an AP budget—here's this story, here's this story, this person is writing this. It makes sense to have something like that—something that says here's where everybody is and so forth. But now, for the first time with the advent of the memo, you're actually getting little bits of guidance here and there.

Would it have been unusual at AP or CBS or ABC to hear that management wanted a story tweaked in a certain ideological direction?

You didn't use to have the direct involvement of the big bosses. But at Fox, it's an everyday thing, a presence in the newsroom. You know, if you make a joke, and it's politically slanted and it's not toward the Republican side, somebody will say to you, "Watch it." It doesn't mean that you would get in trouble, that Roger [Ailes] would be there or something, but there's just that fear at all times.

Are the employees at Fox ideologically aligned with Ailes?

I don't think that's the case. There are probably more people there who tend to be conservative or Republican than I have encountered at other places. And I have to say that they're right when they say that people in journalism tend to be liberal or Democrat. Again, I haven't found that that had much of an effect on the news. But it certainly does at Fox. There are many people who work at Fox, as there are elsewhere, that are much more liberal and Democrat-leaning than management is.

But what's also true is that it's such a young staff of workers. Many of the people who write news copy, for instance, had no experience writing before they started. So there's no background in writing, and as a result they're very easy to mold.

The memo sort of gives you hints. If they [Fox executives] are worried that what we write or what the anchors say might make the wrong point, it will show up in the memo . . . [The line producers] are mostly eager young people. They've got a grueling job hour-to-hour. It's just too much trouble for them to try to buck the system. They've got so much to do that they just don't want to have to explain [why they didn't comply with the direction in the memo]. So everything gets done pretty much the way management wants it.

Can you remember a specific instance in which one of your superiors told you to approach a story with a particular ideological slant?

It was, I would say, about three years ago. I was assigned to do a special on the environment, some issue involving pollution. When my boss and I talked as to what this thing was all about, what they were looking for, he said to me: "You understand, you know, it's not going to come out the pro-environmental side." And I said, "It will come out however it comes out." And he said, "You can obviously give both sides, but just make sure that the pro-environmentalists don't get the last word."

Fair and balanced?

Yeah. I thought about it and thought about it and I went to him the next morning and I said, "I can't do this, I've never started out a project with an idea of what the outcome *should* be—and certainly to be told that. And I'm not going to do it." Fortunately, he was wise enough to know that what he had done was wrong, and he left it alone.

Part of what Fox's message is, and I have to say that to a certain extent I agree with it, is that political correctness is a terrible thing. There are a lot of assumptions that are simply made and not questioned, and a lot of that, liberals like me have perpetrated. And I have to agree that there's too much of that.

But isn't there also a political orthodoxy on the right that Fox enforces?

Yeah, I was going to get to that . . .

I'll give you another example from that memo. When the Palestinian suicide bombings started last year, shortly after they started, one of the memos came down and suggested, "Wouldn't it be better if we used 'homicide bombing' because the word 'suicide' puts the focus on and memorializes the perpetrator rather than the victims?" OK, never mind the fact that any bombing that kills is a homicide bombing. What would you call a suicide bombing where the perpetrator isn't killed? An intended suicidal homicide bombing? It got ridiculous.

It may be ridiculous, but if you watch Fox now, you'll frequently hear suicide bombings described as "homicide bombings," right?

I'll tell you, it's interesting. On that same day [that Fox management distributed a memo suggesting suicide bombings be called "homicide bombings"], the White House had made the same suggestion—well, the Bush administration, whether it was the White House or the Pentagon or whatever. That's the background to it.

By the next day, enough people [at Fox] were saying, "What about this?" So the next day's memo kind of reluctantly said, "Well, you could use either one." But by then, everyone—and again, we're talking about young people who don't have any perspective on this; all they know is that you do what they're told—they know what management's feeling about this is. So . . . it's "homicide bombings." And that's the beginnings of a new P.C.

So people at Fox know what management's political views are—and they know that management wants to see those views reflected on their television screens?

Yes, but it's not because the people on the second floor— Roger Ailes and so forth—come down and say, "This is what we want." It kind of filters down. And very often, the people overreact and take it upon themselves and do things that even management wouldn't expect them to do.

In the case of the California judge who ruled unconstitutional [the words] "under God" in the Pledge of Allegiance, I was sitting there watching our anchor report the story. He was reading the teleprompter, and he was saying, "Because we want you to have as much information [as possible] about this important story, we want you to be able to go right to the source. We're giving you the address and phone number of the judge."

Everybody knew that was a call to harass this guy. Even the poor anchor sees this. I mean, this is the way I saw it because I know the guy. But the point of it is, the guy running the newsroom, he had the control room type up this graphic with the guy's address and phone number on it. And I'm told . . . that when the people on the second floor saw this they said, "Oh, jeez, we can't do that." And they had it taken off. It was this guy down here kind of freelancing, sucking up, thinking he knew what management wanted. And they stopped it.

When [United Nations weapons inspector] Hans Blix was giving his report to the Security Council on what they had uncovered or not uncovered [in Iraq], he began by saying, "We have not found any weapons of mass destruction." He continued to say: "But we think they're hiding them, we want them to be more open and show us, and blah blah blah." Well, you know how it's done on the screen: They'll say Blix: "the first sentence," and then Blix: "the second sentence," and so on. It was going to run through the whole thing.

When [the Fox supervisor running the newsroom] saw this—"We have not found weapons of mass destruction"—I'm told by people in the control room that he went in there and said, "We can't, we're not going to put that on the air like that." But it was too late, it was already in the system, and it went on. And again, it was not because management told him not to, and I don't think they would have said don't put it up. They're smarter than that. But this guy—he still runs the newsroom. Maybe they think, well, he was trying to please them, so he gets to stay there.

Are you aware of times where the reverse happened—that is, where things were happening on the air and someone in management sent a message saying, "I want this to slant more Republican"?

No, I can't say that I've ever known them to do that. But what they have is a middle management that is all too willing to just play ball. They know what they can do, what they should do, what they shouldn't do and so on.

There's just an atmosphere of—I don't want to say "fear," but for some of the young people there that's what it is. You know, I'd rail against this. I never made any bones about it. Right in the middle of the newsroom, I'd say, "Did you see what we did?" The typical thing would be for people to say to me, "So we're not fair and balanced? Like you didn't know that? What are you getting all upset about?"

What else do you remember from the editorial note?

When the war was just beginning or we were just sending troops over there, one of the daily memos made reference to protesters and said that we're going to be seeing a lot of protesters—I think they used the word "whining," yes, whining—about American bombs and American soldiers killing Iraqi citizens. "Whining"—you've got your clue, a hint. They're *whining*. Yeah, tell that to the families of American soldiers that were going to die there.

That was in the memo?

I'm not sure of the exact words, but it was to that effect. So that day I'm down editing lead-ins to tape pieces, and a producer comes down while the editors were putting [one of the reports] together. And the producer says, "No, we can't run that." Why? Because somewhere in the middle of it there was a few seconds of footage of some Iraqi children in a hospital. And he said, "Well, we don't know why they were there." They could have just cut out that clip, but he said to kill the whole thing. This was a report from a reporter on what went on that day. But simply because of that memo, they just killed the story.

Were there other times when you believed the editorial note had a direct influence on the political slant of Fox's news coverage?

I came in one morning, and the first thing I saw on the monitor was our anchor doing a story [about reaction to Sen. Trent Lott's suggestion that America would have been a better place if then-segregationist Sen. Strom Thurmond had been elected president when he ran in 1948]. And it was clear that Fox, through the anchor, was anti-Trent Lott. So I went right to the memo, and sure enough the memo said we should make sure our viewers know that this wasn't even the first time Lott has made such remarks. And I thought, "Wow, I don't understand." So I go to the wires, and sure enough, there it is: Bush has condemned what he had said, and Bush wanted to get rid of Lott as the majority leader.

So it was an unexpected Fox approach to the story—at least until you figured out that it also just happened to be the Bush administration's approach?

That's right.

Did you complain about the bias you saw at Fox?

I reserved my right to rail against what I saw every day practically, and there were times when I would take an anchor to task in front of other people. And I was wrong in doing that, with people I considered friends. But it was just so, so . . . I had just never seen anything like this.

Very often among many of the anchors there, their idea of "fair and balanced" is you have on liberal or Democrat "A" and conservative or Republican "B." You spend most of your time challenging or dismissing rudely what the liberal has to say and lobbing softball questions to the conservative. You'd be sure to give them equal time or give the liberal a little more time even.

You see it day in and day out. For many of these people, the young people, it's par for the course. This is what they see and they let it go. It's hard for me not to comment on things. I've been sitting here for the last six months watching this debate about who's biased and who isn't and whether Fox is this or that. And when I saw this thing about Chris Wallace, I thought, "This is it. This is the last straw."

Wallace said that Fox has received an unfair "rap" as slanting its coverage in a Republican direction. But lots of people associated with Fox have said that. What was it about Wallace's comments that set you off?

The whole idea of throwing him into this debate. Here's a guy who's presumably going to be paid, what? A seven-figure salary, high six figures? What else is he going to say? That's not the guy you should be talking to. Why don't you talk to the people who have to work in this . . . people who can tell you at least privately at least what really happens? You're not going to get the straight story from the people making a million dollars there, not even off the record.

Are your former colleagues at Fox—both the million-dollar anchors and the people working in the newsroom—conscious and aware that they're slanting coverage to the right?

I think many are. A lot of them [aren't.] That anchor that I argued with, I think he sincerely believes that Fox and his work are "fair and balanced. " He would quote from some letters from people who accused him of being liberal. But you've got to understand. When 99 percent of your audience is conservative, you're going to get some raving lunatic conservatives writing in who say you're too liberal.

Even the people who know better . . . well, look, you're working for somebody. I probably should have quit there right away. I stayed on, I had a job, but I reserved my right to yell and scream and not care whether I was considered a malcontent or whatever. And I would not write something that was supposed to be objective that wasn't. You just don't do that.

Well, maybe *you* don't.

Well, you don't in journalism. But now, journalism, a lot of it is viewpoint. Salon, I'm sure, it's, you know, "This is what you can expect from there." But at least you know what you can expect. Fox, you know, you can expect a Republican slant. But just admit it, you know?

And the denial is your biggest frustration?

Yes, it is. Hearing the mantra, you know, "Fair and balanced. We report, you decide." I mean, come on. Don't make me laugh.

"They want to be listened to, protected and amused. And they want to be spanked vigorously every once in a while."
—CNN's Tucker Carlson on women, as quoted by Liz Smith, 3/9/04

Carlson on who he would like to be if he could be a woman:
"[Elizabeth Birch], formerly of the Human Rights Campaign, because you'd be presiding over an organization of thousands of lesbians, some of them quite good-looking."

"Most of the time you can beat a woman in an argument. But what do you win? Nothing. You get short-term pleasure followed by a lot of pain."
—Tucker Carlson

Whatever You Do, Don't Diss the King: When Bush-Backing Bullies Attack

from buzzflash.com (12/24/03)

Maureen Farrell

YOU CAN'T MAKE THIS STUFF UP," Andrew Sullivan announced, referring to Rep. Jim McDermott's most recent controversial comments. "Fresh from Howard Dean's raising of the question of whether President Bush had been tipped off in advance by the Saudis about 9/11 comes Democrat Jim McDermott, not exactly a stranger to conspiracy theories." Citing McDermott's observation that the U.S. could have found Saddam Hussein "a long time ago if they wanted," Sullivan criticized the Congressman for saying that the Bush administration knew Saddam's whereabouts and timed his capture for political gain.

"You begin to wonder if some Democrats have gone nuts—politically as well as psychologically," Sullivan remarked.

Dear God, this is getting old, isn't it? While the "Democrats-as-traitors" smear has run its course (particularly since "Baghdad Jim" was vindicated in the end) "crazy conspiracy theorist" is the Bush-protecting, truth-deflecting insult du jour. But considering that three weeks ago, Illinois Congressman Ray LaHood issued his less-than-subtle hint that the U.S. was "this close" to nabbing Saddam [*Pantagraph*] and last summer's headlines repeatedly made similar claims [Google], McDermott's musings aren't as far-fetched as Sullivan would have you believe.

For those keeping track, the progression went something like this:

- In July, Australia's *The World Today* reported that "former Pentagon insiders say they think US authorities are close to catching Saddam Hussein in Iraq within weeks," while the BBC announced that "US Deputy Secretary of State Richard Armitage said on Monday that troops carrying out such raids in Iraq "were just hours behind Saddam Hussein."
- On August 15, *The Sydney Morning Herald* published comments from senior US commander Col. James Hickey who said, "We're working on a lot of interesting information right now and have good reason to believe [Saddam] is still in this area . . . He's running out of space and he's running out of support. We're going to get him and it's going to be sooner rather than later . . ."
- On Dec. 2, the following quotes by Republican Congressman Ray LaHood were published on Pantagraph.com:
  - "We're this close" [to catching Saddam Hussein]—LaHood
  - "Do you know something we don't?"—Pantagraph editorial board member
  - "Yes, I do."—LaHood
- On Dec. 15, Rep. Jim McDermott told a Seattle radio station, "I don't know that it [Saddam's capture] was definitely planned on this weekend, but I know they've been in contact with people all along who knew basically where he was. It was just a matter of time till they'd find him."

Given this, does Sullivan really consider McDermott's comments "nuts"? Or is it that, once again, the official story doesn't quite mesh with what we've been told, and it's best to head off speculation?

Soon after Saddam's capture, several reports emerged, pointing to inaccuracies within the official U.S. account. The real story, one paper reported, "exposes the version peddled by American spin doctors as incomplete." Though few were swayed by Saddam's sister's observation that her brother had been drugged, less than a week after his capture, a British newspaper stated that "Saddam Hussein was captured by US troops only after he had been taken prisoner by Kurdish forces, drugged and abandoned ready for American soldiers to recover him." [Agence France-Presse] Meanwhile, on Dec. 21, Bloomberg.com reported that "Hussein Was Held by Kurds Before U.S. Capture," [Bloomberg.com] and Scotland's *Sunday Herald* reported that the Kurdish media, which was first to disclose the news, claimed that "Saddam Hussein, the former President of the Iraqi regime, was captured by the Patriotic Union of Kurdistan." [*Sunday Herald*]

Now that contradictory information has begun to trickle in, it seems that the official version of the story, like far too many official versions before it, may not be entirely accurate. And considering that last May, Andrew Sullivan deemed the BBC's deconstruction of the original heavily-propagandized Jessica Lynch story a "smear" told by a "far-lefty" [Journalism.org], he'll have to excuse us for not trusting his insights this time around, either.

Then, too, retired Air Force Colonel Sam Gardiner has openly stated that much of what we're reading about Saddam's capture isn't designed to inform us, but to fool others. "We are seeing an orchestrated media campaign by the administration and a psychological operation aimed at the insurgents in Iraq," he said. "As a former instructor at the National War College, Air War College and Naval War College, I am familiar with the pattern of using the press to conduct psychological operations. . . The technique is straightforward: plant stories or persuade media outlets to slant the news in a way that debilitates your enemy. And so far, media reports on the intelligence significance of Saddam's capture have followed that pattern to the letter."

Citing "the terrible job" *The Washington Post* and *Christian Science Monitor* have done cutting through the spin, Gardiner wondered, "Why are so few real questions raised by reporters when they are confronted with the military's media and psychological operations campaign? Why aren't they helping us get to truth?" [MediaChannel.org]

Good question.

Last time Rep. McDermott was pilloried by pundits, you might recall, it was for telling the truth about Bush's lies. "The President of the United States will lie to the American people in order to get us into this war," he said, in the fall of 2002, right about the time George Bush was telling tall tales about Saddam being "six months away" from developing a nuclear weapon. [CommonDreams.org]

At the time, the Republican National Committee was outraged by McDermott's comments, [RNC.org] as were dittoheads nationwide. *The Weekly Standard*'s Stephen Hayes [MSNBC] was appalled by McDermott's blasphemous assertion that the Bush administration "sometimes" issued "misinformation" and "would mislead the American people." Hayes also took umbrage to other sins, such as McDermott's charitable stance regarding weapons inspections; his refusal to "backpeddle" from the truth; and the Congressman's concerns over the Bush administration's ever-changing rationale for war. [Weekly Standard.com]

It wasn't that long ago (May 7 to be exact) that former White House spokesperson Ari Fleischer told reporters, "One of the reasons we went to war was because of [Iraq's] possession of weapons of mass destruction. And nothing has changed on that front at all." Somehow, in the interim, that imminent threat morphed into a possible weapons program. "So what's the difference?" George Bush asked Diane Sawyer. [*New York Times*] Billions of dollars and thousands of lives later, we might ask, "So what was the hurry?"

As memories of White House denials and fabrications linger, a litmus test begins to emerge: the louder right-wing pundits howl about any given story, it seems, the nearer and dearer the truth.

At times, the media attack machine can be downright comical, however. Unsatisfied with merely taking swipes at Congressman McDermott (making certain to refer to him as "Baghdad Jim," of course), *Newsmax* also recently went after Madeleine Albright for "telling reporters that the Bush administration may already have captured Osama bin Laden and will release the news just before next year's presidential election." Yes, Virginia, the Bush administration's political maneuvers have become so over-the-top, that when our former Secretary of State says it's a "possibility" Karl Rove might be harboring Osama bin Laden, right-wingers believe she's serious and promptly step in to protect our appointed king. [*Newsmax*]

"It's nuts. It's staggering. It's paranoid," Bill Bennett protested and Albright felt compelled to explain. "Last night, in the makeup room at Fox News, I made a tongue-in-cheek comment to Mort Kondracke concerning Osama bin Laden," she said. "To my amazement, Mr. Kondracke immediately went on the air to repeat this comment, which was made to a person I thought was a friend and smart enough to know the difference between a serious statement and one that was not."

The million dollar question throughout all of this, of course, is where does the blame for this bizarre political climate lie? With McDermott and Albright or the Mayberry Machiavellis and the pundits who protect them?

Recent retaliatory attacks may provide the answer. While former psychiatrist Charles Krauthammer dismissed Howard Dean's announcement "that 'the most interesting' theory as to why the president is 'suppressing' the Sept. 11 report is that Bush knew about Sept. 11 in advance" by saying "it's time to check on thorazine supplies," Krauthammer's tact was made even more unethical by the misrepresentation of Dean's words. "But the trouble is, by suppressing that kind of information, you lead to those kind of theories, whether they have any truth to them or not, and eventually, they get repeated as fact," Dean continued. "So I think the president is taking a great risk by suppressing the key information that needs to go to the Kean Commission," he added, though Krauthammer failed to notice.

Dean could have spoken more judiciously, of course, but even so, Krauthammer's attack lost its oomph once Sept. 11 Commission chairman Gov. Thomas Kean admitted that the 9/11 attacks could have been prevented.

And though CBS News reported that Kean "is now pointing fingers inside the administration and laying blame," [CBS News] Kean soon softened his rhetoric before, as the *Boston Globe* pointed out, "the vaunted Bush attack machine," could call its media minions to arms. "One reason the attack machine didn't unload on Kean immediately last week," the *Globe*'s Thomas Oliphant explained, "was that he quickly amended his comments . . . and gave the White House nothing defined to shoot at."

Nevertheless, Kean's initial statement was stunning enough to finally land Sept. 11 widow Kristen Breitweiser a guest spot on the Dec.18 edition of *Hardball*, where she expressed relief that at least one official was at long last saying that someone should be held accountable for 9/11 intelligence failures. When asked what she would do differently had she been president on Sept. 11, she alluded to the President's August 6, 2001 briefing that warned that Osama bin Laden was planning to hijack airplanes in the U.S., and replied:

BREITWEISER: Undoubtedly, I think that I would have told the public. I would have told people like my husband and the 3,000 others that worked in New York City and that decided to fly on planes that day that we were a nation under an imminent threat, that the airlines were a target.

And after the first building in New York City, then you know what?

People like my husband in the second building would have immediately fled. They would have immediately evacuated that second tower, because they wouldn't have thought it was an accident.

People like Donald Rumsfeld may not have sat at his desk for 45 minutes until the Pentagon was hit. People like the president wouldn't have sat there for 25 minutes in front of a group of children.

(CROSSTALK)

BREITWEISER: They would have acted more decisively. Lives would have been saved. I would have informed the public.

MATTHEWS: It sounds like the problem is at the top.

BREITWEISER: It does. [*MSNBC*]

Of course, while Dean is fair game, few pundits would dream of attacking Breitweiser and other Sept. 11 victims' family members for making such assertions or raising questions. Wondering about everything from how the FBI immediately knew exactly which flight schools to search and which A.T.M. videotape would reap Mohammed Atta's mugshot to why NORAD failed to promptly react, Breitweiser and three other Sept. 11 widows were featured in the August 25 edition of the *New York Observer*. "When you pull it [NORAD's 9/11 timeline] apart, it just doesn't reconcile with the official storyline," Lorie van Auken said. ". . .There's no way this could be. Somebody is not telling us the whole story." [911Truth.org]

Lest anyone believe that these widows and Gov. Kean

also need thorazine, the Daily Misleader reminds us that although Bush denies any foreknowledge of the Sept. 11 attacks, once upon a time, the White House conceded otherwise. [Misleader.org]. And as the *Boston Globe*'s Thomas Oliphant announced, "The problem is not Tom Kean's assertion that the terrorist attack on the United States two years ago was preventable, it is President Bush's repeated assurance that it was not." [*Boston Globe*]

"[T]he White House [has] decided to lead a fresh burst of weird propaganda on a nearly two-year-old theme about unconnected dots and intelligence chatter, designed to create the impression that the attacks were literally bolts from the blue instead of evidence that the government had been caught napping," Oliphant continued, reminding us that warnings of a "spectacular attack" [BuzzFlash.com] are not just figments of our collective imaginations.

Else you're beginning to believe the spin, however, this brief retrospective should shock you out of it:

"There were lots of warnings."
—Secretary of Defense Donald Rumsfeld
(*Parade Magazine* interview,
Defense Department Website,
Oct 12, 2001)

"As each day goes by we learn that this government knew a whole lot more about these terrorists before September 11th than it has ever admitted."
—Former Senator and 9/11 commissioner
Max Cleland ("9/11 Commission
Could Subpoena Oval Office Files,"
The New York Times, Oct. 26, 2003)

"I don't believe any longer that it's a matter of connecting the dots. I think they had a veritable blueprint, and we want to know why they didn't act on it."

—Senator Arlen Specter
("FBI, CIA Brass in a Sling,"
New York Daily News, June 6, 2002).

"They don't have any excuse because the information was in their lap, and they didn't do anything to prevent it."

—Senator Richard Shelby, member of
the joint intelligence committee
investigating 9/11 ("Another Dot That
Didn't Get Connected,"
San Francisco Chronicle, June 3, 2002).

"As you read the report, you're going to have a pretty clear idea what wasn't done and what should have been done. This was not something that had to happen."

—911 head Thomas Kean,
("9/11 Chair: Attack Was Preventable,"
CBS News, Dec. 18, 2003)

"[T]he least understandable argument of all is the line first used by Rice in May of 2002, that no one could have foreseen that terrorists would hijack airplanes and crash-fly them into buildings. It is especially odd coming from the coordination person in the White House. . . It is also odd coming from the official who had an administration plan for actions against Al Qaeda on her desk on the day of the attacks."

—Thomas Oliphant
("Prejudging the 9/11 report,"
the *Boston Globe*, Dec. 21, 2002)

"US authorities did little or nothing to pre-empt the events of 9/11. It is known that at least 11 countries provided advance warning to the US of the 9/11 attacks. . . . It had been known as early as 1996 that there were plans to hit Washington targets with airplanes. Then in 1999 a US national intelligence council report noted that "al-Qaida suicide bombers could crash-land an aircraft packed with high explosives into the Pentagon, the headquarters of the CIA, or the White House."

—former British environment minister
Michael Meacher, ("This War on Terrorism
is Bogus," *The Guardian*,
Sept. 6, 2003)

"If you were to tell me that two years after the murder of my husband that we wouldn't have one question answered, I wouldn't believe it."

—Kristen Breitweiser
("9/11 Chair: Attack Was Preventable,"
CBS News, Dec.18, 2003)

"We spent $100 million on Whitewater. Only $3 million has been spent on investigating September 11! It's not about 'getting Bush'—I'm no fan of Bill Clinton either! In a democracy it's always about us—and what we're willing to let people get away with."

—David Potorti, author of *September 11th*
Families for Peaceful Tomorrows,
("Building a War Machine
on the Back of Victims,"
Pulse of the Twin Cities, Dec. 10, 2003)

"Delusions" regarding 9/11 aside, there are countless examples of what happens when anyone questions the official story, as well as what citizens are "willing to let people get away with." So much so, it seems, that when George W. Bush advised that we should "never tolerate outrageous conspiracy theories concerning the attacks of September the 11th," many pundits seemed to think that meant we shouldn't tolerate any diversion from the official script—and should attack anyone else who dares question anything.

Even so, speculating that "Bush knew" about Sept. 11 or Saddam's whereabouts or the real reason we went to war in Iraq (or anything else right-wingers deem "off limits") is akin to wearing a huge "kick me" sign amidst a gaggle of Bush-backing bullies. And as Sept. 11 families spokesman David Potorti pointed out, this is not about "getting Bush" or even a matter of Democrats versus Republicans, but about uncovering truth and preserving democracy.

Considering the ferocity of pundits' attacks, however, truth and democracy are precious commodities. Blessed be those who try to protect both.

Joseph Wilson had the gall to question the lies of George W. Bush. The Bush administration, which values revenge over national security, punished Wilson by revealing that his wife was a CIA operative.

Abrams and Novak and Rove? Oh My!

from *The Nation* (11/3/03)

Eric Alterman

Even though the Joseph Wilson affair has convulsed the capital for many weeks, much of what makes it important is still ignored. Part of the reason is the insider establishment's deep-seated unwillingness to face up to the Nixonian depths of this Administration's moral depravity. A President, Vice President and Cabinet willing to deceive an entire nation for the purpose of war are not going to think twice before destroying the career of a loyal CIA agent in an attempt to smear her husband. Nor is a group so radical that it casts the CIA as the enemy in its plans for world domination likely to worry about the body count of innocent victims on its revolutionary path to neoconservative nirvana. The media treat this case as an aberration. It's the rule.

But another part of the reason this case is so hard to explain in terms that account for why it has taken off is that it involves a shady aspect of the media/government nexus that everyone involved would prefer to leave unexamined. Reporters almost never focus on the sources of their information—even when the leak itself is the most significant part of the story.

The idea that "leaking is wrong" is something that politicians always say but only children believe. Was it wrong for Daniel Ellsberg to leak the Pentagon Papers?

Are whistleblowers evil? Didn't even John Kennedy tell *New York Times* and *New Republic* editors that in retrospect, he wished they had refused his request to keep plans for the ill-fated Bay of Pigs invasion from their readers?

No less naïve is the notion that Presidents and their advisers abhor leaking. What they abhor are leaks they can't control. But they leak all the time as a matter of policy— and here is the key point—even in the most sensitive matters of national security and with the use of classified data. If this surprises you, then you haven't been paying attention. In his most recent book, *Bush at War*, Bob Woodward brags that he was given access to the deeply classified minutes of National Security Council meetings. He also noted, not long ago, that the President sat for lengthy interviews, often speaking candidly about classified information. This surprised even Woodward, who observed, "Certainly Richard Nixon would not have allowed reporters to question him like that. Bush's father wouldn't allow it. Clinton wouldn't allow it." But George W. Bush does it—breaking the law in the process—and nobody seems to care. Why? Because Woodward plays ball—he reports Bush & Co.'s actions in the same heroic, comic-book cadences they use themselves. Moreover, he doesn't bother weighing any competing claims or seeking to determine whether anything he is spoon-fed might actually be true.

The second great fiction of this story is the notion that Robert Novak is a "journalist." Nobody else published this story, because all six of the other reporters given the leak weighed the perceived motives of the leaker and the likely cost of publication to the country and to Plame and Wilson against the value of this hand-delivered scoop. The only person to take the bait was Novak—who published it in the *Washington Post* unedited, because its editorial page apparently sends his copy to the printer without reading it first. In publishing what one "senior administration official" describes as a leak "meant purely and simply for revenge," Novak even refused a request from the CIA not to reveal Plame's identity.

Novak may have acted unpatriotically but not inconsistently. He has never made any bones about the fact that he is an ideological warrior first and a journalist second, if at all. To offer one small but revealing example from a previous decade that appears to have new relevance today, let's go back to October 5, 1986, when Sandinista soldiers shot down a C-123K cargo plane ferrying weapons to the *contras* in southern Nicaragua. Of the four-man crew, the two American pilots were killed, but its cargo kicker, Eugene Hasenfus, also an American, survived and was captured. He revealed to the world that his entire effort had been controlled by the CIA and sanctioned by the US government, sending both into a massive panic.

The *contras'* man in the State Department, Elliott Abrams, took to the airwaves on the *Evans & Novak* program on CNN. Asked whether he could offer "categorical assurance" that Hasenfus was not connected with the government, Abrams smirked, "Absolutely, that would be illegal. . . . This was not in any sense a US government operation. None." This performance was a part of Abrams's plea-bargained conviction for withholding information from Congress by Iran/*contra* special prosecutor Lawrence Walsh.

I interviewed Novak not long after this for a too-kind profile I was writing and asked how he felt about being a pawn in Abrams's deception. His answer: He "admired" Abrams for lying to him on national television because the lie was told in the service of fighting Communism. "He had a tough job and there were lots of people out to get him," Novak averred, expressing zero regrets about misinforming his viewers. "Truth" did not even appear to enter into his calculations. There was his side and there were the other guys, period. That the *Post* and CNN willingly lend space to the man, knowing what they do, is another of the ongoing scandals involving journalistic standards and conservative ideological domination of the elite media.

Finally, regarding the identity of the leakers—well, yes, Karl Rove is obviously a top suspect, given both his power and modus operandi. Ditto Dick Cheney's Rasputin, I. Lewis Libby. But what about Elliott Abrams? A convicted liar and longtime ally of Novak whiling away his time inside the National Security Council, he has played a much larger role in these war plans—and the battles that have accompanied them—than so far has been recognized by the media. Abrams has quite legalistically denied any role in "leaking classified information," according to White House press secretary Scott McClellan. But the last time Abrams pretended ignorance, he was lying. When caught, he found himself celebrated by Novak, pardoned by Bush's daddy and given a spanking new career by Bush himself. I think he knows the drill by now.

ANAGRAM

Brit Hume
Rebut him

RIGHT-WING CONSPIRATORS

with a short take by The Beast *staff*

The Radical Right is supported by a complex and far-reaching conspiracy of corporate and political leaders doing what they can to undermine our democracy so that corporations can rule.

Fox isn't the only overtly right-wing media network, or even the most insidious.

Hillary Was Right

from *The American Prospect* (1/17/00)

Nicholas Confessore

When Hillary Clinton went on the *Today* show in early 1998 to defend her husband against the malefactions of a "vast right-wing conspiracy," she was pitied and disparaged in roughly equal measure. Rightly so: Her husband, it turned out, was dallying with an intern less than half his age. And while the president has garnered more than his share of conservative vitriol, the notion that he was the victim of a conspiracy—a "vast" one, no less—seemed paranoid, the stuff of an especially bad Oliver Stone movie.

But perhaps Hillary's main mistake was her choice of words. Rupert Murdoch's varied holdings, for example, are vast and right wing, but far more concerned with profit as an ultimate end than with ideology. And though the fortune of Richard Mellon Scaife has helped underwrite such enduring conservative institutions as the Heritage Foundation and Kenneth Starr's Whitewater investigation, those relationships are either not very secret (Heritage's funding is a matter of public record) or not very vast (only a half-dozen or so of the lawyers associated with the Paula Jones lawsuit were involved in dishing Linda Tripp's Lewinsky gossip to the Office of Independent Counsel).

A real right-wing conspiracy would have to be more densely networked, more full service. It would need both a fundraising arm and a propaganda arm—and it would have to be below the radar screen, beneath mainstream notice. Such a conspiracy would have to link together not just Murdoch and Scaife, but also the veterans of conservatism (say, William F. Buckley, Jr.) with its youth corps (Ann Coulter, for one), its political operatives (Haley Barbour) with its intellectuals (Dinesh D'Souza), its incumbents (Dick Armey) with its aspirants (Steve Forbes), its eminences (Russell Kirk) with its cranks (David Horowitz), its godfathers (Barry Goldwater) with its wayward sons (Pat Buchanan).

With the publication of Buchanan's *A Republic, Not an Empire*, the wayward son has joined the godfather. Having dropped Little, Brown, Buchanan issued his latest book through a small, Washington, D.C.-based publishing company named Regnery—a development far more significant than Buchanan's latest update on Jewish bankers. Regnery's fold, which has been swelling impressively in recent years, now includes Horowitz, Coulter, Armey, Barbour, Roberts, D'Souza, and even Forbes, whose election-year tome *A New Birth of Freedom* was released by Regnery in October.

Welcome to the world of Regnery Publishing—lifestyle press for conservatives, preferred printer of presidential hopefuls, and venerable publisher of books for the culture wars. Call it—gracelessly but more accurately—a medium-sized, loosely linked network of conservative types, with few degrees of separation and similar political aims. Just don't call it a conspiracy.

Regnery Publishing's right-leaning corporate philosophy actually goes back to 1947, when the late Henry Regnery, Sr., set out to publish "good books," as he wrote in the company's first catalogue, "wherever we find them."

Works by Regnery's friends among the nascent conservative intelligentsia soon followed, including Russell Kirk's
The Conservative Mind, William F. Buckley, Jr.'s *God and
Man at Yale*, Whittaker Chambers's *Witness*, and Barry
Goldwater's *Conscience of a Conservative*. Henry Regnery's
son, Alfred Regnery, who took over in 1986 and moved
the company to Washington, D.C., has likewise been both
a friend to and publisher of conservative authors. After
stints in law school (where he roomed with American
Conservative Union Chairman David Keene) and as college director of Young Americans for Freedom, Alfred Regnery was appointed head of the Office of Juvenile Justice
and Delinquency Prevention by Ronald Reagan in 1983.
While there, as reported by Murray Waas in *The New
Republic*, he helped run Edwin Meese's ill-fated President's
Commission on Pornography; disbursed generous grants
to Jerry Falwell's Liberty College, Meese pal George
Nicholson, and professional antifeminist Phyllis Schlafly;
authored, with then-Assistant Secretary of Education Gary
Bauer, a much-ridiculed report called "Chaos in the Public
Schools"; and in general cultivated an updated version of
his father's network of friends.

But by the time Alfred Regnery took over the family
business, the firm had slipped into semi-dormancy. Regnery Publishing's 1993 purchase by newsletter magnate
Tom Phillips woke it up. Phillips, one of the Republican
National Committee's "Team 100" and a board member
of the Claremont Institute, lavished both money and
attention on his new acquisition. Leaving Alfred Regnery
at the helm, Phillips folded the company into his Eagle
Publishing division, an overtly political enterprise with a
distinguished stable of conservative media: *Human Events*,

a 56-year-old,ultra-right weekly newspaper; the Evans-Novak Political Report; the 75,000-member Conservative Book Club (founded in 1964 as "America was walking down Lyndon Johnson's path to a socialist 'Great Society'"); and a similar operation called the Christian Family Book Club. But perhaps most significant—given the central role direct mail has played in the conservative resurgence of recent decades—is Eagle's list brokerage operation, which rents out Eagle's own customer lists and those of organizations like Newt Gingrich's GOPAC, Empower America, the Western Journalism Center, and the Ronald Reagan Presidential Foundation, not to mention Pat Buchanan's American Cause and the Steve Forbes for President campaign.

By the time Phillips Publishing spun off Eagle last July, an entirely new entity had emerged: a company that treats publishing less as a media enterprise than as a form of political activism. With a new, almost Gingrichian sensibility, Regnery's titles have begun to reflect the particular ideological and policy concerns of foundation-funded, third-wave conservative thinkers. Believe that the American family is in its death throes? Read Maggie Gallagher's *The Abolition of Marriage: How We Destroy Lasting Love.* Worried that American higher education is overrun by radical feminists and licentious left-wingers? Pick up the late George Roche's *The Fall of the Ivory Tower: Government Funding, Corruption, and the Bankrupting of American Higher Education,* or David Horowitz's *The Heterodoxy Handbook: How to Survive the PC Campus.* Believe that corrupt teachers' unions are the bane of the American education system? Read G. Gregory Moo's *Power Grab: How the National Education Association is Betraying Our Children.* If you suspect that the Walt Disney Corporation is out to lead children astray with Miramax films and "Gay Day" at Disney World, have a look at *Disney: The Mouse Betrayed*, by Peter and Rochelle Schweizer. And if you wonder whether more assault rifles equals less crime, imbibe the pithy wisdom of Wayne LaPierre's *Guns, Crime, and Freedom*.

Most of these authors hail from the tight knit world of conservative think tanks and advocacy groups—the ideological heirs of Kirk, Buckley, and Goldwater. LaPierre, for instance, is vice president of the National Rifle Association, and Peter Schweizer is a media fellow at the Hoover Institution. Horowitz, whose career lately consists of writing one book every two years about his personal transformation from left-wing radical to right-wing reactionary, runs the Center for the Study of Popular Culture.

But the Phillips publishing family does not shy away from more direct forms of political engagement: According to the Center for Responsive Politics, Phillips International (then called Phillips Publishing International) gave $125,150 in soft money to the Republican National Committee (RNC) in 1997-1998, while Eagle Publishing gave the RNC another $19,500. (The RNC, not incidentally, was chaired by Regnery author Haley Barbour until January 1997.) The Phillips Publishing PAC has contributed $64,450 to various Republican officeholders and seekers during the same period, while Phillips himself gave $1,000 in contributions to 15 different Republican candidates in 1998. Eagle/Regnery, in other words, is more than just a conservative press—it is a partisan press, with close personal, organizational, and even fundraising ties to the Republican Party. It should thus come as no surprise that a frequent topic in the Regnery catalogue is one William Jefferson Clinton.

Since 1996, Regnery has published no less than eight presidential exposés: Roger Morris's *Partners in Power: The Clintons and Their America*, Bill Gertz's *Betrayal: How the Clinton Administration Undermined American Security*, Edward Timperlake and William C. Triplett's *Year of the Rat: How Bill Clinton Compromised U.S. Security for Chinese Cash*, Ann Coulter's *High Crimes and Misdemeanors: The Case Against Bill Clinton*, Ambrose Evans-Pritchard's *The Secret Life of Bill Clinton: The Unreported Stories*, Gary Aldrich's *Unlimited Access: An FBI Agent Inside the Clinton White House*, and R. Emmett Tyrrell's *The Impeachment of William Jefferson Clinton: A Political Docu-Drama* and *Boy Clinton: The Political Biography*. To date, five of these books have made various best-seller lists.

For all intents and purposes, the eight are interchangeable —with each other and, stylistically, with most of the other political books in Regnery's catalogue. Each posits a nebulous conspiracy centered around the Clinton White House, a murky stew that typically blends one or more of the following ingredients: shady banking and land deals loosely grouped under the "Whitewater" rubric; the murder—or induced suicide—of Vince Foster; Filegate and Travelgate; dalliances with prostitutes and nymphets; rampant drug use; treason via Chinese spies; and an Arkansas-based, Clinton-masterminded drug-smuggling outfit.

Thus constructed, Regnery's Clinton books run from the racy to the absurd. Tyrrell's *Boy Clinton* follows the future president from alleged cocaine benders with Little Rock entrepreneur Dan Lasater to his sojourn with communists in Prague during the late 1960s. ("Inquiries I had made about his trip to Moscow turned up little that was new," Tyrrell writes breathlessly. "People were still wondering where he had gotten sufficient funding for such a trip. Some still suspected a KGB front. Others suggested the CIA.") Coulter, although her tone is even more vicious than Evans-Pritchard's ("We have a national debate about whether he 'did it,' even though all sentient people know he did," she writes. "[O]therwise there would only be debates about whether to impeach or assassinate."), relies mostly on the standard litany: Whitewater, Foster's "mysterious" death, Filegate, and Clinton's Paula Jones deposition. It is Evans-Pritchard who proposes what is easily the most tangled web of Clintonian malfeasance, touching not only on the usual stuff—booze, women, land deals— but also on the Oklahoma City bombing, which he argues was actually an FBI sting gone wrong and one of many Justice Department operations by which Bill Clinton has sought to turn America into a police state.

The most infamous of the Regnery titles is undoubtedly Gary Aldrich's *Unlimited Access*, which included such "revelations" as lesbian encounters in the White House's basement showers, Hillary Clinton ordering miniature crack pipes to hang on the White House Christmas tree, and the claim—backed by anonymous sources—that Clinton made frequent trips to the nearby Marriott to shack up with a mistress "who may be a celebrity." That last bit helped catapult *Unlimited Access* to the top of *The New York Times*'s bestseller list, though Aldrich soon revealed to *The New Yorker*'s Jane Mayer that the Marriott story was "not quite solid" and, indeed, was "hypothetical." But according to Aldrich, it was Regnery editor Richard Vigilante who had moved the Marriott bit out of the epilogue (where it had been presented as a "mock investigation") and into the middle of the book (where it was presented as an actual occurrence). Vigilante, Aldrich told Mayer, threatened not to publish the book if Aldrich didn't agree to the changes.

In fact, the defects of *Unlimited Access*—a reliance on loose or anonymous sourcing; the blending of fact, fiction, and fantasy; the influence of Regnery's anti-Clinton *esprit de corps*—can be found, to varying degrees, in nearly all of Regnery's Clinton books. The drug-smuggling charges in Tyrrell's and Evans-Pritchard's books, for instance, were first aired in the pages of the Scaife-funded *American Spectator*, the hysterically conservative magazine of which Tyrrell is editor, founder, and chief polemicist. "The Arkansas Drug Shuttle," published in the *Spectator* in 1995, was a fanciful tale of cocaine smuggling, the CIA, and black cargo jets told to Tyrrell by former Arkansas state trooper L.D. Brown—who happened to be on the *Spectator*'s payroll at the time. Indeed, Tyrrell's dispatches stirred considerable controversy among the magazine's own staff. "Even within the *Spectator*, people had problems with the [drug-smuggling] stories," says David Brock, the *Spectator*'s star investigative reporter at the time. "People didn't feel that they met the standards of the *Spectator*." Senior editor Christopher Caldwell jumped ship for *The Weekly Standard*, and when longtime *Spectator* publisher Ronald Burr tried to order an independent audit, Tyrrell fired him. "I can't really comment on the *Spectator*," says Alfred Regnery, who stands by all his company's Clinton books. "But a book publisher doesn't have the same obligations as a magazine. We cross-examine the authors to some extent, but publishers do not have the wherewithal to check every single fact."

Yet Regnery Publishing seems not just to encourage conspiracy theorizing from its authors, but to *demand* it. In 1997 Alfred Regnery approached veteran crime reporter Dan Moldea about writing a book on the Vince Foster case. Regnery, says Moldea, hoped that his contacts within the law-enforcement community would shed new light on the case. But Moldea came to the same conclusions as all the official inquiries did. "There were some mistakes, some omissions," says Moldea. "But this was a dead-bang, bona fide suicide." When Moldea turned in *A Washington Tragedy: How the Death of Vincent Foster Ignited a Political Firestorm*, the editors at Regnery "were less than thrilled. There were some real battles that went on between us, between me and the staff," he says. "Things were being cut out of the book that I was really upset about, like this section on Scaife. It got so bad that I was almost hoping that they would reject the book, because I knew that they were just going to seal it and it would never see the light of day."

That, according to Moldea, was roughly the fate of Linda Tripp's own account of the Lewinsky scandal. In January, Alfred Regnery told *The Washington Post* that Vigilante had turned down Tripp's book in 1996 because her asking price of a half-million dollars was too high. "I came away with the impression of a woman who valued her privacy and her professional career," Vigilante said at the time, "and who was distinctly uninterested in writing a book." That wasn't quite the case, says Moldea. Regnery told him that Tripp "had come to Regnery wanting to write a book about Vince Foster and her experiences in the White House." But, says Moldea, she believed that if she ticked off her superiors, "she would have trouble with her job as a federal employee. So she was pulling her punches, and Richard Vigilante decided to reject her book."

It's not clear whether such decisions result from a top-down editorial policy or simply from a sort of reverse vetting process conducted by overeager staff editors. Alfred Regnery himself is no fire-breathing demagogue; Phillips, the more enthusiastically ideological of the two, may be more directly responsible for the direction Regnery's books began to take in 1993. "I always liked Al Regnery, even though we had nothing in common," says Moldea, who credits Regnery with standing by his version of the Foster book in the face of heavy intra-company criticism. Similarly, David Brock says that after criticizing the Aldrich book in *Esquire*, "I got a weird call from Alfred Regnery. He said he agreed with what I had said, and he conceded that there were problems with the book. Then I wanted details, but he didn't want to talk about it anymore." It is Vigilante's name, moreover, that comes up most frequently regarding editorial heavy-handedness.

What is clear, however, is that Regnery's conspiracy theorizing has benefited greatly from Eagle Publishing's web of media enterprises. Sometimes the synergies are transparent, as when *Human Events* published a list of the "10 Best Conservative Books of 1998," five of which were Regnery titles. Sometimes they're more subtle—not to say conspiratorial. *Human Events* editor Terrence Jeffrey had ample time, for instance, to convince Buchanan to switch to Regnery during the 1996 presidential race, when he served as Buchanan's campaign manager. (Jeffrey also failed to disclose his relationship with Buchanan when he penned a lengthy, front-page defense of *A Republic, Not An Empire* in the September 17 issue of *Human Events*). When

Human Events excerpted the "Cox Report" in its June 4 issue, the weekly's lead feature was none other than Caspar Weinberger's introduction to Regnery's edition of the "Cox Report." Regnery's "Cox Report," in turn, was published the same month that Bill Gertz's *Betrayal* hit the stands (and just a few months before Regnery put out a second Timperlake and Triplett book, *Red Dragon Rising: Communist China's Military Threat to America*). Similarly, after Aldrich's *Unlimited Access* was published in June 1996, *Human Events* ran a five-page excerpt of the book in its July 5 issue—followed, in subsequent issues, by eight more articles defending or discussing the book. Tyrrell's *Boy Clinton* was also excerpted that year, while the Schweizers' *Disney: The Mouse Betrayed* was excerpted last spring. Like all Regnery titles, each was heavily hyped by the Conservative Book Club.

Certainly such coordination would not have required many phone calls; *Human Events*, Regnery, and the Conservative Book Club all share the same Washington, D.C., address. "There's no contract that exists that says we have to carry 'x' number of Regnery titles each year," says Brin Lewis, who doubles as vice president of Eagle Publishing and president of Eagle's book club division, which owns the Conservative Book Club. "But we carry a lot of them."

Normally, implausible exposés are relegated to remainder bins and the back pages of *The National Enquirer*. But partly thanks to Eagle's pipeline to the conservative elite, and partly thanks to a powerful direct mail operation that doubles as a de facto Eagle publicity machine, the likes of Aldrich's miniature crack pipes make it into broader forums like *The Weekly Standard* and *The Wall Street Journal*—and from there out into the political ether. Allegations of Clinton-related drug smuggling at Arkansas' Mena Intermountain Municipal Airport, for instance, filtered up from the *Spectator* and Regnery's Clinton books to *The Washington Times* and *The Wall Street Journal*—the latter running favorable reviews of the books as well as numerous editorials about the Mena "scandal"—which led to further recycling by *The Washington Post* and dozens of other newspapers in 1996 and 1997. Indeed, as recently as last March, a *Wall Street Journal* editorial writer used the Juanita Broadrick controversy as occasion to flog, yet again, the Mena connection. Such ludicrous charges might easily be dismissed as rant. Yet in the past three years, Republicans in Congress have opened not one, but two official inquiries into the matter—one under the auspices of the House Banking committee and one by the CIA Inspector General's office.

But if nothing else, attacking Bill Clinton has been a lucrative endeavor. "What's bad for the country is good for Eagle Publishing," gushed Tom Phillips to his audience at the annual right-wing convocation known as "the Weekend" last February. "Seven successful anti-Clinton books! We took six of them and put them in a shrink-wrapped six-pack for $99." When Clinton leaves office, there's always his presumptive heir; released in May, excerpted in *Human Events*—and offered free, via direct mail, to new *Human Events* subscribers—was former ABC analyst Bob Zelnick's *Gore: A Political Life*. And if Gore sells poorly, Eagle can always to go back to the Clinton well: Currently in bookstores, just in time for primary season, is Barbara Olson's *Hell to Pay: The Unfolding Story of Hillary Rodham Clinton*.

After You, My Dear Alphonse

from *The Nation* (10/20/03)

Katha Pollitt

What's the matter with conservatives? Why can't they relax and be happy? They have the White House, both houses of Congress, the majority of governorships and more money than God. They rule talk-radio and the TV political chat shows, and they get plenty of space in the papers; for all the talk about the liberal media, nine out of the fourteen most widely syndicated columnists are conservatives. Even the National Endowment for the Arts, that direct-mail bonanza of yore, is headed by a Republican now. Never mind whether conservatives deserve to run the country and dominate the discourse; the fact is, for the moment, they do.

What I want to know is, Why can't they just admit it, throw a big party and dance on the table with lampshades on their heads? Why are they always claiming to be excluded and silenced because most English professors are Democrats? Why must they re-prosecute Alger Hiss whenever Susan Sarandon gives a speech or Al Franken goes after Bill O'Reilly? If I were a conservative, I would think of those liberal professors spending their lives grading papers on *The Scarlet Letter* and I would pour myself a martini. I would *pay* Susan Sarandon to say soulful and sincere things about peace, I would hire Al Franken and sneak him on O'Reilly's show as a practical joke. And if some Democratic dinosaur lifted his head out of the Congressional tarpits to orate about the missing WMDs, or unemployment, or the two and a half million people who lost their health insurance this year, I'd nod my head sagely and let him rant on. Poor fellow. Saddam Hussein was his best friend, after Stalin died. No wonder he's upset.

For some reason right-wingers do not take this calm and broadminded view. Maybe they didn't get enough love in their childhoods, or maybe they're in more trouble than we know. In any case, they've taken to lecturing the opposition on manners whenever it shows signs of life. Ted Kennedy says the Iraq war was "a fraud made up in Texas" and Bush complains that he's "uncivil." "Not civil," Condoleezza Rice agrees, "not helpful." Well, *excuuuse* me! In *National Review*, Byron York obsesses about anti-Bush websites and the "one long bellow of rage" that is . . . MoveOn.org? David Brooks, the *New York Times'* new conservative Op-Ed columnist, mourns the passing of the culture wars, which were about ideas, and wrings his hands over the "vitriol" of the new "presidency wars," which are just about hating Bush as "illegitimate . . . ruthless, dishonest and corrupt." Exhibit A: Jonathan Chait's eloquent, shrewd and not at all vicious *New Republic* essay on why he hates President Bush (among other things, his triumph is an affront to meritocratic principles—well, it is!). Even Ann Coulter is worried that "the country is trapped in a political discourse that resembles professional wrestling." Gee, is this the same Ann Coulter who wrote that Timothy McVeigh should have driven his truck into the *New York Times* headquarters, whose bestselling polemic *Treason* argues that liberals are Commie-loving traitors who hate America? The Prozac must be working.

As Brooks, at least, acknowledges, the right is in a weak position when it claims to be shocked, shocked, shocked by liberal speech today. Remember when Newt Gingrich blamed Susan Smith's drowning her children on Democrats? ("How a mother can kill her two children, 14 months and 3 years, in hopes that her boyfriend would like her is just a sign of how sick the system is, and I think people want to change. The only way you get change is to vote Republican.") Never mind that Smith had been molested as a young girl by her stepfather, a South Carolina Republican Party activist with close ties to Pat Robertson's Christian Coalition. Remember when Gingrich called the Democratic Party "the enemy of normal Americans," and Dan Burton, chairman of the House Reform Committee, called President Clinton a "scumbag"? (Committee spokesperson Will Dwyer defended this epithet as "straight talk.") During the Clinton years you could turn on the TV and watch Jerry Falwell hawking videos "proving" that Vince Foster was murdered—a view promoted repeatedly by the *Wall Street Journal* editorial page and even entertained by Brooks's *Times* colleague William Safire. (And Foster's was only one of the many murders the President was supposed to have arranged.) You could hear Rush Limbaugh declare, "Bill Clinton may be the most effective practitioner of class warfare since Lenin"— Bill Clinton, the best friend Wall Street ever had!

Ancient history? It was only two years ago that Richard Lessner of the Family Research Council asked in a press release, "What do Saddam Hussein and Senate Majority Leader Tom Daschle have in common?" Answer: "Neither man wants America to drill for oil in Alaska's Arctic National Wildlife Refuge." Just this September, Tom DeLay accused Ted Kennedy of "extremist appeasement," charged that "national Democrat leaders this year have crossed a line and now fully embrace their hostile, isolationist extreme" and called opposition to the Miguel Estrada nomination "a political hate crime." (You'll notice—a small but telling point—DeLay continues the Gingrich-era intentionally rude substitution of "Democrat" for "Democratic.") Coulter's *Treason* sits on the bookshelves alongside right-wing ravings with titles like *Bias, The No-Spin Zone* and *Useful Idiots* (in which Mona Charen cites yours truly as "demonstrating the reliable theme of America-loathing that informs much leftist thinking" because I didn't want to fly the flag after 9/11). Very high-minded, very rational!

Well, they wanted state power, and thanks to the Supreme Court Five, they got it. But unfortunately, running the country turns out to be harder than it looked when Bill Clinton was killing off Hillary's lovers between Cabinet meetings. He made it seem so easy! Now, unemployment is way up, the government's awash in red ink, Iraq is a mess. So, everything has to be someone else's fault—mean liberals who really, really want to win in 2004, Osama-loving pranksters who forward e-mail jokes about the President's IQ, Bill and Hillary, still magically pulling the strings three years after leaving the White House, having thoughtfully arranged for 9/11 before they departed.

They can dish it out, but they sure can't take it.

Fox Broadcasting Network is just one element of a vast empire.

Rupert Murdoch

from *What Liberal Media?*

Eric Alterman

The *Wall Street Journal* editors enjoy the backing of the Dow Jones Corporation and CNBC, and even with their more than five million readers, a few hundred thousand viewers, and the uncounted numbers who read their opinions on the Internet, via www.opinionjournal.com, they have to be considered relative pikers compared to the empire amassed by the veritable Wizard of Oz, Rupert Murdoch. With a net worth hovering in the area of $5 billion, the Australian national's News Corporation has holdings that include:

- Fox Broadcasting Network;
- Fox Television Stations, including over twenty U.S. television stations, the largest U.S. station group, covering more than 40 percent of U.S. TV households;
- Fox News Channel;
- A major stake in several U.S. and global cable networks, including fx, fxM and Fox Sports Net, National Geographic Channel, Fox Kids Worldwide, and Fox Family Channel;
- Ownership or major interests in satellite services reaching Europe, the United States, Asia, and Latin America, often under the Sky Broadcasting brand;
- 20th Century Fox, with its library of over 2,000 films; 20th Century Fox International, 20th

Century Fox Television, 20th Century Fox Home Entertainment, Fox Searchlight Pictures, Fox Television Studios;
- Over 130 English-language newspapers (including the *London Times* and the *New York Post*), making Murdoch's one of the three largest newspaper groups in the world;
- At least twenty-five magazines, including *TV Guide* and the *Weekly Standard*;
- HarperCollins, Regan Books, Zondervan Publishers;
- Fox Interactive, News Interactive, www.fox news.com;
- Festival Records;
- The Los Angeles Dodgers.

While most of Murdoch's corporations are registered abroad to avoid taxes—News Corp. pays a paltry 7.8 percent effective tax rate in the United States—Murdoch gets more for his money as he is able to use the proceeds of one to support the other. Politically and commercially, he is determined to put "synergy" to work. Murdoch's magazines and newspapers support his television programs and movies and vice versa. His reporters make up news that other companies would have to pay public relations firms millions to try to place. No newspaper in America is less shy about slanting its coverage to serve its master's agenda—be it commercial or political—than the *New York Post*. Judging by the *Post*, almost every Fox program is either "jaw-dropping," "megasuccessful," "highly anticipated," or all three. Columnist Gersh Kuntzman once revealed that editors consider page two to be the "Pravda Page." "When there's a major [Murdoch] business deal going down, with no interest to readers," he explained, "it's on page two. Or when [then-conservative New York Senator Alfonse] D'Amato makes a pronouncement of no particular interest to readers, it's on page two." Oftentimes, this tendency turns the paper into kind of an extended inside joke in the media, where it is carefully read because of its obsessive media-oriented gossip. For instance, the *Post* declared the film *Titanic*, a Murdoch property, to have received "the first endorsement of any Hollywood movie by a Chinese official." The paper did not mention just who believed it or why this mattered. The entire article was based on a premise so farfetched— that the entire Chinese nation was agitating to see the sappy film a full month before it was scheduled to open— that the article read as a kind of satiric self-criticism session of the kind that Maoists used to undergo in the days when they plotted to overthrow the evil government of "Amerika."

Once famous for its loveably nutty "Headless Body in Topless Bar"-type headlines in the early 1980s, Murdoch's tabloid has lost him perhaps hundreds of millions of dollars over the years at a rate of $10 million to $30 million per annum. (Actual figures are a closely guarded secret.) But despite its down-market definition of news, the paper still provides Murdoch with an entree to the media elite because of its great gossip pages, and, hardly incidentally, its terrific sports section. Curiously, in a city that is so fierce about its cultural pride, in late 2002 the *New York Post* was run largely by Australian imports. The *Post*'s current editor, hired in 2001, is Col Allan, a man who brags about peeing in the sink during editorial meetings and enjoys the nickname "Col Pot" back in Sidney. Allan took just six weeks to decide to fire the *Post*'s only black editor, Lisa Baird, who was fighting a losing battle with breast cancer at the time. He also fired the paper's only liberal columnist, that feisty New York institution, Jack Newfield, preferring the columns of Victoria Gotti, the sexy daughter of a murderous mob boss. Allan also demonstrated his tin ear for New York politics quite early in his tenure when, upon Jim Jeffords's decision to switch sides in the Senate and vote with the Democrats—thereby giving that party a one-vote majority—he headlined the front page "Benedict Jeffords." New York, someone might have pointed out to him, has two Democratic senators and voted for both Al Gore and Bill Clinton by so large a margin that they barely needed to campaign there. Its denizens were not exactly angry about a switch in the Senate that gave their side more power.

Murdoch made no attempt to hide his paper's political agenda. Rudy Giuliani, who all but forced TimeWarner to add Fox News Channel to its local roster of stations, was second only to Leonardo in the *Post*'s pantheon of heroic Italians. Hillary Clinton, the "rejected wife," who proved the cause of "a veritable crime wave in the White House" and who, while running for senator, "couldn't find the Bronx unless she had a chauffeur, and couldn't find Yankee Stadium with a Seeing Eye dog," was, to say the least, treated rather less generously. To the degree that any racial problems existed anywhere in New York, they were always the fault of black people, who demand special treatment or merely raise a ruckus for its own sake—all of these views shared by many on the right. All Israelis were noble warriors; all Palestinians, vicious terrorists. These, however, were predictable prejudices for a right-wing ideologue. The most interesting bias exhibited by Murdoch media properties was that on behalf of Communist totalitarianism—at least of the variety practiced in Beijing.

Initially Murdoch held conventional views about murderous Communist dictatorships and praised the manner in which modern telecommunications "have proved an unambiguous threat to totalitarian regimes everywhere." But when Beijing shut down his satellite broadcasts, Red Rupert switched sides, telling critics: "The truth is—and we Americans don't like to admit it—that authoritarian societies can work." When the Chinese complained about how the BBC portrayed them, Murdoch booted it off his Asian satellite network, Star TV. "The BBC was driving them nuts," he was quoted as saying. "It's not worth it." Sucking up to the killers soon became a family affair. Murdoch's son James even found some kind words to say about the Reds' enforcement of anti-religious repression.

Murdoch's publishing companies were put to work for the commies as well. Murdoch gave over a million bucks to Deng Xiaoping's daughter for an unreadable propagandist tome that no sane person could ever have imagined would become a best-seller in the West. When Chris Patten's tough-minded memoir of his years as the governor of Hong Kong threatened to upset the Chinese, however, Murdoch canceled the contract and attacked its author. His explanation? "We're trying to get set up in China. Why should we upset them?"

Amazingly, Murdoch would not even take his own (adopted) nation's side in a conflict with the Chinese. During the hostage crisis of April 2001, while the Chinese were refusing to release U.S. soldiers, the paper seemed to undergo a personality transplant, all but ignoring the biggest story in the world. *Post* editorials, which usually declare war every time someone sneezes near the Stars and Stripes, were almost completely mum. John Podhoretz, who later advised George Bush to invade Iraq merely to get the corporate accounting scandals off the front page, was the perfect diplomat. Steve Dunleavy, who, as the *Post*'s almost insanely belligerent columnist, usually thinks of foreign policy as a subset of bar-fighting, proved to be remarkably patient and thoughtful in his discussion of the crisis. "Until happiness is restored to 24 American kids and their families, let's keep our sabers safely and silently sheathed," wrote the newly sissified tough guy. "Careless rhetoric can prove disastrous to freedom, as President Jimmy Carter harshly learned during the Iran hostage crisis."

In 1985 Murdoch acquired 20th Century Fox Studios, in much the same way he acquired the *New York Post:* with lots of cash and some crucial political interventions from the politicians he funded. He combined the company with the fledgling Metromedia television stations to launch America's first new broadcast network since the early days of television. Fox was given every break imaginable throughout the 1980s on the grounds that a new television network should be encouraged. Finally, in 1994, following nearly ten years of indifference, the Federal Communications Commission checked into the network's ownership to see if it was foreign-owned. It was; Murdoch's News Corporation was actually an Australian company, not an American one, as he had portrayed it. But rather than allow the commission to enforce the law, according to Reed Hundt, then the FCC chair, conservative

Republicans "lambasted me for the audacity of having looked into the question."

While some of what the Fox network produced has been genuinely great—most notably *The Simpsons*—much of its programming appears devoted to answering the question "just how low can you go?" Conservatives like William Bennett and Pat Robertson enjoy condemning liberals for the promotion of casual sex and alternative lifestyles at the expense of society's bedrock social institutions like marriage and courtship, but Robertson has no more powerful and influential enemy in this regard than his business partner in the Fox Family Channel. In the spring of 2000, the network that had invented *Studs*, a dating show with stripping men, managed to amaze even its critics with *Who Wants to Marry a Millionaire?* Here, women were invited to prostitute themselves and debase the institution of marriage for the greater glory of Fox's ratings. (It almost didn't matter that the program's producers went about this task entirely incompetently, as the alleged "millionaire" was no such thing, but did have a few restraining orders in his past. The marriage was never consummated but the "bride" did get to pose naked in *Playboy*.) A year afterward, Fox managed to outdo itself in the cultural debasement sweepstakes with the debut of *Temptation Island*, in which four "committed" couples were dumped on an island and filmed "canoodling" in various combinations.

From the outset, the networks "news" programs demonstrated a similarly catholic interpretation of the term "family values" when it came to reeling in viewers (and hence profits). Its original flagship, *A Current Affair*, erased much of the journalistic rulebook. As Burt Kearns, one of its top producers, later recounted, in order to get a copy of a tape alleging to show the actor Rob Lowe having sex with some young women of "jailbait" age, at the 1988 Democratic convention in Atlanta, the producers lifted footage from an Atlanta station and claimed it as its own, paid a club owner for the sex tape even though he had no legal ownership, and physically destroyed the evidence in the face of a lawsuit. As Kearns put it, "The Rob Lowe tape was a milestone for the show and tabloid television. Sex, celebrity, politics, crime, morality and America's obsession with home video cameras were all rolled into one. . . . We were the fucking champions of the world." (In fact, the events caught on tape did not really take place in Atlanta but were filmed in France. There were no underage girls involved and hence, no story. But nobody ever reported that.) Details aside, Kearns was right. The conservative Roger Ailes, the former Reagan/Bush aide who then went on to head Fox News Channel, said he did not believe that such shows even require a defense. "News is what people are interested in," Ailes insisted. "We're just getting the same girls to dance around shinier poles."

Despite this rather tricky track record, family-values wise, when Murdoch began Fox News Channel in 1996 with Ailes at the helm, conservatives fell all over themselves to praise it. "If it hadn't been for Fox, I don't know what I'd have done for the news," Trent Lott gushed during the Florida election recount. George W. Bush extolled Bush I-aide-turned-anchor Tony Snow for his "impressive transition to journalism" in a specially taped April 2000 tribute to Snow's Sunday-morning show. The right-wing Heritage Foundation had to warn its staffers to stop watching so much Fox News on their computers, lest the entire system crash.

The conservative orientation of Fox is invaluable to the right, not merely because Fox offers the spin on reality conservatives prefer to have people see and hear, but also because it helps pull the rest of the not-terribly liberal media in its direction. In Chapter 10, I discussed the key role played by Fox and its election analyst, George W. Bush's loyal cousin, John Ellis, in helping create the media stampede to call the election for Bush. But the hiring of Ellis was no isolated incident; rather it was symbolic of business as usual. For instance, when, just before Election Day, the media discovered that George W. Bush had been hiding a DUI conviction, Fox seemed to spin the incident even more furiously than Karl Rove and Karen Hughes. Morton Kondracke of *Roll Call:* "A footnote." John Fund of the *Wall Street Journal:* "A blip." Mara Liasson of NPR: "Yes, I agree with that. I think it's a blip." The program in question—*Fox Special Report with Brit Hume*—did not even bother to devote much attention to the potentially election-altering news. Instead it focused, once again, on troubles Al Gore had in fighting off Ralph Nader.

When it did return to the story, the FNC spin focused on the Bush campaign's charge that the Gore team had somehow engineered the leak. FNC's Tony Snow went so far as to give credence to "rumors" that the Clinton administration had been involved and predicted that this might help the Bush campaign by creating sympathy for it—and therefore "backfire" on Gore. Snow never cited a shred of evidence for any of these claims, which was wise, as none existed. Meanwhile, FNC's Paula Zahn mused aloud on the question of just how long Maine Democrats had "sat on the story." In fact, it was the local Maine news-paper, where the Bush family compound is located, that sat on the story, for whatever reason we cannot know. As Eric Boehlert noted, all this spin-oriented damage control is, indeed, a far cry from the days during the height of the Clinton scandals, when former FNC correspondent Jeb Duvall, according to his account in *New York Magazine*, was once met by a news producer who "came up to me, and, rubbing her hands like Uriah Heep, said, 'Let's have something on Whitewater today.' "

Such fare is, however, the norm for a station where a spe-cial about foreign policy is hosted by Fox commentator and former Republican House Speaker Newt Gingrich; *Heroes*, an irregular series, is hosted by Gingrich's ex-colleague in the Republican congressional leadership, John Kasich; and on *The Real Reagan*, a panel discussion on Ronald Reagan, hosted by Tony Snow, all six guests were Reagan friends and political aides, plus the ever-present Ollie North. Fox's cov-erage of the conflict in Afghanistan is similarly slanted but also kind of crazily flawed. Most famous, of course, was the incident in which Geraldo Rivera missed the spot of the "hallowed ground" from which he pretended to be reporting by a mere 200 miles.

But most news organizations have displayed a bias toward the American side in covering the events in Afghanistan. Indeed, how could they not? While none beside Rivera brag about "packing heat" and laughably threaten to take out bin Laden themselves, these reporters too are Americans, who saw the tapes of the horror of September 11. Most are not only deeply patriotic people themselves, personally sympathetic to the soldiers and their cause, but also quite understandably hostile and fearful of an enemy that has been targeting journalists with a gruesome (and occasionally bloodthirsty) effectiveness. These reporters are also, in many cases, extremely sensitive to the charge that the media is anti-American, and in the cases of both Fox and CNN have been warned against appearing so. It is a baseless charge, as any quick comparison between U.S. and British or European coverage of the fighting immediately demonstrates. To take just one "for instance," on December 30, 2001, U.S. airstrikes hit the village of Niazi Kala (also called Qalaye Niaze) in eastern Afghanistan, killing dozens of civilians. The attack was major news in several U.K. newspapers, with the *Guardian* and the *Independent* running front-page stories. The headlines were straightforward: "U.S. Accused of Killing Over 100 Villagers in Airstrike" (*Guardian,* January 1, 2002); "U.S. Accused of Killing 100 Civilians in Afghan Bombing Raid" (*Independent,* January 1, 2002); " '100 Villagers Killed' in U.S. Airstrike" (*London Times,* January 1, 2002). In contrast, the *New York Times* first reported the civilian deaths at Niazi Kala under the headline "Afghan Leader Warily Backs U.S. Bombing" (January 2, 2002). Keep in mind that the *New York Times* is usually considered Public Enemy Number One by conservatives. Note also that this antiwar/anti-American accusation, while useful to conservatives seeking to force news organizations to hew to their views, has always been false. In the most famous case, that of the Vietnam War, the media has been exonerated by none other than the official history of the U.S. Army. But as with the overall charge of bias, endless repetition, coupled with a multi-billion dollar propaganda offensive carried out over a period of decades, has had its intended effect. Much of the U.S. media is particularly wary of reporting any news that might be construed as "anti-American," regardless of the merit of the charge. For many, it is simply not worth the hassle.

Yet even in the deeply pro-American, patriotic context in which the U.S. media has been operating since September 11, 2001, Fox still manages to distinguish itself.

Osama bin Laden, its anchors, reporters, and guests explain, is "a dirtbag," "a monster" overseeing a "web of hate." His followers in Al Qaeda are "terror goons." Taliban fighters are "diabolical" and "henchmen." Fox is not interested in covering the civilian casualties of U.S. bombing missions. As Brit Hume explained, "We know we're at war. The fact that some people are dying, is that really news? And is it news to be treated in a semi-straight-faced way? I think not." To a considerable degree Fox's open bias in this case—and in many others—is refreshing. It is perhaps the only news station where news comes with a context, and is therefore made more understandable for consumers than the helter-skelter version to which most Americans have become accustomed. It's unfortunate, both for genuine liberals as well as for the cause of democratic discourse in the United States, that it is the only one available. And fortunately for the pro-war crowd in the United States, Rupert Murdoch has no significant investments in Iraq—nor any desire to convince Saddam Hussein to let his satellite network into that nation.

Because investments almost always appear to trump ideology in Murdoch's world—he supported Tony Blair in England against his conservative opponents and received some extremely curious favors from the government thereafter—the millions of dollars Murdoch pours into the low-circulation conservative opinion magazine, the *Weekly Standard*, is perhaps his most curious invest-ment. Most of Murdoch's properties earn money. The *New York Post* may look like a money-loser, but it buys him a political voice in New York and with the media elite, which is extremely valuable when he needs a favor from one of the city or state's elected politicians. It also allows him to intervene directly in the copy of the newspaper, offering him the opportunity to punish enemies and reward allies. Fox News Channel, has, like its broadcast parent, turned out to be a surprisingly shrewd commercial proposition. Though its older, largely rural audience does not produce the revenues of CNN despite significantly higher ratings, it does give every indication of having become a profitable enterprise with remarkable rapidity.

But the *Weekly Standard*, unlike Fox, will never make a profit, as political opinion magazines never do. And unlike the *New York Post*, the *Standard*'s editors will not allow Murdoch to dictate its politics. When Murdoch's other publications were toadying up to the Chinese during the spy plane crisis of 2001, the *Standard* was denouncing the administration—and by extension, Rupert and James Murdoch, with fire and brimstone. When the kind of deal Murdoch was actively seeking was finally achieved by the Bush administration, William Kristol, together with Robert Kagan, thundered about "The profound national humiliation that President Bush has brought upon the United States." While writing a column on the topic, I made a few calls to the magazine to determine what their policies were with regard to criticizing their owner. Kristol, executive editor Fred Barnes, and senior writer Christo-pher Caldwell were all apparently too busy to get back to me. Opinion editor David Tell was helpful with critical pieces about China but also demurred on the question of Murdoch per se. Senior editor and best-selling swami David Brooks was all charm and no information: "I'm sorry. I'm having some computer problems. At first I thought you were asking me to comment on the son of my employer. Must be some garble." Murdoch could not have liked that.

Perhaps the owner was suckered in. In its original inception, the magazine, edited by Kristol, appeared to be exactly the same wavelength as its sugar daddy. Murdoch, recall, was trying to pay then-House Speaker Newt Gingrich more than $6 million for an unreadable book of speeches much in the fashion that he paid Deng's daughter. (The Murdoch "advance" was ruled out of order by the House ethics committee and was never paid. The book was an easily predicted flop.) The *Standard*, as it was originally conceived, appeared to be a kind of Newt Gingrich fanzine. The cover of its first issue, published in April 1996, portrayed Gingrich as Rambo, bravely swinging on a vine above a burning Capitol, and featured four pieces on Newt of the Jungle. Within two years, however, it was Gingrich and company who seemed bound for the nuthouse—or at least for disgrace and retirement. The *Standard* transferred its affection to Republican dissident and media darling John McCain, with Kristol and Kagan acting as a kind of unofficial brain trust during McCain's heady 2000 run. When Bush won, however, that was fine, too.

There is no question that the *Weekly Standard* has been home to many of the most talented political writers anywhere, conservative or no. Bill Kristol, David Brooks, Christopher Caldwell, and Tucker Carlson would have enjoyed considerable success no matter what politics they practiced. Even though the *Standard* had been a bastion of the McCain mutiny, the Bush administration swallowed its collective pride and raided it upon coming into office. Among the staffers who moved over to the administration were John Dilulio (to head up the president's faith-based initiative), Matt Reese (to work for U.S. Trade Representative Robert Zoellick), and David Frum and Ed Walsh (to join the White House speechwriting shop).

Of course things did not always work out perfectly. Dilulio quickly ran afoul of the Republican thought police when he seemed to take seriously his mandate to involve inner-city clergy to address real problems. Warned publicly for his apostasy by Grover Norquist, he was the first significant member of the administration to quit his job. David Frum lasted a bit longer, but also left under clouded circumstances. He was working as a supposedly anonymous White House speechwriter. But his wife, novelist Danielle Crittenden—who has a sideline in instructing women to use their husband's name professionally but used her own—could not bear to see hubby's genius go unrecognized. Following Bush's famous "Axis of Evil" State of the Union in 2002, Crittenden sent out a mass e-mail proudly proclaiming her husband's authorship of the phrase. Timothy Noah, Slate's gossip columnist, published the offending e-mail. ("It's not often a phrase one writes gains national notice . . . so I hope you'll indulge my wifely pride in seeing this one repeated in headlines everywhere!!") Noah also quoted Crittenden's stepfather's Canadian newspaper telling the same tale. And he cited other possible authors. Later Frum, thinking twice, decided it was Bush's idea after all. As speechwriters are not supposed to take credit for anything, even incoherent geopolitical formulations, Frum decided it would be a good time to, as the saying goes, "return to private life." Republican pooper-scooper Robert Novak blamed Crittenden's e-mail for the decision, but Frum said it wasn't so. Still, Frum did not improve his credibility with his announcement, in early 2002, that W. had already "proven himself to be one of the great presidents of American history."

Under the rhetorically challenged Bush, the *Standard*'s most important function was to become the primary public voice of America's war party, no matter who was the enemy. China, the Palestinians, the Iranians, the Syrians, the Cubans, and, of course, Al Qaeda and the Iraqis would all have qualified. When, for instance, some Republicans, including some of ex-President Bush's closest advisers, dissented from the policy of a U.S. war against Iraq in the summer of 2002, Kristol and company shot back—in the language of Joe McCarthy—that "an axis of appeasement—stretching from Riyadh to Brussels to Foggy Bottom, from Howell Raines to Chuck Hagel to Brent Scowcroft—has now mobilized in a desperate effort to deflect the president from implementing his policy." Those on the left who opposed an invasion of Iraq did so not out of pragmatic considerations about its effectiveness, lack of allied support, effect on the region and its inhabitants, or moral considerations about the launching of a pre-emptive war. Rather, they were "queasy about American principles." Others, "mostly foreign policy 'realists,'" opposed it because "they're appalled by the thought that the character of regimes is key to foreign policy." A few "cosmopolitan sophisticates of all stripes," Kristol noted, using the word that Stalin chose for Jews, were on the wrong side because they "hate talk of good and evil."

Kristol was hardly alone in this tactic. As John Judis noted in the *American Prospect*:

> The *Wall Street Journal* identified Scowcroft's views with those of the "anti-war left." The *New York Sun* enumerated Scowcroft's current business ties and his founding of a "front group" that includes a "PLO apologist" on its board. As for Hagel, the *Wall Street Journal*'s editorial page accused him of trying to "grab a fast headline." And in an article titled "Sen. Skeptic (R., France)," the *National Review* insinuated that the Nebraskan was more European than American in his views. But the hawks didn't expend most of their ammunition on Scowcroft and Hagel. Instead, they took aim at the *New York Times* and its new executive editor, Howell Raines. The *Wall Street Journal*, The *Weekly Standard*, the *Washington Times* and columnists Charles Krauthammer and George Will charged that the *New York Times* was promoting opposition to the administration's Iraq plans by publishing false information about the dissenters in its news pages.

The idea of honest, principled, and intelligent opposition to a war against Iraq was ruled out of order by most conservative pundits, no matter what the credentials of those giving voice to it. Note also that the very idea of reporting dissent—be it within the military, the Congressional Republican Party, or the Republican foreign policy establishment who had crafted George H. W. Bush's war with Iraq—was equated, once again, with the dreaded liberal bias, as if Brent Scowcroft, James Baker, Lawrence

Eagleberger, Republican Chuck Hagel, and even House Republican Whip Dick Armey had somehow switched to the "liberal" side so that they might be charged with making common cause with the *New York Times*. Krauthammer even concluded, "Not since William Randolph Hearst famously cabled his correspondent in Cuba, 'You furnish the pictures and I'll furnish the war,' has a newspaper so blatantly devoted its front pages to editorializing about a coming American war as has Howell Raines' *New York Times*." Too bad for the pundit, Hearst never said this. It is a tale that ten minutes worth of research might have prevented his repeating, but never mind. (Curiously, Krauthammer, who is partially paralyzed, and Kristol—like most of the outspoken journalistic war hawks with regard to Iraq, including Bob Kagan, George Will, Rush Limbaugh, Marty Peretz, Andrew Sullivan, Jacob Heilbrunn, Christopher Hitchens, and Michael Kelly—share with George Bush, Dick Cheney, Republican Majority Whip Tom DeLay, the hawkish defense official Paul Wolfowitz, Senate Majority Leader Trent Lott, and the DOD adviser Richard Perle the quality of having managed to avoid military service of any kind during their entire lives. Hence, they are entirely innocent of any understanding of its character from the ground up. In the case of the vice president, who required four separate deferments to stay out of harm's way while the unlucky amongst his generation went off to fight and die to defend "freedom in South Vietnam," he has explained that he "had other priorities in the 60s than military service.")

It should surprise no one that when both the *Times* and the *Washington Post* egregiously underreported a massive antiwar demonstration in Washington in late October

2002 with a crowd estimated by local police to be well over 100,000 people, not one of the above pundits bothered to complain. The *Times* was forced to run an embarrassing "make-up story" in which it admitted its earlier (buried) story on the demonstration, which claimed merely "hundreds" of demonstrators, had been profoundly misleading. The *Post* received a hard slap from its ombudsman, Michael Getler, who complained that the paper had "fumbled" the story of the biggest antiwar demonstration since the 1960s. Hypocrisy aside, the apparent lack of sympathy evinced by the editors of both papers would appear to put a crimp into the arguments of anyone accusing these media titans of an antiwar bias, which is perhaps why the hawkish pundits who focus obsessively on the coverage of Iraq in both papers, decided to ignore it entirely.

No one—not even *Times* superhawk William Safire—was more important in the media debate over Iraq than the *Weekly Standard*'s William Kristol, McCarthyite language or no. When, in late August 2002, Vice President Cheney finally laid out a case for war, the *Washington Post*'s Dana Milbank quoted Kristol and Kristol alone for analysis. "The debate in the administration is over," he declared in apparent triumph. "The time for action grows near." Of course it did not hurt that the pro-war side also had Howard Kurtz, asking this dumb question on its behalf: "By the way, do you think there were any Hill hearings on removing Adolf Hitler?" (Mr. Kurtz does not seem to be aware that it was Hitler who declared war on the United States, not the other way around.) As James Capazzola nicely put it on the Web log Rittenhouse Review, "That's the liberal media at work."

Short Take

Rupert Murdoch
The Beast staff
from BuffaloBeast.com

That's right, the Aussie outcast is now an American citizen. Only someone as vile as Murdoch would use "The 700 Club" as a template for an entire news network. Seizing the opportunity to be a fixer for his ultra rich pals hampered by pesky facts in their quest to dominate the world, Rupert created a 24/7 "world affairs for dummies" channel. Predictably, Fox News rapidly became the ratings leader, scoring particularly well with the lucrative 'dipshit' demographic. We sometimes watch this atrocious propaganda orgy for inspiration, but advise non-satirists against it, as long-term exposure can lead to mental degeneration and an irrational fear of information.

We See That Now

from *The American Prospect* (February 2004)

Tony Hendra

We confess. It's all true. Everything you say. We trafficked in hate. We did it in anger. Just as you said, Mr. Kristol, Mr. Krauthammer, Mr. Brooks: We poisoned the airwaves and befouled the sheets of our nation's most august publications. We attacked a sitting president, impugned his integrity, smeared his family, invaded his privacy, tried desperately to drag him down to our own filthy, rock-bottom, sewer-dwelling level.

There is no parallel between your measured criticism of Bill Clinton and our vile attacks on George W. Bush. Bill Clinton deserved everything thrown at him because a corrupt and evil man who gains the White House by underhanded means *should* be attacked with every weapon at the disposal of a free press. And yes, it's true, just as your more sagacious radio hosts have maintained: Hillary Clinton *does* owe her success to the practice of witchcraft. And no, it's not true that ridiculing Chelsea at the most vulnerable stage in her development was the media equivalent of child molestation. Chelsea Clinton was fair game because she is the spawn of Satan. Scurrilous of us to suggest that the tirelessly moderate and civil proponent of these and so many other truths, Robert Bartley, now resides in the circle of hell reserved for hate-mongers and bigots! Mr. Bartley dwells in the bosom of his Republican creator. We see that now.

George W. Bush cannot be, as we've screamed till we're blue in the face, the cretinous finger puppet of

an incalculably cynical and malevolent cabal *and* a ruthless neo-Confederate, bent on creating a plutocratic
ruling class at home and a rapacious corporate imperium
abroad. He's one or the other. We cannot have it both
ways. We see that now.

Similarly, we can hardly denigrate Rupert Murdoch and
his "gutter press" while at the same time carping that
without him the right would be a marginalized mob of
obscurantist paranoids kept on life support by retrograde
trust-fund nut jobs. Mr. Murdoch is a great populist.
Lowest-common-denominator programming is an honorable tradition in both the United States and the United
Kingdom. Taking such programming to China, where he is
equally solicitous of a proto superpower whose interests
are frequently inimical to ours, does not mean that Mr.
Murdoch is giving aid and comfort to the enemy, or that
NewsCorp's money is somehow "tainted." It's despicable
of us to suggest that all those hardworking journalists—
from Bill O'Reilly to William Kristol—who take his supposedly dirty money are likewise tainted! We see that now.

What demon put into our so-called minds the idea that
the ghastly tragedy of that bright morning in September
2001 might have been prevented because the Bush administration had received warnings for a month that some sort
of attack might be coming? And that the president and his
advisers had ignored that intelligence and then made use
of the tragedy to seize the draconian emergency powers
they craved and get the economy back onto a perpetual-
war footing? How could we even entertain such thoughts?
What venom flowed through our hate-infarcted hearts?

We're sorry for our endless ranting about oil being the
lifeblood of the Bush family circle, and The Carlyle Group

existing as nothing more than a gigantic corporate kick-back to its members for faithful service while in office, and the Bush team comprising the selfsame men who supported Saddam Hussein to the hilt while he was committing most of his genocidal atrocities and therefore making them his guilty accomplices. These are vicious, hateful untruths. We see that now.

The First Amendment does not give us the right to screech that young Americans are dying in Iraq so that George W. Bush can get himself legitimately elected president. It's a bald-faced lie that his bald-faced lies about weapons of mass destruction cost them their lives. Our brave men and women in uniform know when they enlist that there is always the chance they may have to pay the ultimate sacrifice. Their motives are never—as we so squalidly claimed in the wake of the Jessica Lynch affair—to get a higher education because the military is now the sole conduit to it for the two-thirds of Americans who can't afford it. What a despicably mercenary motive to impute to our heroes! And in any case, why *isn't* the re-election of an epochal president a lofty patriotic aim, worth the sacrifice—as our great defense secretary has implied—of a few lives? Why would this aim fill us with rage and hate, instead of quiet pride?

We were wrong to call George W. Bush's huge tax cuts legalized looting, wrong about the replacement of a $5 trillion surplus with a $3 trillion deficit. No, that is *not* $8 trillion down the drain in three short years. We arrived at that ridiculous conclusion by juggling the figures. If you're as egregiously partisan as we, you can make figures prove anything. We see that now.

We apologize from the bottom of our hearts for our

unfounded suspicions about the plane crash that killed Minnesota Sen. Paul Wellstone and his family. Only a wild-eyed conspiracy nut would link it to the crash had killed Missouri Gov. Mel Carnahan. Nostra culpa! Grief unhinged our better judgment. Hey, Democrats die in planes around election time. That's life. We better get used to it.

What drives us to ask—so shrilly, so annoyingly—why Ken Lay *still* isn't in prison? Are we really *certain* that he deprived hundreds of thousands of people of their savings? That he helped hatch a plot to bring down the Democrats in California by destabilizing that state's power supply? So what if that's now happened? Has Mr. Lay done *anything* that is technically wrong?

Realizing now the awesome power of prayer, we'll stop praying every moment of every day that Tom DeLay gets snatched up in the rapture. We realize, too, that the sign in his office—"This Could Be The Day" (i.e., Judgment Day)—does not utterly disqualify Mr. DeLay from assessing the best long-term interests of the nation. We believe, with him, that the poor *are* entirely to blame for their own poverty, and that if—sorry, *when*—our savior returns, he will indeed own a concealed-carry permit. We know now that Mr. DeLay is not precisely the kind of religious lunatic the Founders had in mind when separating church and state; that he and his co-religionists are in no way brutish, heathen, hate-driven humbugs whose fundamentalism makes Osama bin Laden look like the archbishop of Canterbury. We hope and pray that Mr. DeLay will guide the destiny of America till the trump of doom. Even if it is next Tuesday.

Looking back on the decade-plus of our boundless ill will and partisan fury, we've come to understand something absolutely vital about that glorious year 1989, the year you won the Cold War: The reason the Cold War *had* to be won was that it made the world a *two-party system*. One of them had to go. It's the same in our great nation. What's the point of having two (or even one and a half) parties when it leads to nothing but unending conflict, frustration, stagnation and despair? For America to bring the message to the world that ours is the best and only way, we must have *unanimity*. One party indivisible under God.

Yet ever since 1989, we've been fighting a new Cold War—in Congress, in the culture, in the media, in the nation's schools and courts and bedrooms.

It's time for us to . . . *surrender*. We're tearing down the Berlin Wall of rage and malice we've erected between you and us. We do this before it is too late, before you reach the point where you will be forced—however reluctantly—to investigate us, confiscate our property, search our houses, seize our personal records, detain us sine die, suspend habeas corpus, take reprisals against our loved ones, hold show trials, send us to re-education camps—whatever you in your impeccable judgment deem necessary to preserve the homeland from, well, the likes of us.

But—a huge "but," we know—if in your great hearts you can find the room to forgive us, if even the meanest of positions can be found for us in the new dispensation, let us serve you. We'll do anything you want, no matter how menial: deleting hard drives, wiretapping journalists, delivering bags of cash to senators, transporting assets to the Caymans, firing pregnant Mexicans, evicting the disabled, laying bets for virtuous windbags, beating up young gay men, escorting Muslims to the border, performing sexual favors for The Heritage Foundation—whatever you need we'll do it, and for free.

Some of us even have advanced skills to put at your disposal. We could help discredit Europe's socialistic health and welfare systems and nonprofit public utilities so The Carlyle Group can privatize them. We could produce inspiring movies about the great Americans who are ushering in the thousand years of prosperity that are just around the corner. We could create upbeat news stories for the Ministry of Truth you plan for George W. Bush's second term.

We come to you not just as sinners but as supplicants, begging not just forgiveness but *inclusion*. There's a reason God named the right the right: Because it's *right*. You have a monopoly on the truth, and you always have and you always will.

We see that now. We really do.

TALK SHOW
TRASH

with quotes by Sean Hannity, G. Gordon Liddy, Tammy Bruce,
and Pat Robertson;
short takes by The Beast *staff;*
and anagrams

They poison the airwaves with their mean-spirited lies, twisting the truth on behalf of the powerful in hopes of becoming powerful themselves. Pity them: they have sold their souls to the Radical Right. They're already in Hell, and they'd like the rest of us to join them.

Leering, hatchet-faced, mean-spirited hypocrite Sean Hannity pretends to be a patriot, but his only real allegiance is to himself.

The Blowhard Next Door

from Salon.com (8/26/02)

Ben Fritz and Bryan Keefer

I f you don't already know who Sean Hannity is, you will. If you are already familiar with the ubiquitous conservative pundit, prepare to see a lot more of him. The 40-year-old co-host of Fox News' "Hannity and Colmes" (as the conservative foil to liberal Alan Colmes) is a young, telegenic face in a graying-man's game. His show is already the third-highest cable news show, trailing only Fox's "O'Reilly Factor" and CNN's "Larry King Live." His radio show, which went into syndication late last year and airs in the crucial 3-to-6 p.m. "drive time" slot, draws 10 million listeners. And he seems poised to follow the gilded paths of Fox colleague Bill O'Reilly and, quite possibly, Rush Limbaugh, who has been the standard-bearing conservative spokesman for nearly two decades.

Eventually, Hannity will "be bigger than Limbaugh," Michael Harrison, the publisher of the radio industry's *Talkers* magazine, predicted to *People* magazine earlier this year. It's not difficult to see why. While no less partisan, Hannity's scrappy, boy-next-door delivery would seem to have a broader appeal than that of the more dour Limbaugh.

So now comes his next step. Following the multi-bestselling Limbaugh and O'Reilly, Hannity has decided to make the leap to print with his new book, *Let Freedom*

Ring. The climate, it appears, could not be better. Already this year, Ann Coulter's *Slander* and Michael Moore's *Stupid White Men* have been runaway No. 1 bestsellers, proving that ink on paper is one foolproof way to break out as a partisan pundit. And sure enough, Hannity's book, released just last week, has already made its way to the top of Amazon.com's nonfiction bestseller list.

But in *Let Freedom Ring*, Hannity seems to be following another regrettable trend in modern punditry: Never let facts stand in the way of a good partisan screed. That was the dirty truth behind *Slander* and *Stupid White Men*, and Hannity continues it with his book, a poorly researched effort full of blatant falsehoods and highly distorted versions of the truth.

Early in the book, Hannity grants that the "vast majority of liberals are good, sincere, well-meaning people. They love their kids. They love their neighbors. I am sure most love their country." The rest of *Let Freedom Ring*, however, is devoted to attacking liberals as a threat against America. Indeed, Hannity frames a war against liberals as part and parcel of the war against terrorism: "The Left may be sincere, but they're sincerely wrong. And they must be challenged and defeated if we are to win this war on terror and preserve our way of life for this and future generations."

But Hannity's claims often stray into the realm of myth. He scores some points with his criticism of the outrageous rhetoric thrown by some liberal commentators, such as James Carville and Bob Herbert, but Hannity gets his facts wrong again and again, especially, and not surprisingly, when it comes to Democratic politicians.

Numerous lies abound, for instance, about former

President Bill Clinton. Hannity cites an oft repeated lie that in a speech at Georgetown University, "Clinton seemingly blamed the vicious terrorist attacks on you and me and all Americans." Citing a passage from the speech in which Clinton noted that Europeans and Americans had engaged in atrocious acts in the past, such as the Crusades and slavery, Hannity says Clinton is providing a "justification for radical Islamic terrorism" and an "apology for terrorism." This criticism had a bold, but short-lived, life span last fall, when conservative critics leapt to attack Clinton based on a slanted article in the Washington Times before actually reading what he had said. The speech itself makes it clear that the former president didn't note these historical events to excuse the attacks of Sept. 11 but merely to illustrate that killing innocent noncombatants has a long history. Other conservatives who picked up this tick had the class to correct their attacks with the truth. Now, 10 months after this myth was corrected, truth doesn't seem to be much of a concern for Hannity.

"Let Freedom Ring" also accuses Clinton of "not effectively going after Osama bin Laden" and suggests Clinton should have sent "a covert team over to the Middle East to take out bin Laden." But Clinton, of course, did attempt to kill bin Laden with a cruise missile attack in 1998 and authorized several other overt and covert measures targeting the terrorist leader. He just failed. But such a claim could also be made thus far against President George W. Bush.

Without citing a reference, Hannity also states on the first page of his chapter on taxes that "the tax burden on American families is at a record high, having skyrocketed during the Clinton-Gore years." Hannity most likely arrived at this figure—and this is a guess; footnotes are irregular and sometimes incomplete—using deceptive calculations that simply divide total taxes collected by the government by the number of families. But the progressive nature of our income tax system means that the national tax burden is not evenly divided among families. Tax receipts naturally went up in the 1990s as the economy grew rapidly and more citizens were pushed into higher tax brackets. Yet a study from the left-leaning but well-respected Center on Budget and Policy Priorities found that the share of income paid in federal taxes by the middle 20 percent of families declined from 1995 to 2000, when it stood at its lowest level since 1979.

Hannity continues this faulty logic in repeating the canard spread by the Tax Foundation that, under Clinton, "tax freedom day" (the day when Americans have paid off their tax bill for the year) was pushed back from April 20 to May 1. Once again, this is a lazy use of averaging to make higher incomes (that is, more people moving into higher tax brackets) look like an increase in tax rates for average citizens.

In other cases, Hannity can't even interpret the data from his own sources correctly. In a discussion of President Ronald Reagan's economic policies, he claims that "had all of Reagan's budgets been adopted federal spending would have been 25 percent less on a cumulative basis." This statement is immediately followed by a chart, reproduced from a Web site that shows that the total difference between federal budgets enacted from 1982 through 1989 and those proposed by President Reagan was $197.3 billion, or 2.7 percent (the 25 percent number on the chart is based on a flawed method of compounding the difference between each year's budget).

When discussing Democratic opposition to Bush's tax cut, he accurately quotes House Minority Leader Dick Gephardt, D-Mo., who stated in April 2001 that "at a time when key indicators tell us that there is an economic slow-down, the president has sent a plan that ignores the needs of average Americans and provides a blueprint to fulfill a campaign promise to cut taxes first no matter what." Amazingly, Hannity follows this quote with an accusation: "Can you believe these statements? Not even the most lib-eral of economists will argue for tax increases during a recession."

Gephardt, however, didn't argue for a tax increase in that quote—or in any others during the Bush tax-cut debate. This is a blatant distortion designed to equate opposition to Republican tax cuts with support for a tax increase. And in an attack that would certainly come as a shock to those who took part in the radical New Left movement of the '60s, Hannity devotes eight pages to his contention that Senate Majority Leader Tom Daschle is "a New Left Democrat" and "arguably the most ideologically intransigent New Left liberal to ever serve in the Senate leadership."

The New Left was, as Hannity himself admits earlier in the book, a radical movement that wanted to largely dis-mantle capitalism and the U.S. military. To back up his use of this label on Daschle, Hannity cites only a list of 10 votes over a 23-year career in which Daschle voted against increased defense spending and missile defense, against the Persian Gulf War, and for a nuclear freeze. One of the cuts Hannity cites Daschle voting for is a minuscule $329 million. Missing from the list, of course, are all of the defense budgets Daschle voted for, including this year's, which included nearly $30 billion in increased spending—hardly the action of a New Left radical.

The lies continue in Hannity's chapter on the environment, where he focuses on the dispute over the Arctic National Wildlife Refuge. He states that the U.S. Geological Survey said ANWR could yield up to 16 billion barrels of oil. But in March a *Washington Post* reporter interviewed a geologist at the USGS who said the total was closer to 3.2 billion barrels. Even the highest estimate given by Sen. Frank Murkowski, R-Alaska, during the congressional debates was 10.2 billion barrels.

But then, Hannity is repeatedly at odds with reality in this chapter, stating that ANWR oil would make the United States "far less dependent on foreign oil" and noting Teamsters president Jimmy Hoffa Jr.'s assertion that drilling would create 735,000 jobs. A *Miami Herald* article citing data from the USGS, the Department of Energy and the Congressional Research Service, however, stated that, at its peak, ANWR would produce less than 5 percent of daily U.S. oil consumption and create between 60,000 and 130,000 new jobs. Yet Hannity, in typical style, uses these falsehoods to make the broad claim that "it is difficult to point to another issue in modern American history where a major political party's rhetoric is so divorced from reality."

Distortions and lies are par for the course throughout "Let Freedom Ring" because, without them, Hannity wouldn't be able to make the continual stream of over-the-top accusations against liberals: They "loathe and ravage so many of our core values and traditions"; they "told us global warming and gays in the military were top priorities, well above securing our nation"; and "after we defeat our last foreign enemy, we will still face threats to our freedom, largely from left-wing extremists in our own country."

On "Hannity and Colmes," Hannity often seems to roll over the timid Colmes with his bluster. When his words are frozen on the page, though, there is no disguising what they are: poorly argued propaganda.

With the 51-year-old Rush Limbaugh's profile fading, and only the 53-year-old Bill O'Reilly (who doesn't toe Limbaugh's conservative line nearly as well as Hannity) equaling him in popularity, Hannity seems on the brink of becoming America's leading conservative pundit. "Let Freedom Ring" is troubling evidence that Hannity won't let a little thing like truth get in the way of his rapid ascent.

He Said It . . .

"Anyone listening to this show that believes homosexuality is a normal lifestyle has been brainwashed. It's very dangerous if we start accepting lower and lower forms of behavior as the normal."
—Sean Hannity, 1989

"I feel sorry for your child."
—Sean Hannity to a lesbian woman who had given birth through artificial insemination.

Sean Hannity

from deal-with-it.org

Gus DiZerega

On October 3, 2003, an important study was released, analyzing Americans' beliefs about the war in Iraq. Three mistaken impressions were common, and a majority of Americans had at least one of them. They were:

* U.S. forces have found weapons of mass destruction in Iraq.
* There is clear evidence Saddam Hussein worked closely with the Sept. 11 terrorists.
* People abroad either backed the U.S.-led war or were fairly evenly split between supporting or opposing it.

According to the Program on International Policy Attitudes at the University of Maryland, 60 percent of Americans believed at least one of these falsehoods. PIPA also correlated these mistaken beliefs with what media outlets they watched. Eighty percent of those who said they relied on Fox News held at least one of these misconceptions, substantially more than respondants who got their news from other media outlets. [1]

Of course, George Bush is primarily responsible for betraying America's trust. But when 80 percent of Fox News viewers were misinformed, versus only 47 percent of newspaper readers and 23 percent of those who relied on PBS or NPR the responsibility is not his entirely.

Sean Hannity, one of Fox's media stars, must take

significant responsibility for betraying the Founders' faith that freedom of the press would lead to informed citizens. He combines a contempt for the facts with vicious attacks on those with whom he disagrees. For example:

> "Forty-eight hours we're sending our men and women in harm's way, and there's the leader of your party [Tom Daschle] in the United States Senate disgracefully attacking our president at a time we're going to war." (May 18, 2003)

> "Here we are in a conflict, in a war, and the President is trying to direct things, and they just can't put aside their partisanship for five minutes and support the troops and support the President, and these are the leaders of the Democratic Party." (April 6, 2003)

Patriotism, Hannity style, is an on-and-off kind of thing. During another time when American troops were in harm's way, he had these words of wisdom to say (We take these two quotations from page 130 of Al Franken's devastating demolition of Hannity in *Lies and the Lying Liars Who Tell Them*):

> "Explain to the mothers and fathers of American servicemen that may come home in body bags why their son or daughter have [sic] to give up their life." (April 6, 1999) [2]

> "They haven't prepared for anything in this. And they're running out of weapons to do it. And frankly, I don't think Clinton has the moral

authority or ability to fight this war correctly." (May
10, 1999; Al Franken, *Lying Liars*, p. 129)

Hannity is another of the Radical Right chicken hawks
who attack people like Tom Daschle who have served their
country in uniform. For Hannity and his ilk, wrapping
themselves in the flag seems an adequate substitute for
serving in the military. The English language has a word
for people like Hannity: hypocrite.

Like so many on the Radical Right, Hannity parades his
supposed religiosity as evidence of his moral superiority
over those he criticizes. But anyone even mildly conver-
sant with Scripture would quickly see the deep contradiction between his hard hearted contempt for the poor and
weak, his relentless attacks on the moral failings of those
with whom he disagrees and his solicitude for ideological
allies like Bob Livingston and Newt Gingrich. Gingrich
has been married twice. He went to his first wife's hospital
bed where she was recovering from cancer surgery, to discuss the terms of divorce. Later he dumped his second wife
to marry a much younger Congressional aide, with whom
he had long had an extramarital affair. Hannity's approval
of Gingrich and loud and incessant disapproval of
Clinton's far tamer affair with Lewinsky seems just
another instance of his hypocrisy.

If Hannity is sincere about his religion, which frankly
we doubt, perhaps he should meditate on Matthew 25:31-
46 ("In as much as ye have done it unto one of the least of
these my brethen, ye have done it unto me"). But taking
those words seriously would alienate himself from his
huge salary and the powers of Mammon, which seems
really to attract his allegiance. [3]

Hannity is now trying to cash in on the right wing book bonanza that has done so much to spread lies throughout our country. Hannity's book, *Let Freedom Ring* is as well-researched and accurate as Ann Coulter's work, as full of truth and integrity as Bill O'Reilly's. In other words, it is a mélange of half-truths, misleading statistics, and simple lies. *Spinsanity* has done a devastating online review,[4] and Al Franken pulverizes Hannity's book in *Lying Liars*.

1. See: http://www.philly.com/mld/philly/news/special_packages/iraq/6918170.htm
2. See: http://www.fair.org/extra/0305/kosovo-doves.html
3. See: http://www.therationalradical.com/talk_shows/sean-hannity.htm
4. See: http://www.spinsanity.org/columns/20020826.html

Short Take

Sean Hannity
The Beast staff
from BuffaloBeast.com (2002)

Misdeeds:
Without question one of the most smarmy, vile, hypocritical talking heads on television. Has the uncanny ability to vilify those who disagree with him, and then state that he's not a partisan person. Exploits his devout Catholicism and patriotism to the point that it makes you think he's selling something—like his book, whose cover features his giant head in front of one of the glossiest, waviest American flags ever. Much of his wrath can probably be traced to his displeasure that Reagan never could remember his name although the men met many times.

Aggravating Factor:
Since 9/11, pretends to be genuinely convinced that anyone who disagrees with the Bush administration does not want America to be safe.

Aesthetic:
Repressed kid from Long Island who got to college, was scared of sex, discovered other

repressed white kids in conservative student group, joined them, devoted rest of life to blasting people who didn't.

ANAGRAMS

Sean Hannity
Ate his nanny

Sean Hannity
Easy, thin Ann

Real therapists put their patients' needs first. Dr. Laura Schlessinger—whose degree is in physiology, not psychology— exploits her callers' vulnerabilities to score points with listeners who think she's a shrink. Her favorite pastimes include bashing gays, bashing women and finding ways to get young single mothers to cry on the air. Dr. Laura will do anything for a buck; her faceless unforgiving voice redefines evil, American-style.

Dr. Laura, Be Quiet!

from *The Nation* (5/15/00)

Katha Pollitt

D r. Laura Schlessinger has said a lot of hurtful and irresponsible things on the radio during her many years as a right-wing religious "therapist" and yenta. She mocks and humiliates her callers, some of whom have serious problems. She never misses a chance to bash feminists, working mothers, unmarried or divorced parents, women who have abortions, people who engage in nonmarital sex and anyone who hesitates to whip them through the streets. While she's not entirely a fraud—like "Dr." Henry Kissinger she has a PhD, but in the irrelevant field of physiology— when she ventures into therapeutic territory she's an ignorant meddler. A recent convert to Orthodox Judaism, she hectored one Jewish mother who had qualms about circumcising her son, insisting that there was "overwhelming medical evidence" of the benefits of circumcision, which is false, and that those who said otherwise were members of hate groups pushing anti-Semitic propaganda. She told another mother, who felt guilty about not including a disruptive autistic child in a special restaurant outing, that it was time to think about placing the child in an institution. Maybe so, but who asked her?

For years groups on the receiving end of Dr. Laura's tirades and black-and-white judgments about people she's never met and situations she knows nothing about have grumbled as her show's ratings soared: With 14.25 million weekly listeners, she's almost tied with Rush Limbaugh for the nation's most popular radio personality. Not bad for a woman whose naked photos—product of a youthful pre-conversion liaison with fellow radio host Bill Ballance— are plastered all over the Web. From time to time, a controversy surfaces: The American Library Association, for example, has strongly objected to her smear campaign against them for their opposition to Internet filtering. But it took gays and lesbians to make a fuss loud enough to make the news, and more power to them, I say. Antigay remarks have long been a Dr. Laura staple—the Gay and Lesbian Alliance Against Defamation (GLAAD) first tried to get a meeting with her in 1997, when she referred to homosexuality as a "biological faux pas"—but recently she's stepped up her attacks. Homosexuality is "deviant," a "biological disorder" or "biological error." Gays are sexual predators who do not deserve rights and should not be left alone with children: "How many letters have I read on the air from gay men who acknowledge that a huge portion of the male homosexual populace is predatory on young boys?" She advocates "reparative" therapy and uses the Family Research Council, Gary Bauer's outfit, as her main source of information on homosexuality.

With Viacom's Paramount unit preparing a Dr. Laura daytime TV show for September—more than 160 stations, reaching over 90 percent of the nation's households, have already signed up—enough was clearly enough. Gays have fought back with letters, ads in *Variety* and the *Hollywood Reporter*, a demonstration at Paramount's gates and a spiffy website, StopDrLaura.com, which claims 14 million hits. In response, Dr. Laura hired a "crisis management" firm, issued a weaselly "apology" ("words that I have used in a clinical [!] context have been perceived as judgment"), fired the crisis management team and relabeled the "apology" a "clarification."

Gay activists want the TV show canceled, which seems unlikely, despite the sympathy of David Lee, producer of Paramount's *Frasier*, who has said he's ashamed of his employer. Dr. Laura is not just the most successful woman in radio history (sigh), she's a multimedia franchise, with more than 3 million copies of her various books in print;

her own foundation, which makes grants to groups that fight abortion and "teen sexuality"; a new magazine called *Dr. Laura Perspective*; and a website crowded with innumerable kitschy and self-promoting tie-ins, from books by others praising her show to teddy-bear tea-sets for children. But the gay protests are at least raising the right question: A major studio would never give a flagrant racist or open anti-Semite his own show, no matter how popular he was—Pat Buchanan, who came close, was always one pole of a debate—so why does Paramount find it more acceptable to promote antigay bigotry?

I used to think focusing on Dr. Laura was a waste of time for feminists. After a week of listening to her mad and prurient diatribes, I think we should take a leaf from gay activism and get busy. When Rush Limbaugh burst onto the national political scene, Fairness & Accuracy in Reporting got right on his case, even publishing a clever paperback, *The Way Things Aren't*, dismantling his fake statistics and fractured anecdotes. Maybe it's time for a similar exposé of Dr. Laura, who says women who have abortions are murderers and that mothers always can—and always should—choose not to work, who falsely describes emergency contraception as "dumping out a pregnancy" and causing "disease," and who urges her callers not to help women leave bad marriages because it's all their own fault (see Noy Thrupkaew's article in the May *Sojourner* for a good introduction). Feminist pickets and protests and demands for equal time might not matter to Dr. Laura's core audience—half lost sheep, half graduates of the Taliban School of Female Deportment—but it would give Paramount another good reason to rethink the show.

Are you a rotten radical left-winger? Mike Savage says you're part of a terrorist network. Let's hope he doesn't tell John Ashcroft.

Savage with the Truth

from Salon.com (2/19/03)

Ben Fritz

Conservative radio hosts have come to dominate the airwaves with ferocious rhetoric that's often filled with ad hominem attacks and blatant untruths, but Michael Savage is easily the worst of the bunch. Savage, who makes Rush Limbaugh look reasonable, isn't just a radio personality anymore. His book "The Savage Nation: Saving America From the Liberal Assault on Our Borders, Language and Culture" has reached the top of the *New York Times* bestseller list, and Savage has been rewarded with his own weekly MSNBC show as part of that struggling cable network's efforts to improve its ratings.

Criticizing the rhetoric on Savage's radio show, which has about 5 million listeners and airs on over 300 stations, is a relatively easy task, as evidenced last week when MSNBC announced Savage's new show. The liberal media watchdog group FAIR, for instance, immediately responded with a press release pointing out that Savage often refers to Third World nations as "turd world nations." In addition, Savage has said the U.S. "is being taken over by the freaks, the cripples, the perverts and the mental defectives," and said of poor immigrants, "You open the door to them, and the next thing you know, they are defecating on your country and breeding out of control."

But there's more to Savage than the sum of his hateful

quotes. Known before his radio career began as Michael A. Weiner, he's also an ethnobotanist with a Ph.D. from the University of California who wrote a number of books about natural healing and nutritional supplements with titles like "Herbs That Heal." Savage became an author after he failed to get an academic position, a result he blames in his book on affirmative action and his status as a white male: "For here I was, a 'manchild in the promised land,' denied my birthright for matters of race."

In 1995, in the aftermath of the Republican takeover of Congress, which many credited to Limbaugh and other conservative talk radio hosts, Savage launched his show on San Francisco talk station KSFO, eventually landing a national syndication deal and becoming, according to *Talkers* magazine, the fifth most popular talk-radio host in the country.

It's worth noting, however, that Savage attempted to return to academia in 1996, when he applied to be dean of U.C. Berkeley's School of Journalism based on less than two years of experience in radio and his Ph.D. in epidemiology and nutrition science. When he wasn't granted an interview, Savage filed a lawsuit that, unsurprisingly, didn't go anywhere.

Unlike Limbaugh and the increasingly popular Sean Hannity, Savage spends little time in his book praising President Bush or the Republican Party, or spreading false tropes that circulate in the conservative media. Unlike Hannity's *Let Freedom Ring*, for example, which often reads like a collection of Republican talking points, "The Savage Nation" is an almost unreadable amalgamation of virulent attacks on liberals, feminism, Islam and gays. It wouldn't be much of a surprise if people like MSNBC president Erik Sorenson, who called Savage "brash, passionate and smart" in a press release, haven't actually opened the book.

If Sorenson did read "The Savage Nation," one has to wonder what he thought of Savage's description of MSNBC correspondent Ashleigh Banfield, whom he calls "the mind slut with a big pair of glasses that they sent to Afghanistan," adding, "She looks like she went from porno into reporting." Those aren't the only kind words Savage has for successful women, though. "Today in America," he writes, "we have a 'she-ocracy' where a minority of feminist zealots rule the culture." In Savage's mind, this "she-ocracy" includes not only the usual conservative targets like Sens. Hillary Clinton and Barbara Boxer, but even right-leaning Supreme Court Justice Sandra Day O'Connor, a Reagan appointee.

One can only hope Sorenson didn't refer to Savage as "smart" based on his insights into the fight against terrorism or, as he calls those who took down the World Trade Center, "pirates in filthy nightshirts." Savage states flat out in his book what several mainstream conservative commentators, like Hannity, have only dared to hint— that American liberals are a threat equal to terrorists. "To fight only the al-Qaida scum is to miss the terrorist network operating within our own borders," he states. "Who are these traitors? Every rotten radical left-winger in this country, that's who."

Lest one think Savage is only talking about the truly radical left, he makes clear that he includes most Democratic leaders and center-left foreign leaders on that list. Former President Bill Clinton, Senate Minority Leader Tom Daschle, German Chancellor Gerhard Schröder and

British Prime Minister Tony Blair are all "New World Order Socialists" to Savage, with Blair earning the extra moniker of "Third Way Führer Blair."

Savage's rants against liberals also occasionally include the obsession of radical right-wingers with a one-world government. "[The liberal agenda] is all about one oppressive central government ruling the whole world," he says. "This is the utopia the left has in mind for us." Savage is fiercely bipartisan when it comes to one-world government, though, adding later on, "I've said for a long time that we have a 'Republicrat' or 'Demican' oligarchy in America and that most of our politicians are pawns controlled by their one-world puppet masters behind the scenes."

Most of the book consists of fact-free rants such as these; "The Savage Nation" doesn't bother with notes, and doesn't even have an index. Like Ann Coulter, Michael Moore and Hannity, when Savage does bother with facts, he often gets them wrong. He says that "the divorce rate has doubled since 1970," but according to federal statistics, while the divorce rate was 3.5 per 1,000 people in 1970, it never came close to doubling, and was 4.7 in 2000.

Using a study by Tokyo University scientists as data, Savage mocks former Vice President Al Gore's efforts "to combat the evils of global warming and the ozone depletion [sic]" and asks "Why won't Al, the global warming bogeyman, back down?" That study, however, found only that the ozone hole in the Southern Hemisphere would heal itself by 2040 thanks in part to regulatory controls of CFCs and other chemicals. Savage, whose biography calls him an "ardent conservationist," seems unaware that ozone depletion and global warming are in fact separate phenomena.

As part of an attack on the use of Ritalin by children,

Savage quotes then-first lady Hillary Clinton at a White House conference calling the drug "a godsend for emotional and behavioral problems for both children and their parents." He fails to mention, however, Clinton's next comment: "We do have to ask some serious questions about the use of prescription drugs in all children . . . What about the effects on our very youngest children who haven't been tested for these prescription drugs and whose brains are in their most critical stages of development?" Hardly the words of someone who, as Savage alleges, is "calling Ritalin a miracle drug."

Just how does a book like this get published? The answer can be found on a network of conservative Web sites. "The Savage Nation" is one of the first books published by WND Books, a partnership between the conservative site WorldNetDaily and Thomas Nelson, a publisher of Christian books. All WND books are not only heavily publicized on WorldNetDaily but also made available for sale there first, giving direct access to a loyal audience most authors would kill for.

Much of Savage's content, meanwhile, can be traced directly to columns he published on the conservative site NewsMax.com. The book itself is divided into two- to four-page sections, many of which are near-exact replicas of Savage's NewsMax columns with the same name. Most of the content in the book, in fact, can be found in the columns archived on the site. Of course, there's nothing wrong with collecting a series of columns into a book. It's noteworthy, however, that Savage doesn't tell his readers they're primarily reading recycled material, and it's revealing that a book containing so many errors is primarily a cut-and-paste job.

The easiest response to all of this, of course, is one that Savage himself partially makes early in his book: "Comedy is what I sometimes do." Does taking Michael Savage seriously play right into his hands? It's certainly important to point out the hypocrisy of a bestselling author who says of himself, "I want to elevate the dialogue, if I can, to some level that's civil."

More fundamentally, in a world where people like Savage are rewarded with their own shows on a major cable news channel, close scrutiny is absolutely necessary. Either MSNBC executives have listened to Savage's show and read his book and believe his brand of vitriol and distortions make him, as Sorenson said, "brash, passionate and smart," or they don't care about anything other than his ratings and his book sales. Either way, they have a lot to explain. Michael Savage may be one small step up in the ratings for MSNBC, but he's one giant leap down for our political discourse.

**"Head shots, head shots . . . Kill the
sons of bitches . . . Shoot twice
to the belly and if that does not work,
shoot to the groin area."**
—G. Gordon Liddy on how people
should deal with Bureau of Alcohol,
Tobacco and Firearms agents.

When did Dennis Miller stop being funny?

Dennis Miller's Monkey Business

from Salon.com (2/9/04)

Heather Havrilesky

It's Miller time (again)

Dennis Miller has a chimp on his desk and a button that
replays Howard Dean's now-infamous "Hooah!" from
the night of the Iowa caucuses, but he wants us to know
that on his new show, he won't be relying on irony or
snide gimmicks to make his deathly serious points. "It
will not be Dennis Miller's Ironypalooza business as
usual," he enunciates emphatically. "Excoriation has been
my milieu up to this point, but on this show, I'm going

to be a smartass with the smartasses, and heartfelt with the sincere people. I hope you'll eventually come to think of this show as an ombudsman: fair and insistent."

Yes, Miller admits, he's less liberal and far more outraged than he was before. "9/11 changed me," he says. "Quite frankly I'm shocked that it apparently didn't change everyone out there." According to Miller's logic, we may have been open-minded, even-handed folks on the 10th of September, but on the morning of the 11th, we all earned the right to surrender to our least enlightened selves, to fall prey to our worst impulses, to vent enough spleen with such righteous outrage that it almost matches the fury of our fundamentalist oppressors.

Miller's worst impulses include a resident chimp, a live-show format without an audience, a watered-down "Weekend Update" that resorts to jokes about Dean's sanity and Kucinich's creepy looks for its weak laughs, and a "Varsity" panel so awkward and unprofessional that the words "Junior Varsity" spring to mind more often than the chimp presses the "Hooah!" button.

Since Miller is relentlessly self-serious and wildly over-confident, he confuses his worst impulses with really bold, daring choices. Thus, the opening current-events segment wins only scattered laughs, not only because it's not that funny but also because those are members of his staff laughing. You see, Miller refuses to ship in "tourists" to fill his audience, so instead, two or three producers and network executives guffaw loudly, and we're meant to think the key grip and the gaffer just can't get enough of Miller's love. And that's bold? Aside from the obvious fact that executives constitute more of a fraudience than honeymooning couples from Michigan ever could, when paired with mediocre jokes that I'm betting are all written by Miller himself (and if they're not, he should replace his entire writing staff), you've got one of the most painful, awkward segments of television ever produced.

"Kraft Foods says it will eliminate good jobs, 6,000 of them, due to more than a year's worth of disappointing losses," Miller quips. One nervous chuckle can be heard, faintly. "All right, who's not eating Velveeta. Is it you?! You slackers! Eat your damn Velveeta!" The studio is deathly silent. I don't think I'm the only one longing for some good old-fashioned tourist laughter about now.

Another bold choice? Invite rambling pundits and TV amateurs to be guests on your show, perch them on bar stools a couple of inches from each other, and do little to herd them toward a discernible point. "For the most part, I'll let people talk until they're talked out," Miller explains, and you just know there's a Big Idea behind it. "I think talk show guests sometimes bank on the host's intercession to save them. I say let them finish, see what's next, what's on the other side of all that bluster. Also, I believe constantly trying to break into their answer with my next question is a particularly precious form of preening that I hope to avoid."

No preening? No live audience? Guests talking until they're talked out? Someone needs to remind Miller that this is *television*. Getting all thoughtful and self-conscious about what makes most talk shows ring false is all well and good, but it doesn't necessarily produce a more entertaining show. Thanks to Miller's ill-considered purist impulses, we find him cringing his way through weak jokes in an empty studio, or wringing his hands as Naomi Wolf and David Horowitz attack each other in 5,000 words or less, sidestepping any recognizable issue or topic for minutes at a time.

In short, Miller *has* changed. Despite his talk of pragmatism, he's evolved into exactly the kind of semi-intellectual who's so boxed in by ideas, he can no longer entertain. Miller says he would like his show to be the headquarters of a "common-sense revolution." Unfortunately, that revolution's not likely to begin until Miller himself demonstrates a little common sense.

 ## Short Take

Dennis Miller
The Beast staff
from BuffaloBeast.com

Once upon a time Dennis Miller was a great funnyman, but in the latter half of the nineties he made a barely noticeable descent into the bowels of conservatism, which was brought to an ugly, pus-filled head by the September 11th attacks. Having recast himself as Bush's own personal Monica Lewinsky, he seems to have undergone an operation to have his political sophistication removed. It's always sad when someone we once admired reveals himself to be a xenophobic buffoon, but not so sad that he shouldn't be stifled with his own viscera. Miller's switch to the right may have made him feel safe, but it turned his once impressive career into a bag of infectious waste. After his last unremarkable HBO special, Dennis will be lucky to get a role in a car wax infomercial.

She Said It . . .

"I wouldn't say that these people [Martin Luther King, Jr. and Rosa Parks] are the villains of the current Left, [but they showed a] preference for deceit in pursuit of power . . . [Rosa Parks] pushed us into the maze of thought police totalitarianism that we face today."
—self-described "progressive" Fox contributor Tammy Bruce, in her book *The New Thought Police.*

Pat Robertson thinks that you and I are termites, and believes that it's time for a "godly fumigation".

Pat Robertson

from deal-with-it.org

Gus DiZerega

Pat Robertson is spectacular proof of Abe Lincoln's observation that you can fool some of the people all of the time. He claims to be a religious leader, yet he invests millions with bloody handed dictators. He says Christians should rule America—but also says millions of Americans who think of themselves as Christians are agents of Satan. He praises the corrupt big city machine politics of Tammany Hall as the best model for *Christian* political influence, and even blamed America for 9/11 while wrapping himself in our flag. We could go much farther, but we don't want to write a book.

PAT AND DICTATORS

Charles Taylor was the Liberian president indicted for war crimes and responsible for much of the bloodshed and suffering that has afflicted Liberia and its neighbors for years. For Robertson he is also a Christian, a Baptist, and therefore in need of American support. According to Robertson, Taylor is a freely elected president. He does not mention that Taylor came to power violently in 1996, and "won" a suspect election only a year later by threatening further violence if he lost. An exhausted electorate figured things couldn't get worse. Things got worse.

Robertson also neglected to tell his listeners that he had invested $8 million in a gold mining venture with Taylor's government, which receives 10 percent of the venture's profits. Defending his investment, Roberston said "Freedom Gold [his company] has found freedom of religion, freedom of movement, freedom of expression, and what appears to be a judiciary dedicated to the rule of law." Even the US Government disagrees. A State Department representative said the US "has not encouraged either trade or investment in Liberia due to the absence of the rule of law and President Taylor's support for armed insurgencies."[1]

CHRISTIANS AND AMERICA
Robertson says he wants America to return to her Christian roots—but his definition of Christianity would make most Christians uneasy. Consider the following quotes together:

* "The Constitution of the United States, for instance, is a marvelous document for self-government by the Christian people. But the minute you turn the document into the hands of non-Christian people and atheistic people they can use it to destroy the very foundation of our society. And that's what's been happening." ("700 Club," 12/30/81)
* "You say you're supposed to be nice to the Episcopalians and the Presbyterian and the Methodists and this, that, and the other thing. Nonsense. I don't have to be nice to the spirit of the Antichrist." ("700 Club," 1/14/91)
* "The people who have come into [our] institutions [today] are primarily termites. They are into destroying institutions that have been built by Christians, whether it is universities, governments,

our own traditions, that we have . . . . The termites
are in charge now, and that is not the way it ought
to be, and the time has arrived for a godly fumigation." (*New York* magazine, 8/18/86)
* In a closed door session of Christian Coalition
leaders, Robertson observed he was seeking to
create "the power of every machine that has ever
been in politics. You know, the Tammany Halls and
Hague and the Chicago machine and . . . all the rest
of them. . . . this is what we've got to do." (*Church
and State*, October, 1997, pp. 4-5.)

His appreciation of dictatorship becomes much more
clear now.

So also does the wisdom of our Founders in separating
religion and politics—wisdom Robertson denies. For
example, the advertisement for his "Regents University" in
U.S. News and World Report centers on a supposed statement by James Madison: "We have staked the whole of
our political institutions upon the capacity of mankind for
self-government, upon the capacity of each and all of us to
govern ourselves, to control ourselves, to sustain ourselves
according to the Ten Commandments of God."

Robertson's claim is about as true as saying the Constitution is based on the teachings of Confucius. Americans United demonstrated far greater understanding of
history when they observed that Madison "opposed tax
funding of religion, publicly funded chaplains in the
Congress and the military and even expressed regret for
issuing proclamations declaring official days of prayer
during his presidency."[2]

If we claim to be a "Christian Nation" rather than

simply a nation where the majority are Christians, people like Robertson would argue (as he does now) that Christians different from himself aren't really Christians and are subverting our heritage. They are "termites," as he so kindly characterizes millions of us. A few hundred years ago Europe fought a 30-year war over who was and wasn't a "Christian" in a "Christian nation." Millions died. Roberston's reasoning takes us back to those fun times.

BLAMING AMERICA

Immediately after 9/11, Jerry Falwell said: "what we saw on Tuesday, as terrible as it is, could be miniscule if, in fact—God continues to lift the curtain and allow the enemies of America to give us probably what we deserve . . . . I really believe that the pagans, and the abortionists, and the feminists, and the gays and the lesbians who are actively trying to make that an alternative lifestyle, the ACLU, People For the American Way—all of them who have tried to secularize America—I point the finger in their face and say "you helped this happen."

Robertson replied: "Well, I totally concur, and the problem is we have adopted that agenda at the highest levels of our government. And so we're responsible as a free society for what the top people do. . . ." ("700 Club," 9/13/01)

Such is how truth, Christianity, and patriotism fare in the hands of Pat Robertson. Significantly, he takes credit for the Republicans' political victories and the success of the radical Republican Right. There is much truth to his boasts. And much reason for good Americans to worry.[4]

1. See: http://www.christianitytoday.com/ct/2002/002/14.18.html
2. See: http://www.escape.com/~drew/wwwboard/messages/267.html
3. TAKE A QUIZ! Can you separate the words of Pat Robertson and Jerry Falwell from those of Osama bin Laden? Think you can? Go ahead! http://funnystrange.com/quiz/

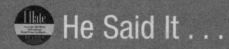

He Said It . . .

"This man was an absolute wild-eyed fanatic. He was a robber and a brigand. And to say that these terrorists distort Islam . . . they're carrying out Islam . . . This man was a killer. And to think that this is a peaceful religion is fraudulent."

—Pat Robertson on the prophet Muhammad

An I Hate Ann Coulter, Bill O'Reilly, Rush Limbaugh, Michael Savage, Sean Hannity . . . *Timeline:* 1947–2004

Nate Hardcastle

Henry Regnery, Sr. founds Regnery Publishing, future publisher of assorted right-wing wackos. Titles to come include R. Emmett Tyrrell's *The Impeachment of William Jefferson Clinton: A Political Docu-Drama* (which suggests that the KGB paid for Clinton's college trip to Russia), Ann Coulter's *High Crimes and Misdemeanors* ("We have a national debate about whether [Clinton] 'did it,' even though all sentient people know he did . . . otherwise there would only be debates about whether to impeach or assassinate"), and Gary Aldrich's *Unlimited Access* (lesbian orgies in the Clinton White House showers; Hillary hanging crack pipes from the Christmas tree).

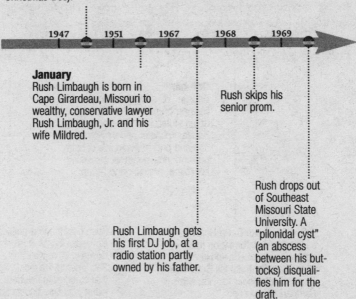

1947   1951   1967   1968   1969

January
Rush Limbaugh is born in Cape Girardeau, Missouri to wealthy, conservative lawyer Rush Limbaugh, Jr. and his wife Mildred.

Rush skips his senior prom.

Rush Limbaugh gets his first DJ job, at a radio station partly owned by his father.

Rush drops out of Southeast Missouri State University. A "pilonidal cyst" (an abscess between his buttocks) disqualifies him for the draft.

AN *I HATE ANN COULTER . . .* TIMELINE

Rush lands his first full-time radio gig—then gets fired. Rush is fired from radio gigs several more times during the next thirteen years.

Rush marries a second time.

Rush marries for the first time. Divorces less than two years later.

| 1971 | 1974 | 1977 | 1980 | 1983 | 1984 |

October
George Will secretly helps Ronald Reagan prepare for a debate, using notes stolen from the Carter White House. Will later appears on *Nightline* and praises Reagan's debate performance—without disclosing his role in prepping the Gipper.

Left-wing wacko David Horowitz begins his transformation into right-wing wacko David Horowitz after Black Panthers kill Betty Van Tanner, bookkeeper for Horowitz's *Ramparts* magazine.

Rush gets his first political slot replacing Morton Downey, Jr. at KMBZ in Sacramento. He discovers that catering to listeners' worst impulses boosts his ratings.

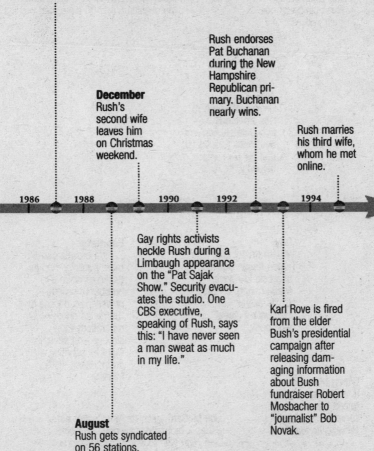

A cargo plane carrying weapons for the *contras* is shot down in Nicaragua. State Department official Elliott Abrams (later GWB's National Security Council envoy to the Middle East) lies about it on CNN: "This was not in any sense a U.S. government operation," he tells "journalist" Robert Novak. Novak later says he admired Abrams for lying to him, because the lie furthered the fight against communism.

December
Rush's second wife leaves him on Christmas weekend.

Rush endorses Pat Buchanan during the New Hampshire Republican primary. Buchanan nearly wins.

Rush marries his third wife, whom he met online.

1986   1988   1990   1992   1994

Gay rights activists heckle Rush during a Limbaugh appearance on the "Pat Sajak Show." Security evacuates the studio. One CBS executive, speaking of Rush, says this: "I have never seen a man sweat as much in my life."

Karl Rove is fired from the elder Bush's presidential campaign after releasing damaging information about Bush fundraiser Robert Mosbacher to "journalist" Bob Novak.

August
Rush gets syndicated on 56 stations.

November
Seventy-three Repub-
lican freshmen are
elected to Congress;
the group credits
Rush Limbaugh for
their success.

March
George Will admits that he provided
George W. Bush with an advance
list of questions before interviewing
the candidate on ABC's program
"This Week."

July
George Will on ABC
News defends a
Bob Dole speech—
but doesn't mention
that his own wife
helped write it.

1994   1996   1998   2000

July
William Kristol and
Robert Kagan publish
an article in *Foreign
Affairs* calling for the
U.S. to exercise
"benevolent global
hegemony."

February
David Horowitz garners
more publicity than he
deserves when a
number of college
newspapers decline to
run his ad opposing
reparations for
slavery—an advertise-
ment he submits
during Black History
Month.

Rupert Murdoch
hires William Kristol
to edit his new con-
servative rag, *The
Weekly Standard*.

Joe McCarthy acolyte Ann Coulter publishes a factually-challenged rant entitled *High Crimes and Misdemeanors:
The Case Against Bill Clinton*.

February
"The O'Reilly Factor" hosts Jeremy Glick, whose father died in the World Trade Center attacks. O'Reilly responds to Glick's criticisms of U.S. foreign policy with such *bon mots* as "I don't really care what you think"; "That's a bunch of crap"; and "Shut up! Shut up!". O'Reilly cuts Glick's microphone; after the interview O'Reilly tells Glick, "Get out of my studio before I tear you to fucking pieces."

September
Jerry Falwell, on Pat Robertson's "The 700 Club," blames 9/11 on—who else?— "the pagans, and the abortionists, and the feminists, and the gays and the lesbians . . . the ACLU, People For the American Way . . ."

July
A "senior administration official" tells "journalist" Robert Novak that Valerie Plame, wife of Bush administration critic Joseph Wilson, is an undercover CIA operative. Novak publishes the revelation over the CIA's objections, destroying Plame's usefulness as an operative and endangering her contacts.

September
Ann Coulter issues her now-infamous call to arms against Muslims: "We should invade their countries, kill their leaders and convert them to Christianity."

2001   2002

September
Andrew Sullivan writes "The decadent left in its enclaves on the coasts . . . may well mount . . . a fifth column." (The *Encyclopedia Britannica* defines "fifth column" as a "clandestine group or faction of subversive agents who attempt to undermine a nation's solidarity by any means at their disposal.")

June
Coulter publishes another hateful, factually-challenged rant. She calls this one *Slander: Liberal Lies about the American Right*.

December
Sean Hannity says Al Qaeda "obviously has the support of Saddam."

December
Bernie Goldberg publishes *Bias: a CBS Insider Exposes How the Media Distort the News*—a collection of unsupported assertions that the media is liberal. The book attributes to a former CBS News employee the following statement: "Anyone working at CBS News who is not a leftist knows how it must have felt to be a black kid in a white school in Tuscaloosa, Alabama, back in 1938."

AN *I HATE ANN COULTER* . . . TIMELINE

February
Bill O'Reilly claims never to have asked watchers to boycott Pepsi for hiring rapper Ludacris—apparently forgetting broadcasts in which he said "I'm calling for all Americans to say 'Hey, Pepsi, I'm not drinking your stuff. You want to hang around with Ludacris, you do that, I'm not hanging around with you,'" (8/27/02) and "Because of pressure by 'Factor' viewers, Pepsi-Cola late today capitulated. Ludacris has been fired" (8/28/02).

March
Fox News runs headline banners falsely asserting "Huge Chemical Weapons Factory Found in Southern Iraq."

March
O'Reilly says the following: "If the Americans go in and overthrow Saddam Hussein and it's clean, he has nothing, I will apologize to the nation, and I will not trust the Bush Administration again, all right?"

June
Ann Coulter publishes yet another hateful, factually-challenged rant. She calls this one *Treason: Liberal Treachery from the Cold War to the War on Terrorism.*

2003

March
George Will extensively praises newspaper scion Conrad Black in a *Washington Post* column, without disclosing that Black recently paid him a $25,000 one-day speaking fee.

May
Bill O'Reilly repeatedly screams "shut up!" at Al Franken during the Los Angeles Book Expo.

August
The Fox Network sues Al Franken, claiming that his book's title, *Lies and the Lying Liars Who Tell Them: A Fair and Balanced Look at the Right,* infringes on its trademark of the phrase "Fair and Balanced."

March
Bill O'Reilly says that "a load of weapons-grade plutonium has disappeared from Nigeria," and attempts to link the claim to Iraq's alleged nuclear-weapons program. The substance he refers to actually is Americium-241, which isn't useful for making weapons—and the stash in question was simply misplaced by Halliburton.

September
ESPN fires Rush after he says about struggling
Philadelphia Eagles quarterback Donovan McNabb:
"I think what we've had here is a little social concern
in the NFL. The media has been very desirous that a
black quarterback do well . . . There is a little hope
invested in McNabb, and he got a lot of credit for the
performance of this team that he didn't deserve."
(Rush fails to mention that the three-time Pro Bowler
was returning from a broken leg.)

August
U.S. district judge
Denny Chin throws
out Fox's lawsuit
against Al Franken,
saying: "There are
hard cases and there
are easy cases. This
is an easy case. The
case is wholly without
merit both factually
and legally . . . It is
ironic that a media
company that should
seek to protect the
First Amendment is
instead seeking to
undermine it."

May
Rush compares
the torture of Iraqi
prisoners at Abu
Ghraib prison to
fraternity hazing.

November
Rush returns
from detox.

2004

October
Rush, who once said
". . . too many whites are
getting away with drug
use. . . . The answer is to
go out and find the ones
who are getting away
with it, convict them and
send them up the river,"
admits to his listeners
that he is addicted to
prescription painkillers.

June
Rush announces
his third divorce.

September
Ann Coulter says
"Saddam Hussein has
harbored, promoted,
helped, sheltered Al
Qaeda members. We
know that."

January
Anti-tax gadfly
Grover Norquist
compares people
who support the
estate tax to Nazis.

Acknowledgments

Many people made this anthology.

At Thunder's Mouth Press and Avalon Publishing Group: Thanks to Will Balliett, Maria Fernandez, Nate Knaebel, Linda Kosarin, John Oakes, Dan O'Connor, Michael O'Connor, Paul Paddock, Susan Reich, David Riedy, Mike Walters, and Don Weise for their support, dedication and hard work. I owe particular thanks to Neil Ortenberg for his support and inspiration during the past seven years.

I am especially grateful to Nate Hardcastle who, with help from Nat May, did most of the research for this book. Nate participated fully in all editorial decisions and created *The I Hate Ann Coulter, Bill O'Reilly, Rush Limbaugh, Michael Savage, Sean Hannity . . .* Timeline that begins on page 335.

Thanks also are due to the dozens of people who generously took time to help Taylor find and obtain rights. Special thanks to Amelia Nash at Salon.com, Habiba Alcindor at *The Nation*, Sarah Gurfein at *The American Prospect*, Soyoung Ho at *The Washington Monthly*, and Laura Obolensky at *The New Republic*.

Finally, I am grateful to the writers and artists whose work appears in this book.

Permissions

Bibliography

The selections used in this anthology were taken from the sources listed below

Alterman, Eric. "Abrams and Novak and Rove? Oh My!" Originally appeared in *The Nation*, November 3, 2003. Portions of each week's Nation magazine can be accessed at www.thenation.com.

Alterman, Eric. "What Liberal Media?" Originally appeared in *The Nation*, February 24, 2003. Portions of each week's Nation magazine can be accessed at www.thenation.com.

Alterman, Eric. *What Liberal Media?* New York: Basic Books, 2003.

The American Prospect staff. "Fact Check Ann Coulter, a Special Edition." Originally appeared in *The American Prospect, Tapped* (www.prospect.org/weblog), July 26, 2002.

Bayard, Louis. "A Dying Breed." This article originally appeared in Salon.com (www.salon.com), October 3, 2002. An online version remains in the Salon archives.

Beato, Greg. "Anabaptist Coulter." Originally appeared in Soundbitten (www.soundbitten.com), October 6, 2002.

Beato, Greg. "Word of Oaf." Originally appeared in Soundbitten (www.soundbitten.com), September 22, 2002.

Bivens, Matt. "Little Miss Treason." Originally appeared online at *The Nation* (www.thenation.com), February 17, 2004.

The Beast staff. "*The Beast*'s 50 Most Loathsome People." Originally appeared in *The Beast* (www.buffalo beast.com), September/November 2002.

The Beast staff. "*The Beast*'s Vilest People in America." Originally appeared in *The Beast* (www.buffalobeast.com), January 26, 2004.

Chait, Jonathan. "Right Reverent." Originally appeared in *The New Republic*, March 25, 2002.

Cohen, Richard. "Blaming of the Shrew." Originally appeared in *The Washington Post*, August 15, 2002.

Confessore, Nicholas. "Hillary was Right." Originally appeared in *The American Prospect*, vol. 11, no. 5: January 17, 2000.

Corn, David. "Ann Coulter Goes to the Movies." Originally appeared online at *The Nation* (www.thenation.com), November 5, 2003.

Crenshaw, Kimberle Williams. "Rush Limbaugh and the Hypocrisy Smokescreen." Originally published by CommonDreams.org (www.commondreams.org).

DiZerega, Gus. "A Rogue's Gallery of the Radical Right." Individual essays originally published by Deal-With-It! (www.deal-with-it.org), 2003.

Farrell, Maureen. "Whatever You Do, Don't Diss the King." Appeared on BuzzFlash (www.buzzflash.com), December 24, 2003.

Fritz, Ben. "10 Great Moments in Jingoism." This article originally appeared in Salon.com (www.salon.com), April 18, 2003. An online version remains in the Salon archives.

Fritz, Ben and Bryan Keefer. "The Blowhard Next Door." This article originally appeared in Salon.com (www.salon.com), August 26, 2002. An online version remains in the Salon archives.

Fritz, Ben. "Savage with the Truth." This article originally appeared in Salon.com (www.salon.com), February 19, 2003. An online version remains in the Salon archives.

Grieve, Tim. "Fox News: The Inside Story." This article

originally appeared in Salon.com (www.salon.com), October 31, 2003. An online version remains in the Salon archives.

Havrilesky, Heather. "It's Miller Time (Again)." This article originally appeared in Salon.com (www.salon.com), February 9, 2004. An online version remains in the Salon archives.

Hendra, Tony. "We See That Now." Originally appeared in *The American Prospect*, vol. 15, no. 2: February 1, 2004.

Mooney, Chris. "Rush Don't Know Dittoheads." Originally appeared in *The American Prospect Online*, April 1, 2002.

Orr, Christopher. "Rush to Judgment." Originally appeared in *The New Republic*, December 1, 2003.

Pollitt, Katha. "After You, My Dear Alphonse." Originally appeared in *The Nation*, October 20, 2003. Portions of each week's Nation magazine can be accessed at www.thenation.com.

Pollitt, Katha. "Dr. Laura, Be Quiet!" Originally appeared in *The Nation*, May 15, 2003. Portions of each week's Nation magazine can be accessed at www.thenation.com.

Safire, Paul. "Animal House Meets Church Lady." Originally appeared in *The American Prospect*, vol. 7, no. 25: March/April, 1996.

Saletan, William. "White Whine." Originally appeared in Slate (www.slate.com), March 29, 2001.

Sirota, David. "The Fox of War." This article originally appeared in Salon.com (www.salon.com), March 30, 2004. An online version remains in the Salon archives.

Solomon, Norman. "George Will's Ethics." Appeared in CounterPunch, January 2, 2004.

Steinreich, Dale. "A Pox on Fox: Latest Lies From Fox News." Originally appeared on Antiwar.com, December 29, 2003.

Talbot, Stephen. "The Wizard of Ooze." Originally appeared in *Mother Jones*, May/June 1995.

Taylor, Charles. "When Right-Wing Fembots Attack." This article originally appeared in Salon.com (www.salon.com), June 27, 2002. An online version remains in the Salon archives.

Thrupkaew, Noy. "Scold Move." Originally appeared in *The American Prospect Online* (www.prospect.org), April 3, 2002.

Tomasky, Michael. "Breaking Kristol: The Propaganda and Lies of *The Weekly Standard*'s Editor." Originally appeared in *The American Prospect Online* (www.prospect.org), April 2, 2003.

The Washington Monthly staff. "The Wisdom of Ann Coulter." Originally appeared in *The Washington Monthly*, November 2001. Web site: www.washingtonmonthly.com.

CLINT WILLIS has edited more than thirty anthologies, including *The I Hate Republicans Reader*, *The I Hate George W. Bush Reader* and (with Nathaniel May) *We Are the People: Voices from the Other Side of American History*. He lives with his family in Maine.